THE LIFE

of

FREDERICK BATES

EDITED BY

THOMAS MAITLAND MARSHALL, PH.D.

Secretary of the Missouri Historical Society

and

Professor of History in Washington University

VOLUME II

MISSOURI HISTORICAL SOCIETY

Sᴛ. Loᴜɪs, 1926

EDWARD BATES

From an engraving, the property of the Missouri Historical Society.

PART III—Continued

The Régime of Governor Lewis

THE RÉGIME OF GOVERNOR LEWIS

ROBERT FORSYTH TO BATES

CHICAGEAUX 10th June 1808

DEAR SIR

I arrived here a few days ago and expect to leave this in the Course of Six days for Detroit, I Hope my Dear Sir you have had the Goodness to drop me a few lines in answer to mine of March last, and that the information you may think proper to Communicate to me, may be favorable — You will Confer particular obligation on me by interesting yourself with Govr Lewis, and making me aquainted with his answer, and Ideas on the Subject, be assured I Shall feel myself Ever grateful for the friendly attention you have uniformly shewed me, and particularly in the present instance. — I am Sorry to give you so much trouble, but Hope you will excuse it, as it proceeds from a Heart that will always be Happy to reciprocate, if Ever in his power — . . .

N. B. this will be handed to you by my brother Thos. by whom I Hope you will favor me with an answer

---

THOMAS F. RIDDICK TO BATES, NEW MADRID

DR. SIR   SAINT LOUIS 2nd July 1808

Your favor from Cape Girardeau arrived safe to hand. It gave your friends In S Louis much pleasure to hear from you; & hope that you will return the Doctors Medicine Chest untouched, and continue your expedition with eaqual Success as to the greatest of all blessings, *Sound Health*

Genl. Clark and family have arrived, and bring with them the *beautiful and accomplished Miss Anderson,*[111] a niece of the Genl. Great agitation In St Louis among the bachelors, to prevent fatal consequences a Town meeting has been proposed for the purpose of disposing of her by lot, no meeting has yet been had. *Your Friend Tom* however does not mean to contend for the prize, a little girl not far distant has been so dextrous with her eyes as to completely make *him* Indifferent to all the fair beside, we have been coquetting, untill I believe both her and myself begin to be *serious;* some good or other must come of it.

There has been for the last five or six days before the first of July a great number of land claims entered for record, Mr. Bouis[112] however would not attend to his business In the Office & I found it was a folly to persist in employing a man by the month that would not write more than three days. I settled up with him to the first of July, and have since made another bargain with him, he to be

111 Elizabeth, daughter of John and Ann Rogers Clark, and sister of William Clark, married Richard Clough Anderson, a Virginian, about 1787. Anderson was a colonel and was appointed principal surveyor of lands granted by Virginia in 1783 to soldiers of the continental line. He opened headquarters at Louisville in July, 1784. He represented Jefferson County, Kentucky, in the conventions at Danville in 1784 and 1788. Elizabeth Clark Anderson died in 1795, leaving a son and three daughters, Ann, Cecelia, and Elizabeth. William Hayden English, *Conquest of the Country northwest of the Ohio River, 1778-1783, and Life of Gen. George Rogers Clark,* II, 1006-1008.

112 Pascal Vincent Bouis was one of three young Frenchmen appointed from St. Louis to West Point by Jefferson in 1804. He resigned his commission of 2nd lieutenant in the United States artillery in 1808. Later he became a planter in Louisiana.

paid at the rate of five cents for recording every 100 words
plats Included, you will thereby gain something and if he
is Industrious he can easily make from one to two and a
half dollars per day, under the old arrangement calculating all I could get him to do at the rate of 12½ Cents, he
did not earn his wages, I have received the land warrants
from Gov. Lewis, also fifty dollars from Mr. Dorr; *all your
business* shall be attended to. Nothing more new, strange,
or Interesting. . . . Mr. Carr & Ladys, compliments.

TO ALBERT GALLATIN

FORT MADISON,

SIR,   Village of Arkansas[113] July 22. 1808.

I had the honor of addressing you, early in the month
of June from Cape Girardeau, since which I have visited
all the intermediate settlements. —

The claimants of Arkansas not having attended generally at Hope Field,[114] I thought it proper, altho not specially required by the resolution of the commissioners, to
come on to this place. —

The business here was completed in one week, since which

[113] Cuming, who visited Arkansas Post in 1808, says, "The settlement
of Arkansas or Ozark is about fifty miles above the junction of that
river with the Mississippi. It consists chiefly of hunters and Indian
traders, of course is a poor place, as settlers of this description never
look for any thing beyond the mere necessities of life, except whiskey."
The post dated from 1686 when Tonti left a detachment of six men
there under Couture. The place was maintained as a trading post and
Jesuit mission throughout the French period. During the Spanish régime
it was one of three principal centers for control of the Indians. Laclede
had a branch warehouse there and died there in 1778. It should not be
confused with Fort Madison, Iowa. Cuming, *Tour*, in *Early Western
Travels*, IV, 298-299; Herbert E. Bolton, *Athanase De Mezières*, I, 74.

[114] Hopefield, Arkansas, was originally Fort Esperanza.

I have been detained by the sickness of my men & other un-
toward circumstances.

Mr. Le Duc,[115] the Translator, accompanied me no farther than the Chickasaw-Bluffs.[116] He had been taken sick
at New Madrid,[117] but by an exertion of that fortitude for
which he is remarkable, he had continued regularly, and
promptly to discharge the duties of his office, until his
indisposition became so seriously alarming that I thought
it imprudent for him to proceed. The illness of Mr. Le
Duc compelled me to employ another Translator — and on
the recommendation of Capt. Armstead,[118] the Comdt. of
this Post, I engaged Andw. Fagot, Clerk of the late Spanish
Comdt. and since commissioned a Notary Public by the
Governor of this territory. He is believed to possess the
requisite qualifications and deserves this confidence *for
the occasion.* His demand is three dollars Per day, which
I shall take the liberty of putting into the next contingent
account.

The claims in this part of the country have been brought
forward with much irregularity. The People are for the
most part so entirely unacqainted with every kind of business, except of that of the chase, it is not at all to be won-
dered at that affairs requiring method, order and an observance of legal forms, should be totally unintelligible to
them. Contrary to my expectations, a great number of
claims remained to be entered when I arrived on the 2d
instant. The next day the People appeared to be ignorant
that the time for receiving them had expired, and having

---

[115] Marie Philip Leduc.

[116] Neighborhood of Memphis.

[117] For an excellent description of New Madrid in 1808, see Cuming,
Tour, in *Early Western Travels,* IV, 281-282.

[118] Probably George Armistead.

procured Agents, presented themselves very generally with their Papers. These Agents thought proper to date all the notices of his clients on 29th June. But they could not *now* be received. I however thought myself justified in becoming the depositary of them, at the same time informing the Agents explicitly that in doing so, I could be considered only as a private individual ,and by no means as a public Agent. Considering the remote and sequestered situation of these claimants I was even induced to receive and reduce to writing the testimony in relation to these antedated and illegal entries. The Papers and the testimony will be carefully preserved, subject to those Orders which you may think proper to give with respect to them.—

Had these People attended at Hope Field as contemplated by the commissioners, these embarrassments might have been avoided.

The large surveys of Messrs. Winters which lie in this vicinity are very valuable.[119] No where in the western country have I seen lands so fertile, and which lie so well as the tract of 250,000 acres claimed by Gabriel Winter between the St. Francis & White River. But the principal reliance appears to be placed on the validity and completeness of the grant of William Winter, which has been

[119] This grant was made in 1797 to Elisha, William, and Gabriel Winter, William Russell and Joseph Stillwell. The grant was invalidated in 1847-1848 on the ground of indefiniteness. For many years the region about Arkansas Post was retarded by the uncertainty of the title. Nuttall says, "Several enormous Spanish grants remain still [January, 1819] undecided; that of Messrs. Winters, of Natchez, called for no less than one million acres, but the congress of the United States, inclined to put in force a kind of agrarian law against such monopolizers, had laid them, as I was told, under the stipulation of settling upon this immense tract a certain number of families." Thomas Nuttall, *A Journal of Travels into the Arkansas Territory during the Year 1819* . . . , in *Early Western Travels*, XIII, 106-107.

located in the Prairie adjacent to this place. The People appear to be very anxious for the confirmation of this grant, under an expectation of purchasing at more reasonable prices from the Proprietor than from the United States.

Mr. Donaldson, the late Recorder has asserted in the public Papers that these Titles are complete. Yet it appears to me very questionable. The conditions have surely not been complied with in such manner, as the Spanish Government[120] had a right to expect. Either the pretensions of Mr. Winter, are in his own estimation not well founded, or he has given extraordinary fees for management: For I understand that one Gentleman, for procuring the survey and smoothing if possible, the passage of the claim; and another for collecting and arranging testimony, have acquired interests almost equal to the original claimant.

At Cape Girardeau and at New Madrid, the Corps of Witnesses were well organized and disciplined: Whenever I suspected a wandering from the fact, I endeavoured to detect and expose it — but it was not always in my power —

About the 10th of next month I hope to give to the commissioners at St. Louis, a satisfactory account of my Mission. — Every possible diligence and attention have been bestowed. Indeed during this whole tour, I have endeav-

120 For the whole subject of Spanish land law, see Houck, *History of Missouri*, II, 214-230. Also *American State Papers, Public Lands*, II, 605-606; III, 607-608; V, 59, 251, 704-705, 709; Stoddard, *Sketches of Louisiana*, 251-252; Scharf, *History of St. Louis, City and County*, I, 321; Eugene Morrow Violette, "Spanish Land Claims in Missouri," in Washington University, *Studies*, VIII, 167-200. For important cases, see Mackay vs. U. S., 10 Peters, 341; Chouteau's Heirs vs. U. S., 9 Peters, 145, 147; Menard's Heirs vs. Massey, 8 Howard, 305; Chouteau vs. Eskhardt, 2 Howard, 349.

oured by the most patient assiduity to remove those prejudices against myself, in common with the other commissioners which some of the settlements have been taught to
entertain. — They complain of delay in the adjustment of
their claims, and of the continual expence which this pro-
crastination occasions. I accounted for the first; to the
satisfaction of the liberal minded and intelligent; and in
order to give them pledges of my own disinterestedness
declined, at this place to receive those recording fees which
I might by Law have demanded. —

TO GABRIEL DUVAL, COMPTROLLER OF THE TREASURY

Sir,   St. Louis 13th Aug 1808.

I had not until yesterday, on my return from the Arkansas the honor of receiving your letter of 28 May last.
The reproof and admonition which it contains shall not be
forgotten in the future settlements of the contingent accts.
of my office. While exercising this government in the
absence of Gov Lewis I was subjected to considerable extra
expenses without additional emolument, and was so far
mistaken as to imagine, that fuel & candles merely for the
Office would be considered as part of the Office rent. I
lament the error & will in future, adhere to the literal
expressions of Mr. Gallatin's orders.

TO THE LAND COMMISSIONERS

Gentlemen,   St. Louis Aug 15. 1808. —

In discharge of the duties imposed on me by your resolution of the —— day of —— last, being a modification of

your previous resolutions on the same subject, I have made the circuit of the lower settlements of this territory. — When descending the Mississippi, the business at Cape Girardeau, at New Madrid and at Camp Esperance was taken up in prime conformity to your order of mission: but not being completed for want of time, and on account of obstacles thrown in my way by factious individuals, I thought it substantially correct to hold an extra session on my return. Your object was to obtain the testimony, and I could not think of disappointing those just expectations by an unnecessary observance of minute forms. Your resolution contemplates my receiving testimony in relation to the claims to lands which lie in the neighbourhood of the Arkansas; but it was also expected that those persons or their Agents, would have attended at Camp Esperance for this purpose. Joseph Stillwell[121] was the only person from that part of the country who met me there, and I conceived it my duty as I was now within 200 miles of their village and about 2/3 of the distance from St. Louis to their principal settlements, to proceed to Fort Madison, where the evidence could be collected with little additional expense to the U States and with no possible inconvenience to the claimants. — I submit to you herewith, the Papers which have been laid before me by the parties concerned as well as those which I have collected from the Public Offices of New Madrid: — together with the oral testimony reduced to writing principally by myself.

There is an Affair, which, to prevent misconstruction I beg leave to mention to you altho' it in no wise concerns the business which you have confided to my management. On my arrival at the Arkansas after the first day of July

[121] Joseph Stillwell was one of the five grantees of Winter's grant,

last, Jno. G. Clark of Natchez and Perly Wallis of Oua-chita[122] Agents for the claimants presented a number of notices to the Recorder dated 29th June. In my private capacity merely I received these Papers, recorded the testimony in relation to them, and informed Mr. Gallatin that they would be carefully preserved subject to any future arrangement which Congress might think proper to make.

M. P. LeDuc, the Translator accompanied me as far as Camp Esperance and performed with diligence and promptness every duty appertaining to his office. On my departure from that settlement, a pleuretic affection which he had sometime previously contracted became so alarming that he found himself unable to prosecute the voyage and remained under the care of Doct Stewart of Fort Pickering.[123]

At the Arkansas I employed Andrew Fagot as a Translator or rather an Interpreter for the occasion. He was recommended to me by gentlemen of the most respectable standing, in that part of the country and is believed to have discharged this temporary trust with fidelity.

***

TO JAMES ABBOTT

SIR,   ST. LOUIS 19. Aug 1808

I take the liberty of enclosing you the record of a demand

---

[122] Ouachita or Washita was located on the Arkansas River in latitude 32° 29′ 37.25″. For an excellent description of the post and the surrounding country, see "A Description of the Washita River, in Louisiana, and the Country bordering thereon, compiled from the Journals of William Dunbar Esq. and Dr. Hunter," in *American State Papers, Indian Affairs*, I, 733.

[123] Fort Pickering was on the Mississippi River two miles below the Fourth Chickasaw Bluff. It was originally called Fort Adams. For a few months in 1797 Merriwether Lewis was in command there.

agt. Mr. William Robison of the House of Robison & Martin for $32.93cts.

The history of the transaction is this — The beginning of last winter Mr. Robison hired a Horse of Joseph Morin[124] to ride to the Belle Fontaine Races; a number of us staid that night at the Cantonments on the Missouri, from which place the horse of Mr. Robison escaped. On his leaving this country, the horse not being then found, he spoke to Major Christy, Capt. Clemson[125] and myself to adjust the business in a proper manner with Morin. *I* agreed to do so — And Christy gave his personal assurances to Morin, who sometime thereafter presented an account of $44, — *I* also lately declined to adjust so exorbitant a demand, and advised Christy to stand a suit. Judgment was recovered as you will find in the record — I then paid the money in the name of Major Christy and obtained his assignment. Be so obliging as to ask of Mr. Robison, the amount of this Judgment. He cannot hesitate in paying it; altho' I must confess that there has been already, a greater delay than I had expected. Probably Major Christy's letters written both before, and after the judgment was rendered, may never have reached him.

Colo. Thomas Hunt died two days ago.[126] The melancholy event has aroused the sympathies of every individual of these settlements who had the pleasure of an acquaintance with his worthy and amiable family. He will be

124 Joseph Morin was a carpenter. In 1795 he was living near St. Louis.

125 For biography of Eli B. Clemson, see Luttig, *Journal of a Fur-Trading Expedition on the Upper Missouri, 1812-1813* (Stella M. Drumm, ed.), 145-146.

126 Billon *(Annals of St. Louis in its Territorial Days*, 225) gives July 17, 1808 as the date of his death.

buried this day at the Cantonments. Most of the Citizens
of St. Louis left town early this morning in order to pay
the last honors to this respectable veteran. I am truly
sorry that the fatigues of a three months excursion to the
lower country from which I have just returned, prevent
my attendance. — I have never heard from you since I
transmitted the powers of Atty that I recollect. — No difficulties have occurred? I congratulate you on the confirmation of your appointment. It was not in my power to be
instrumental in it. —

A PROCLAMATION[127]

Whereas, by the 5th section of an act of the Congress of
the United States entitled 'An act further providing for
the government of the district of Louisiana' passed the 3d
day of March 1805 it is provided that for the more convenient distribution of justice the prevention of crimes
and injuries, and execution of process, criminal and civil,
the Governor shall from time to time, as circumstances
may require, lay out those parts of the territory, in which
the Indian Title shall have been extinguished, into districts, subject to such alteration as may be found necessary, and that he shall appoint thereto such magistrates
and other civil officers as he may deem requisite:

Now therefore, I have thought proper, for the promotion
of these objects to divide the at present too widely extended district of New Madrid, by à line commencing on
the Mississippi, opposite the 2d Bluff, and running, indefinitely, in a due west direction: And I do hereby declare
all that portion of country lying to the south of said line,

[127] Original in the Department of State, B. R. L., 3449.

as far as the 33d degree of north latitude to be, and the same is hereby established as a separate district, to be known and denominated, for all judicial purposes, 'The District of the Arkansas' prohibiting the exercise of the district authorities of New Madrid, beyond, or to the southward of the said East and West line, so as aforesaid established as the northern boundary of the newly created district of the Arkansas.

In testimony whereof, I have caused the seal of the territory to be hereunto affixed. —

Given under my hand at Saint Louis, the twentieth day of August, in the year of our Lord, one thousand, eight hundred and eight, and of the Independence of the United States of America, the thirty third.

By the Governor   Meriwether Lewis

— Seal —   Frederick Bates
                Secy of Louisiana

GEORGE HOFFMAN TO BATES

Dr. Sir,   Michilimackinac, Augt. 23d. 1808.

Many applications will no doubt be made this fall to Gov. Lewis by British subjects for permission to trade with the Indian tribes residing on the West side of the Mississippi. A Mr. Crookes[128] purchased goods at this

---

[128] Ramsay Crooks was born at Greenock, Scotland, in 1787. At the age of sixteen he entered the service of the North West Company. In 1806 he was trading in Wisconsin. In 1807 he came to St. Louis where he entered into partnership with Robert McClellan. In their first trading venture they were balked by the Teton. Crooks became famous because of his connection with the Astoria project. After the failure of that

place — applied to me for a License — The oaths necessary by the tenor of the 15. Sec. of the last Embargo Law was tendered to him — He refused taking it — alledging that he conceived himself an American Citizen, that he was concerned with one Mc.Cleland, an American born, in the Illinois, and that he was in no wise interested or concerned with the Macinac Company, I, therefore, thereupon, granted him a *Common* Clearance.

Mr. Bouthillier[129] also called for a Clearance & made oath that he resided in this Country antecedent to the 1st of July 1796 and has ever since considered himself a Citizen of the U. States, He therefore also obtained a *Common* Clearance — It will I suspect be stated & urged to the Governor that this Crooks is a British subject (which circumstance was not suggested to me until this morning). And that if *he* is allowed to go into Louisiana it will be reprehensible & unpardonable partictily [*sic*] to prevent other Br. subjects trading in that Country — Much Clamour may ensue — I state these facts in order that misrepresentation shall not prevail.

The contents of Gov. Lewis' letter of the 2d June last to the late Mr. Campbell[130] has been communicated to the Macinac Company — therefore in case of infractions they cannot profit by the plea of ignorance — As to Laws, rules & regulations on the subject of Indian trade & intercourse generally they had early, full & correct information. Herewith I transmit to you for your & the Governor's informa-

enterprise, he was long identified with the Astor enterprises. For sketches of him, see *Early Western Travels* (Thwaites, ed.), V, 36-37; *Wisconsin Historical Collections*, IV, 95-102.

[129] Probably François Bouthillier, fur trader and early resident of Prairie du Chien.

[130] John Campbell who was killed in a duel with Redford Crawford.

tion a List of Clearances granted at this Custom house
this year.

R. Dickson[131] has started for the states — It is said for
the purpose of applying at Washington City for the appointment of Indian Agent for the Upper Mississippi — I
have seen & read a paper which you granted him giving
him permission to trade in Louisiana, & have also been
informed that Gov. Lewis feels very thankful & grateful
towards Dickson on account of services rendered by him
to our Government — I fear that neither of you know the
man — He has done what has perhaps advantaged the U.
States — But believe me not from any love he bears our
Country. He is better known here than *elsewhere.* He is
a Br. subject in heart & sentiment — connected in trade
with two powerful & almost overbearing British fur trading
companies — He possesses not the smallest wish for the
happiness of the American people — understands the Indians well; and has great influence over many in the quarter where he heretofore traded & at Laprairie du Chien —
Such an appointment will certainly be an alarming and
dangerous weapon in the hands of an Enemy — Will it
then think you be wise & prudent for our Gov. to appoint
R. Dickson Indian Agent   I have myself no personal or
private antipathy or malice to this man — He will probably
apply to you & the Governor for letters of recommendation — Or perhaps use the testimonials of your high opinion
of him which he now possesses — I write this merely that
you may put your selves on your guard so that our Govt.
shall not be imposed upon. As you understand the duties
of a Collector perfectly it is almost useless to inform you
that the Collector whose application is made for a Clear-

[131] **Robert Dickson.**

ance can have no eye to the Laws on the subject of trade or intercourse with the Indians — This is hinted at because it has been & perhaps will again be pretended by British fur traders that the Clearance of a Collector is all they need — Mr. Reid[132] is just about to depart — I write in haste — I expect to get to Washington City about the 15 of Nov. — On the subject of the duel between Mr. Campbell & Mr. R. Crawford Mr. Reid can give you a detailed account of the whole affair — You may hear false & contradictory reports — Campbell was always an eye sore to some one or all of the Br. traders here. Mr. Reid's information may I think be relied on — . . .

Mr. S. Abbott's[133] compliments to you.

The production, by D., of your Licence to him commenced the quarrel between Campbell & Crawford — Your conduct in having granted it was however neither canvassed nor censured — I haven't time.

[P. S.] We (Mr. Abbott & myself) have also written to Gov. Lewis & Gov. Harrison

---

TO ALBERT GALLATIN

SIR,   ST. LOUIS Aug 28. 1808

I have this day taken the liberty to draw on you in favor of Messrs. Falconer & Comegys for the sum of Three hundred & Sixty dolls. the amount of my travelling allowance while performing a circuit of twelve hundred miles by order of the commissioners for ascertaining & adjusting the titles and claims to Lands in the Territory of Louisiana.

132 James Reid, Mackinac merchant.
133 Samuel Abbott, Mackinac pioneer.

The Certificate of the Coms. accompanies the Draft. In that certificate they have thought it sufficient to state the distance from St. Louis to the Arkansas — and that all my travelling allowances collectively do not exceed the distance between the northern & the southern settlements.

TO ALBERT GALLATIN

SIR,   ST. LOUIS Augt. 28. 1808.

On the 12th of this month I returned to St. Louis, and on the 15th submitted the Report, a copy of which I have now the honor to enclose —

I ask your indulgence while I state some unpleasant incidents which have lately occurred.

Judge Lucas was opposed to the mission of a single member, tho' I hope he had no objections to myself — I had his vote. It is not recollected that he assigned his reasons at the Board. In his subsequent conversations with the People, many arguments were employed to shew the impropriety of the arrangement. I was hurt at *this;* because, if those dissatisfactions had been expressed at a proper time and place, they might have had weight; at least from the very great respect which I have never ceased to feel and to express for his *superior* good sense, and integrity of principle, I should have attended to his observations with the utmost deference. They *might* and probably *would* have over ruled those preferences which I then gave to the plan which was adopted. But left to my own reflections in this business, I considered that our time was now passing away, and that it ought to be economized in every possible manner, consistently with the due dis-

charge of that great trust which the government had confided to us. Indeed, for some days previously to the revision of the first resolution on this subject, I had taken up
an idea that the minds of Judge Lucas and Mr. Penrose,
were made up, and that the Recorder alone would be sent
on this circuit. Besides, I had witnessed during our former visits to the neighbouring settlements the extreme
impatience of the Commissioners to return to St. Louis
and foresaw that should we make this distant tour *collec-*
tively the object would not, in all probability, be accomplished. Permit me to make you the assurance, that the
People are satisfied with the attention, which I have
bestowed on their business, and that I confidently expect
the future approbation of the Board, when it has leisure
to examine critically, the performance of those duties, with
wch. I was charged.

Some few days after my return, I laid on the Table a
resolution for meeting *every day,* instead of every *third*
day. The necessity of this was too obvious to leave room
for reasonable opposition. The proposition was treated
by Judge Lucas with much oblique asperity; but, at length,
after undergoing some amendments was reluctantly acquiesced in. I have been since reproached, as being no better
prepared for decision than my Colleagues. It is very true;
but surely if we intend to do the business at all it was time
that we had commenced it. —

The Judge has frequently spoken of the possible non
extinguishment of the native right, and of other embarrassments, with respect to which we ought to ask information or instruction from you. The suggestion, at this late
hour of the day has not been attended to, and never regularly submitted to the Board. —

I took an early occasion, after several warm and unpleasant conversations to make to the board professions of cordiality, and expressed a wish, that we might as men of business, labor in that great work the accomplishment of which appeared to be expected from us. Judge Lucas reciprocated my conciliatory dispositions with a warmth of feeling so peculiar to him; and I had, at *that moment* no doubt, that the business would go smoothly on. I am willing *still* to *hope* so.

The Recorder has been desired to compile all the Ordinances, Official Letters, Instructions &c. which have relation to the Land Subject. My mornings and evenings are now employed in this research. I shall transcribe them in a bound Book, and accompany the Report with an Index. —

In May last, when going down the river I appointed the Clerk of the Board, my friend Thomas F. Riddick to act in the Recorder's office in my absence. He received previously to the first of July, a considerable number of Claims in addition to those which were made with myself in the lower districts. It is impossible that all these should be yet actually recorded. The work goes on industriously, and I presume that in the meantime, the Board will consider them as sufficiently recorded in contemplation of Law.

Since the arrival of Gov Lewis, I have had no interference in the business of Lead Mines — In one of the Letters which I had the honor to receive from you, it appeared to be expected that the Recorder would still act in that affair under the direction of the Governor. He has, however, with great propriety, I think, and I hope, with your approbation, assumed the whole **management**.

TO GEORGE HOFFMAN

S̄ir,   St. Louis Aug 30. 1808.

.   .   .   .

You desire me to forget those unpleasant occurrences, which for a moment interrupted our harmony. I was surprized at this request, as the differences to which you allude, could not, in their very nature create a permanent alienation. At any rate they have had no such operation on my mind. The interest which I feel in your advancement (because I know that you deserve it) would induce me without hesitation to exert myself in your behalf, if I had influential friends to whom I could without a breach of decorum, address myself on such a subject. But my dear Sir, I have already been admonished on this score — in gentle terms it is true; but in a style sufficiently peremptory, to prevent my making again the fruitless experiment. At Washington these things are not expected from me, except when they relate to that quarter of the country in which I reside — and *then sparingly.* —

You complain of my neglect. That I never answer your letters — In this you wrong mé. I believe I have answered every line which you have done me the favor to write. I recollect particularly well that I chatted with you, for half an hour at least in February last, and even threw out some suggestions, which I believed you would avail yourself of in procuring an exchange of Office.

PERLY WALLIS TO BATES

Dear Sir —   Septr. 1st 1808

Together with every acknowledgement of gratitude For your politeness and attention while at Arkansas I would observe I had a tolerable prosperous Journey to Ouachita and from thence to this place[134] although I have been exercised with the fevre Both then and since I return,d as you will Discover by the shaking of my hand we have had serious work and hard swearing here last week capt Armistead has had his hands head & heart full Burnet has been apprehended for the murder of Patterson and many others have been arraigned for felony and bound to the Peace Burnet is sent to New Madrid gaol I have lent capt Armstead every assistance in my Power which Perhaps was very imperfect as we have not the Laws of the Teritory I should Take it as a singular favour if you would favour us with a coppy of the Juditiary sistem of the Teritory as soon as you conveniently can if one could be furnished for my self bound I will Pay all necessary expence I likewise would observe the People are anxious for our seperation and organization I hope you will Take the earliest opportunity To inform us what is Done concerning our country and if it will not be too great a task amidst a multitude of complexed business which I know you to be ingaged in I would ask the Particular favour of a line to inform me how you Prospered on your Journey up the River when it is Probable the land claims will be adjusted and concerning other matters, whic[h] I have before mentioned Time fails.

TO HENRY DEARBORN

Sir,

St. Louis Sept. 3. 1808.

I have the honor to enclose the copy of an Account rendered to General Clark, on his return to this country. It

----

134 Probably Arkansas Post.

embraces all the money transactions in which I was employed, on his behalf, and has been provisionally accepted by him as correct.

He has been good enough also, to suffer me to include in this account some other bills and disbursements which do not fall properly within his department, as balances had been carried from these latter settlements to the Cr of the Indian Account. By this arrangement he has taken upon himself, the final adjustment at the War Office, of all my disbursements and drafts, as well those, which you have done me the honor to accept, as others which were negociated at Louisville. My absence to the lower settlements of this territory prevented an earlier communication on this subject. —

APPOINTMENTS TO MILITIA OFFICES BY GOVERNOR LEWIS
APRIL 1—SEPTEMBER 30, 1808[135]

Ap 4   Mackay Wherry
      Captain
    Joseph Beaty[136]
      Lieutenant
    James Calloway[137]
      Cornet
    Benjamin Allen
      Burser

Of a troop of Cavalry, in the District of Saint Charles 3d Regiment —

May 16   John E. Hart Lt. Colo. Comdt. of 5th (New Madrid) Regiment
    Stephen Ross Major 1st Bat: of 5th Regiment

[135] Original in Department of State, B. R. L., 3449.
[136] Beatty.
[137] Callaway.

James Trotter Captain in 1st Bat: of 5th Regiment
Robert Trotter Lieut. — 1 Bat: of 5th Regiment
Amos Rawls — Captain — in 2 Bat: of 5th Regiment
Franklin J. Smith Surgeon of the 5th Regiment
Joseph N. Amoureux[138] Pay Master of 5th Regiment
Jacob Jacobs[139]Quarter Master of the 5th Regiment
Thomas Ward Caulk Lieut. in 2d Bat: 5th Regiment
James Faris[140] Ensign in 2d Bat: of 5th Regiment

[May 17]   Alexander McNair Aide de Camp to the Comr.
in Chief with the rank of Major, vice Edwd. Hempstead resigned
Nationiel Pope Judge Advocate for 2d Regiment

June 10   Daniel Richardson[141]
        Captain   of Compy. in 1st
    James Brown Lieutenant   Regiment.
    John Maupin Ensign,

July 11   Zephaniah Sappington Captain in 1st Regiment
Uri Musick[142] Lieutenant in 1st Regiment
Thomas Sappington Ensign in 1st Regiment
Mary Philip Le Duc Lieutenant in 1st Regiment
Andrew Andreville[143] Ensign in 1st Regiment
J. Cottle Captain in the 3d Regiment
John McConnell[144] Lieut. in the 3d Regiment
Peter Teaque[145] Ensign in the 3d Regiment

[138] See letter of Amoureux to Bates, June 6, 1810.
[139] Jacob Jacobs moved from the District of Columbia to the District of Cape Girardeau in 1799.
[140] Farris.
[141] Richardson settled in the St. Louis District in 1803. In 1818 he was one of the representatives of St. Louis County in the assembly.
[142] Uri Musick settled in the St. Louis District in 1805.
[143] Andre Andreville.
[144] John McConnell settled on the Dardenne in 1801.
[145] Pierre Teaque, a resident of St. Charles in 1801.

James (Jacques) Fietto Lieut. in the 3d Regiment
David Bocher Ensign in the 3d Regiment

25 Sylvestre Labbadie[146] 1st Lieut of St. Louis-Dragoons
Francois Valois[147] 2d Lieut of ditto
John Alexr. Mechan jr Cornet of ditto
Peter Chouteau jr Burser of ditto

Aug 4 John Dougherty ⎫ of the 2d troop of
       Burser ⎬ Cavalry in district
    Joseph Baker Cornet ⎭ of Cape Girardeau

Blank Commissions for the following Organization of a
Battalion of militia at the Arkansas, were signed by the
Governor, on the 18th May, and filled by the Secy. when
he visited those settlements in July

Francis Vaugine Major ⎫
Daniel Moony[148] Captain ⎪
Harrold Stillwell Lieu- ⎬ of 1st Company
   tenant ⎪
Tenace Racine Ensign ⎭

Baptiste Cailliot[149] ⎫
   Captain ⎪
Peter Lefeve[150] Lieu- ⎬ of 2d Company
   tenant ⎪
Charles Bougy Ensign ⎭

[146] Sylvestre Labadie, Sr., was a native of Tarbes, France. He came
to St. Louis in 1778. He was a merchant, an extensive landowner, and
preceded Pierre Chouteau as Spanish Indian agent. His son, Sylvestre
Labadie, Jr., was born in 1778. The son speculated extensively in land.

[147] François Valois settled in the St. Louis District in 1790.

[148] Daniel Mooney, captain in the New Madrid regiment in 1812,
major in the Arkansas County regiment in 1814.

[149] Probably Caillot.

[150] Probably Lefevre.

Stephen Vaugine Pay Master	of the Arkensas
Andrew Fagot Judge Advocate	Battalion

Sep 8 Benjamin Wilkinson
Captain
Risden H. Price Lieu-
tenant
John Voorhis Ensign
Francis V. Bouis Burser

of a volunteer com-
pany of Infantry in
town of St. Louis

Secretary's Office
St. Louis September 30th 1808
Frederick Bates
Secy.

APPOINTMENTS TO CIVIL OFFICES BY GOVERNOR LEWIS
APRIL 1—SEPTEMBER 30, 1808[151]

Ap 4 Elisha Goodrich,[152] Justice of the Peace, township
St. Charles, Dt. St. Charles

Jno. E. Hart, Sheriff New Madrid, vice Saml. Hammond declined

Andw. Scott, Justice of Peace, township Big Prairie,
Dt. New Madrid.

Thos. Evans, Justice of Peace, township & Dt. of
New Madrid

151 Original in the Department of State, B. R. L., 3449.

152 In 1799 Elisha Goodrich settled on the Missouri in the District of
St. Louis.

Gèo. Ruddle,[153] Justice of Peace, township little Prairie, Dt. of New Madrid

May 16   Jos. Lewis, Sheriff of Dt. of New Madrid, vice Hart declined to accept

Robert Mc Coy Coroner of the District of New Madrid

John Baptiste Olive Treasurer of District of New Madrid

Thomas Clarke Justice of Peace township Tywapity, Dt. of N. Madrid

Joseph Lafernait Juste. Peace township & Dt. of New Madrid

June 6   John G. Heth[154] Clerk of the Courts of Common Pleas and quarter Sessions, Dist. of St. Charles, vice Robert Spencer removed.

July 7   John G. Heth Justice of Peace townsp. St. Charles, District of St. Charles, vice Janis resigned. —

Andrew Kincade, Justice of Peace for townp. Bon Homme Dt. St. Louis

8 John G. Heth, Treasurer of the District of St. Charles.

25   Mánuel Andre Roche Justice of Peace, township of St. Charles District of St. Charles, vice Francis Duquette resigned. —

Aug 5   Stephen Byrd, Judge of the Courts of common pleas & quarter sessions & of oyer & terminer for the

---

[153] George Ruddell or Ruddle in 1796 had a farm north of Little Prairie. He was a son of Isaac Ruddle of Ruddle's Station, Kentucky.
[154] John G. Heath.

district of Cape Girardeau vice Christopher Hayes deceased.

Benjamin Fooy Justice of the Peace, township of Arkensas District of New Madrid.

George Armistead Justice of the Peace for the township of the Arkensas, District of New Madrid —

The *two* foregoing commissions were dated 18th May — left blank by the Governor, and filled by the Secy. when he visited the Arkensas in the month of July. —

Civil organization on the reestablishment of the district of the Arkensas

Aug 20 Francis Vaugine,	Judges of the Courts of Common Pleas and Quarter Sessions & of oyer & terminer for district of the Arkensas during good behavior for four years.
22 Joseph Stillwell	
22 Charles Refeld	
23 Benjamin Fooy	

Jno. Honey Clerk of the Courts of Common Pleas, Quarter Sessions & of oyer & terminer — District of the Arkensas

John Honey, Treasurer, Recorder and Judge of Probate for the District of the Arkensas

Harrold Stillwell, Sheriff of the district of the Arkensas

Andw. Fagot, Coroner, Just. Peace & Noty. Public, Dist of the Arkensas

Aug 23 John Burk Treat, John Honey and Benjamin Fooy Esquire *directed,* and impowered by dedimus, to administer oaths of office, within and for the district of the Arkensas. —

George C. Sibley, Justice of the Peace, for township of Bon Homme district of Saint Louis. — He resides at Fire Praire. —

Secretary's Office

. St. Louis September 30. 1808

Frederick Bates

Secy.

LICENSES TO TRADE WITH AND TO HUNT AMONG THE INDIANS GRANTED BY GOVERNOR LEWIS, APRIL 1ST — SEPTEMBER 30, 1808[155]

May 2 Ramsay Crooks, partner of Robert McClellan; to ascend the Missouri with provisions for their trading establishment.

11 Charles Dorion; to trade with the Sieux and Iowas at the river Le Moin and on the Missouri.

25 Augte. Chouteau by Agent Henry Deroulier; to trade with the Sieux Bands.

Aug 23 Louis Coignard; to trade on the St. Francis; on White River at the Arkansas, not above Fort Madison; at Little Praire

Sept 1 Francis Robidoux;[156] to trade at the Fire Praire, and (with the permission of the Agent or sub Agent at that place) with the Ottos & Panis. —

---

[155] Original in the Department of State, B. R. L., 3449.
[156] Francis Robidoux for many years was in business in St. Louis.

3   Baptiste Vallet;[157] Joachim Vallet, Baptiste Derwate
and —— Gerlerno; to hunt on the Missouri not higher
up than Fire Praire unless with permission of the
Agent or Sub Agent; to take no more than 15 lb. Powder — & not to go into the Osage River

14   P. Vial,[158] Bapt. Le Beau,[159] Amable Quesnel, Bapt.
Jeamdt, Gab. Morleau; to hunt on the Missouri, on the
same terms limitations as the foregoing —

Sepr 14   F. Piqueure, Jos. Piqueure, J. M. Cardinal,[160]
Ant Lafranchise;[161] to hunt on the Missouri on the
same terms and with the same limitations as the foregoing.

Louis Berthelet, Joseph Quesnel, Francis Embroise,
Bapt. Alary & Bap. Laurens;[162] to hunt on the Missouri — on same terms & with same limitations as the
foregoing.

Francis Ragotte & Chs. Bissonett: to hunt on the
Missouri on same terms & with same limitations as
the foregoing.

Peter Montardy; to trade at the Fire Prairie — and
(if the Agent or Sub Agent at that place *permit)* with
the Sieux, Ottos, Missouris and with the well disposed
Panis. —

24   Etienne Cadron, Patron, Peter Decelle, Jos. Dayon,
Louis Chatelereau, Jacques (Sauvage) Ranga (Sau-

[157] Probably Jean Baptiste Valle, who was made civil commandant
of Ste. Genevieve by Stoddard.
[158] Probably Pedro Vial, who made the trip from Santa Fé in 1792.
For the journal of that expedition, see Houck, *Spanish Régime,* I, 350-358.
[159] In 1809 Baptiste Le Beau had a tavern in St. Louis.
[160] Jean Marie Cardinal.
[161] Antoine La Franchaise.
[162] Probably Jean Baptiste Laurain.

vage) Baptiste Gouniville, Louis & Jos: Le Blanc,
Castor (Sauvage) Peter Plante, Baptiste Greza,
Joseph Rivar, Joseph Greza, Peter Quesnel, Francis
Belford, Joseph Gobey, Baptiste Le Court, & Nathl.
Soucier, to hunt on the Missouri not higher up than
the rock of Arrows on the *right* bank — nor on the *left,*
higher up than the place opposite the Fire Praire;
not to pass westward of a line drawn south from the
Rock of Arrows to the Arkansas, nor to take collec-
tively more than 100 lb. of Powder.

Sep 24 Peter Berger; to hunt on the Missouri, on the
same terms and with same limitations as the foregoing.

Robert Mc Clellan & Compy; to trade at the Fire
Praire, with authority to the Agent or Sub Agent of
that place, so to extend the licence, as to embrace such
portion of the upper country as he (said Agent) may
judge proper. —

Secretary's Office

St. Louis September 30. 1808

Frederick Bates

Secy

TO PIERRE ANTOINE LA FORGE,[163] NEW MADRID

St. Louis Oct 3. 1808.

SIR,   Secretary's Office

Your letter complaining of the unlawful issue of certain

---

[163] Pierre Antoine La Forge was exiled from France during the
French Revolution. With other Frenchmen he settled at Gallipolis, but
in 1791 moved to New Madrid where he acted as interpreter, commissioner of the police, syndic, and officer of militia. After the acquisition
of Louisiana he was appointed civil commander and judge of the New

executions from the Office of the Clerk of the General court,[164] has been received by the Governor. —

His Excellency instructs me to say that you are probably mistaken in the statement which you have made of the transaction. Those suits are said to have been instituted under the Spanish government, and placed on the docket of the general court by order of Captain Stoddard.[165] — At any rate it is an affair in which the Governor is not disposed to interfere. If any wrong has been done or suffered, the general court will, on proper application award an ample redress.

MERIWETHER LEWIS TO JOHN PERRY

SIR,   ST. LOUIS Octo. 10. 1808. —

Complaints of violence and a contempt of the Laws have been lately exhibited against you, and so conclusively sup-

Madrid court of common pleas and quarter sessions. He was ill at the time of the earthquake (1811) and died from exposure.

[164] Section 8 of a law establishing courts of judicature, passed October 1, 1804, provided that, "There shall be holden and kept twice in every year a supreme court of record which shall be called and styled the general court, the sitting of which court shall commence at St. Louis on the first Tuesdays in May and the last Tuesdays in October, yearly and every year." *Mo. Territorial Laws*, I, 60. For amendments, see *ibid.*, I, 59-64, 105-125, 183-184.

[165] Amos Stoddard was born at Woodbury, Connecticut, on October 26, 1762. He served in the Revolutionary War during 1779-1782. After the war he became clerk of the supreme court of Massachusetts. He practiced law at Hallowell, Maine, during 1792-1798. He became a captain of artillery on June 1, 1798. He was appointed to receive Upper Louisiana and acted as governor until the creation of the District of Louisiana. He attained the rank of major in 1807 and in 1812 was appointed deputy-quartermaster. He was wounded at Fort Meigs, and died of tetanus on May 11, 1813. His *Sketches, Historical and Descriptive, of Louisiana* is an invaluable work.

ported, as to render it highly improper, that you should be longer continued in the discharge of public duties.

When an Officer acts in direct opposition to the best and principal objects of his appointment, and perseveres in that opposition, after being warned, cautioned & admonished, it is surely time to inform such misguided Officer, that his services are no longer required.

I do therefore revoke your commission as a Justice of the Peace for the township of Breton, district of St. Genevieve.

TO JOHN BURKE TREAT,[166] TEMPORARY INDIAN
AGENT AT FORT MADISON, VILLAGE
OF THE ARKANSAS. —

Secretary's Office
St. Louis October 1808. —

Sir,

Notwithstanding all the precautions which the Governor has taken for the suspension of intercourse with the Osages, he regrets to be informed that they are still supplied, from your quarter, with military stores. It is particularly said, on authority which cannot be questioned, that a trader of your village, has lately taken into their country two barrels of gunpowder.

I am instructed by his Excellency to require of you, a rigid compliance with the orders formerly transmitted; and to desire that you will employ every exertion, for the detection and punishment of those persons, who either have, or may hereafter, violate those orders. —

The Governor has indeed taken under the protection of

---

[166] The Arkansas factory was established in 1805. Treat became the factor in 1810. *American State Papers, Indian Affairs,* I, 768, 769.

the U. S. those of the great and little Osage who are about to establish themselves at the Fire Praire,[167] on the Missouri. But those arrangements have, for the present, only a local operation: They do not change those hostile relations, which lately subsisted and which still continue, except with respect to those who manifest an amicable temper by joining the Osage-Villages in the Fire Praire, where a garrison is now building[168] for their Security. All others remain out of the protection of the U. S. and the Govr. reiterates those prohibitions of intercourse, which I had the honor to deliver you in July last.

When these differences are adjusted, I shall lose no time, in advising you of so desirable an event.

GEORGE HOFFMAN TO BATES

Dear Friend: Chilicothe, Oct. 21st, 1808.

.   .   .   .   .   :   .

I am just now on my way to Washington City. I have no news to communicate. There is much talk in the State

[167] The region about Fort Osage was known as Fire Prairie. In the treaty with the Osages of November 10, 1808, Fort Osage was to be located on the Missouri, "a few miles above the Fire Prairie." *American State Papers, Indian Affairs*, I, 766; Kappler, *Indian Affairs, Laws, and Treaties*, II, 95.

[168] In June, 1808, General Clark was ordered by the secretary of war to fix on a suitable site for a factory. The place selected was on the south side of the Missouri River about 300 miles from its mouth, near modern Sibley, Jackson County, Missouri. Captain Eli B. Clemson with his company of regular troops, accompanied by George C. Sibley, the factor, ascended the river to erect Fort Osage, or as it was subsequently called, Fort Clark. On September 4 General Clark arrived with a detachment of militia. For the Indian situation and negotiations with the Osages, see Clark to Eustis, February 20, 1810, *American State Papers, Indian Affairs*, I, 765.

about the Embargo. The word Embargo issued from the mouth of almost every Woman & Boy I have met since I entered the settlements, and was often used by men who did not know whether it related to Vessels, Horses or Cornfields. . . .

It is with a good deal of reluctance I make the following request. You are already informed of the death of Mr. John Campbell. After my return to Detroit I was persuaded to become a candidate for the office of Indian Agent for the Upper Mississippi. Sensible that I am far from being perfectly qualified for such an appointment I hesitated long before I agreed to it. The Governor, Major Atwater, brother-in-law to S. R. Bradley, Mr. Sibley,[169] & the officers of Detroit Garrison gave me almost unasked for, very flattering recommendatory letters. Judge Griffin has also written to Governor Harrison requesting him to use his influence in my behalf. Will you venture to befriend me? From your representations Gov. Lewis will perhaps write in my favor. I wrote to you from Macinac soliciting letters but be assured that I did not think of applying for this office until after I had been a week at Detroit. The office of Factor with the usual salary was what I then intended applying for. I have not yet seen Gen'l Worthington nor Doctor Tiffin from both of whom I expect letters ere I leave this place.

Excuse me for having written to you on the subject contained in the latter part of this letter at the same time that I have been acknowledging the receipt of your friendly favor.

The third judge had not reached Detroit when I left

[169] Solomon Sibley.

there, and no one had heard from him since he was appointed.

I have no doubt but that everything the late Mr. Campbell told you respecting James Aird was true. Aird certainly is a British subject, and I know him to be one of the members of the Michilmackinac Company.

He may perhaps from his having resided in the Indian Country previous to the time of the evacuations of the Western & No. Western Posts by the British claim under Jay's treaty all the rights & privileges of an American citizen. But still his interest is connected & interwoven in that of many powerful British fur traders, and he considers himself as one of the King's loyal subjects.

Write to me soon if you please, directed to W. City.

MERIWETHER LEWIS TO JAMES AUSTIN

Sir,   St. Louis Nov 10. 1808.

I have lately received the depositions of St. Gamine Beauvais,[170] Amable Partnay[171] and Louis Grenier[172] in relation to a riot, on the 2d of this month, in which John Perry jr, Saml Perry and others were principally concerned. It would appear to me, from the evidence which has been transmitted, that it would be the duty of a Jus-

---

[170] St. Geminin or St. Gemenin Beauvais was born near Montreal about 1770. He came to St. Louis in his early manhood. On December 5, 1799 Delassus granted him a vacant half block at the north end of the village, and there he built a blacksmith shop. It stood on what is now the northwest corner of Main and Cherry streets. He sold this and in 1807 moved to Ste. Genevieve, but eventually returned to St. Louis.

[171] Probably Amable Partenais who moved from Kaskaskia to Ste. Genevieve. He was living at the latter place as early as 1797.

[172] Louis Grenier was at Mine à Burton as early as 1802.

tice of the Peace to issue his process for the arrest of the offenders. You will therefore be pleased to review the subject, and compel the execution of your warrant, by the aid of the militia of the neighbourhood, if necessary. The delinquents should be bound in heavy penalties to keep the peace, and answer for its late violation, at the next court for the district of St. Genevieve, or otherwise they should be committed to jail.

I desire that you will cause an estimation to be made, of all the Lead Mineral which has been raised on the Lands of the United States, adjacent to the lands of Moses Austin Esquire. After an account has been made of this estimation, you will permit the proper owners, that is, the persons who have dug and raised it, to take it away. And if any resistance be made by an armed force, the militia, are to be called to your assistance, and in the event of a continued forcible opposition, they are hereby ordered to fire on the lawless Banditti, employed in the resistance.

GEORGE HOFFMAN TO BATES

Dear Sir,   Washington City Nov. 15th. 1808.

I reached this place two days ago, and yesterday received your letter of the 30. of August last — the style & contents of which gave me infinite pleasure. My feelings on the subject alluded to by the second paragraph thereof were never other than those of sorrow & regret — for I never entertained dislike nor ill will towards you — On the contrary I felt exceedingly unhappy whenever the circumstance occurred to my recollection, which was frequently, that any part of my conduct should have ever given you cause to suspect either my candour, or my friendship for you — However, thanks to fortune, all, it appears, is now fairly understood; and, we can again go on with the same unreserve & free interchange of idea, & information that we ever did or could have done — And I pray most fervently that all remembrance of the affair may be hurled into oblivion ere this reaches you.

Your reply to my request for letters to your friends is plain, candid and generous — And I believe that I feel as grateful for it as I could have done had you written a quire full in my behalf. I was wrong in soliciting your interference for me — But what is much worse the impropriety was repeated by a letter I wrote to you from Chilicothe in October last. When I wrote from Macinac I had no *particular* object in view — But when I came down to Detroit the argument, flatteries & persuasions of my friends induced me to become a candidate for an office for which I never thought myself sufficiently qualified — Under a belief that you had not only the ability but also the disposition to aid me, whenever you could consistent with propriety, I ventured to invoke your friendship once more. Your last letter is, however, a sufficient and *satisfactory* answer to both my requests.

Yes, my dear friend, I feel very anxious to make an exchange of office — But I have no reason to expect such good luck — I was with the Secy. at War yesterday, who, after reading my letters, informed me that the President did not intend to appoint another Principal Indian Agent for the Upper Mississippi — that he conceived it unnecessary at this time to run the Govt. to the expence incident to such an appointment — that he means to send to that Country merely a Sub-agent with a salary of 5 or 600$. And that a Frenchman of your Country, recommended by Genl. Clarke, was already fixed upon for that purpose —

Of course I said no more on that head — He treated me politely — The residue of the letters I brought, altho' they might possibly be of service in other ways, I shall not deliver. I was at the Treasury office also, but did not see Mr. Gallatin. I set the people there to work at my Accounts which I expect will all be adjusted in the course of two or three days — They are obliged to pass through so many different officers hands that it requires much more time to settle them than one would at first imagine — I shall, before I leave this place, pay into the Treasury all I owe to the Govt. — But whether I shall return to Mac-inac, or what else I shall turn my hands to for an honest livelihood is to me as yet perfectly unknown.

I neither expect nor deserve thanks for this letter for I have written nearly three pages altogether concerning my-self — As to the business of Congress I can give you no more information than the public prints contain — For even the Members of Congress, individually, know no more — They find themselves in a very intricate path. They hardly know what is best to be done — For we can't make successful war against either of the damn'd nations who have so wantonly & grossly insulted & invaded our rights & sovereignty — And the operation of the Em-bargo, it seems, has not brought and is not likely to bring either to a right sense of justice. A total non-intercourse law with both the belligerent powers and their respective dependencies making it felony for any American to have Commercial intercourse with either, or the subjects of either, or to be found aiding or supplying either in any manner, it is thought will be resorted to as the most likely to produce the desired effect — There is little doubt but our Govt. will do France & England all the injury it can —

A Motion is now pending to permit free trade to & from the West India Islands and the Canada's — It will hardly grow into a Law — The subject of the Embargo will hardly be argued before Monday — The Documents which accompanied the President's Message will not all be printed until Saturday.

R. Munroe is here writing in the office of the Treasurer.

OBannon the celebrated heroe of Derne I am informed lies under imputations not very honorable — Such as immense and unwarrantable speculations & peculation during his Command at Macinac — Selling public property of considerable value without authority & disposing of the proceeds to his own private use — Hiring out the Soldiers under his command to Citizens & receiving wages for their services to his use — and of being guilty of many other acts equally dishonest, low and mean — Having seen depositions on the subject I can't well doubt the truth of these charges until he disproves them or some way destroys the credibility of the deponents which I suspect is impossible for him to do — I guess the Laurels he gained under Eaton have withered & faded.

I shall quit this place for Chilicothe in the course of ten or 14 days — I shall be happy to hear from you at Detroit —

JOHN B. C. LUCAS, CLEMENT B. PENROSE, AND FREDERICK BATES TO ALBERT GALLATIN[173]

Sir,   Saint Louis 26th November 1808.

The Board conceive it to be their duty to inform you of the progress made in the business which Government have

[173] The original manuscript is in House Files, 3451.

confided to them. In a great majority of claims in which testimony will be offered all the witnesses have been examined, and the claims laid over for decision, this was conceived by the Board to be the most correct method until the records were completed and before them, as they would then have at one view all the claims of each individual, indeed it was indispensably necessary in the claims of persons under the 2d Section of the Act of 1805 that it might be ascertained whether they claimed any other land in their own name in the Territory: the Recorder has not yet been able to complete his entries in his books, of course he cannot lay his records before the Board. It has been stated to the Board by him that the claims & the written evidences thereof which were entered for record in the course of last June, will on the most moderate computation cover seven hundred and fifty pages of eighteen inch record books. The Recorder having been himself, during the months of June and July engaged in a mission from the Board to the Districts of New Madrid & Arkansas to receive the testimony, hath not been able to return to Saint Louis before the middle of August, it is obvious that some more time hath elapsed before he could have made the necessary arrangements in his office, with respect to the claims that have been entered at his office during his absence, and those that had been put in his hands while he was taking testimony in the before mentioned districts. This together with the increase of business which necessarily followed a revision of all former proceedings will exclude the possibility of making a report this Session of Congress, as was by them contemplated.

It will probably occupy three months to complete the testimony, about nine to make decisions and give certificates, & to make monthly returns, and not less than six to close the business and make report; perhaps it is unnecessary to observe that the provision for compensation of the Commissioners Clerk & Translator ends on the first of January next.

GEORGE ARMISTEAD TO BATES

DEAR SIR   FORT MADISON[174] 30th Novr 1808

Your letter by Mr Honey[175] was handed me by that young Gentl. Mr Mc Farling[176] arrived some time after him   he is now waiting the return of the Arkansas Indians from hunting I presume to give them a talk; he then proposes assending this river with a party of Indians and Militia to bring down the white hunters and traders I believe he will find but very few traders and not one has gone as far as the Osage Indians. I wrote you some time since inclosing a talk of the Osage Indians they have since left this as the Indians East of the Mississippi could not attend to hold a talk untill the spring. I have since been informed by Mr Mc Farling that the Governor is determined to have them drove off this river if they do not of there own accord move to the Mesura in all there talks at this place their was and evident determinat in them never to return they

------

[174] See note 113 above. In his list of government fòrts, Heitman does not mention the Arkansas Fort Madison. *Historical Register and Dictionary of the United States Army, House Docs.,* 57 Cong., 2 Sess., Doc. 446, II, 521.

[175] John W. Honey in 1814 was a partner of Christian Wilt in the ownership of a shot tower near modern Illinois Station. In 1816 he was one of the representatives from St. Louis County in the Missouri territorial assembly.

[176] James McFarlane, McFarling, or McFarlin.

complain much of a Mr Shoto[177] and observed that, it was his wish for them to return that his son would have the benefit of there hunts. It appeared to be the wish of those that visit this post to be at peace with the U. S. and all the Indians. Mr Treat gave them a few presents and they took there leave appearently much pleased, promised to return the horses taken from the hunters last spring and never again to stain the path with blud — I am realy pleased to think that a Verga. will be our next president I have ever herd the amiable accomplishments of Mr Madison an no doubt but what he will follow the amiable qualities of Mr Jefferson god grant he may. A soldier should never interfer or hasard an opinion relative to politiks that they are in duty bound to esteem merit and the virtuus carrectors who are placed at there head

The judges have Excepted there commissions and nex monday we shall have a cort — Mr Mc Farling has excited much allarm among the inhabitants from his threats and bosting authority &c &c the particulars of which I do not realy think worth mentioning as I presume you are acquainted with him — I shall leave this in a few days for Washington I have only to assure you that it will at all times give me pleasure to hear from you, and, beg you to present my respects the Governor

PERLY WALLIS TO BATES

DEAR SIR —   ARKANSAS Decr. 18th 1808

After my compliment to you I send you by Mr Mc Farlin who goes to St. Louis with Claremont[178] an Ossage Chief

[177] Pierre Chouteau.
[178] He was variously known as Clermont or Clermore. His Indian

to gether with a number of his fellows an acount of the Situation of the Inhabitants of this Place The Difficulty occationed by the Depredations of the osage indians and their being Declared out of the Protection of the United States has occationed Serious alarm among those inhabitants who have been acostomed to Depend upon hunting for their subsistance Some few of them I understand have ventered up the river to hunt how far they went I cannot say but most of them returned when the aforsd. Indians came Down there was Ten or Eleven of them came here soon after you lef this Place and Taried considerable Time which would inevitably have been killed by the Chactaws and other Indians had it not been for the vigilanc care and Perservereanc of captain Armistead together with the other gentlemen of this Place they returned and thus have came which were very obstinate about going to St Louis they Declare they have been betrayed cheated and belied but this was the channel through which they would wish to Treat and no other That they were the True and Substantial friends of the white People and they implored their Pity and Protection but the agent have Declared he could not Treat withem Claremont which I believe to be a great and a good man says White Hare and Shoto are his mortal enemies the one be cause his father was the only great Cheaf of Ossages and that Dignity belonged to him (Claremont) and the other because he wished him to leave his village on the Arkansas River and move over to Missori which he never would in consequence of which he had been striped of his Dignity and incapasitated to render that Service to the white People which he other

name was Tawagahe, Builder of Towns. He was the lawful chief of the Osages, but his right was usurped by White Hair while Clermont was an infant.

ways could, for the Truth of which his assertions he call God and the ground to witness who he said were the two greatest Powers That they both heard him and knew he spoke truth but with much perswasion he has agreed to go which I hope may come to a favourable issue and he Permitted to retain his Dignity and return in Time to his village I think this man Deserves attention and has been illy Treated by white hair the People of this country say he has never suffered injury to be Done to the white People when he could Possibly Prevent it and has often risqued his life for that Purpose the People of this Place impatient Desire me to write to you concerning their claims If you have Leisure from business I wish you would write me something concerning them I have sent you a line before concerning The laws of the Territory we have them in manuscript in Part which was sent by Mr. Honey I wish you to inform me by the Earlyest oportunity The event of the Indian Negociation I hope it will soon be so that the Por hunters of this Place may return to the wods (without a breach of the Laws of the United State) to Procure themselves food and cloathing and some thing to Pay their Debts They think it hard to brak of all of a sudden Agriculture will be their object as soon as the Land claims are adjusted and hunting of Little consequence many families have no claims to Land in this country I hope a Land office will soon be open for the sale of land that all may Purchase Time fails.

TO ALBERT GALLATIN

Sir,   St. Louis Dec. 25. 1808.

I fear that in obtruding myself so frequently upon you I have counted too largely on your indulgence. The embarrassing situations in which I have been occasionally placed, appeared to require some explanations; in making which I hope that official decorums have not been violated. With the sincerest personal respect, and a just sense of what is due to the first Officer of the Treasury, I never have adventured to trouble you, with misunderstandings merely personal. If they have ever been mentioned, it was because I thought them so interwoven with the public business as not to be susceptible of a separation from it.

The consciousness of acting under the dictates of the purest convictions is not a sufficient reward: I aspire to the approbation of those who have reposed in me so liberal a confidence. —

Until very lately, the right of the Spanish Lt. Governor as Sub Delegate to make orders of survey after the promulgation of the Intendants' Regulations,[179] was never questioned. The late Board was unanimous in a confirmation of claims of this description. A difference in opinion arises now, for the first time, on this subject, and like all former differences, have degenerated into personal hostility. These regulations were published at St. Louis on

[179] The regulations of the Intendant Morales were put forth at New Orleans in July, 1799. They are in translation in *American State Papers, Public Lands*, V, 731-734. Under the regulations of O'Reilly (February 18, 1770) and of Gayoso (September 9, 1797) the commandants of St. Louis and New Madrid, as sub-delegates of the Governor General at New Orleans, made land grants. The regulations of Morales placed the granting of lands in the hands of the Intendant. Several of the Spanish officials insisted that the Morales regulations were never in effect in Upper Louisiana, and certainly many grants were made by the officials of Upper Louisiana after the promulgation of the Morales instructions. The question of the legality of these grants was one of the knotty problems which had to be solved by the commissioners. For excellent discussions of the entire subject, see Houck, *History of Missouri*, II, 214-230; Violette, "Spanish Land Claims in Missouri," in Washington University, *Studies*, VIII, 167-200.

the 6th Feby 1800 from which time until the 1st of October following I have been of opinion that the Lt Governor, in capacity of Sub Delegate of the Intendency (as recognized in the preamble to the 38 articles of Morales) *did possess the power to order the survey.* In this opinion Mr. Penrose concurs, tho', as he is pleased to say, for very different reasons from those which I have assigned. I do not know what his reasons are, but *this,* with a thousand other circumstances of a similar kind, afford me the painful assurance, that tho' we agree in sentiment an unhappy spirit of repulsion, or perversity of temper will incessantly divide us. Judge Lucas is greatly and decidedly opposed to these orders, and has employed all the vast resources of a fertile fancy, in combating them.

I take the liberty to enclose you the translation of one of those orders, which so far from being a contradiction of the Articles, is, as I think, a practical commentary, demonstrative of the course marked out by the Intendant, as far as circumstances permitted that course to be trodden. —

The 15th Article,[180] on which the Judge principally relies, says 'All concessions shall be granted in the name of the king, by the General Intendant, who will order the surveyor &c.' I take this Article, however, merely as a declaration of the manner, in which the *complete title* will issue, and not as a restraint of that power, which the Sub Delegates

---

[180] Article 15 read as follows: "All concessions shall be given in the name of the King, by the general intendant of this province, who shall order the surveyor general or one particularly named by him to make the survey, and mark the land by fixing bounds, not only in front but also in the rear; this ought to be done in the presence of the commandant or syndic of the district, and of two of the neighbors, and these four shall sign the *proces verbal,* which shall be drawn up by the surveyor." *American State Papers, Public Lands,* V, 733.

(formerly the subordinate officers of the civil and military government) were expected to exercise. These officers formed a part of the Intendancy, and transacted matters of detail within their respective limits. They *commenced,* but did not *perfect* the title and the head of the department might, no doubt, order a re survey, if he was dissatisfied with the original. If all the requisites of this Article were complied with, the claimant would have nothing to ask from our government. His title would have been complete without its interposition. But it is now our business to do that which the Intendant would have done, under the late order of things: to foster and mature those germs which our Predecessors planted; to grant confirmations to those who by three years residence and cultivation had acquired the right of domain.

The Lt. Governor, as Sub Delegate had the initiative, by virtue of his office, as appears by the 2d Article[181] of the Regulations; and this *initiative,* tho' not a *'Concession'* as mentioned in the 15th Article, assumes the language of one, as a bill assumes the language of the Law, before it acquire the constitutional sanctions.

If this construction be a false one, the Regulations of Morales are impracticable. The policy of the Spanish Government was to create in Louisiana, population, industry and a market, which might relieve them from a precarious

[181] The second article read: "To obtain the said concessions [grants for newly arrived families], if they are asked for in this city [New Orleans], the permission which has been obtained from the governor to establish themselves in the place ought to accompany the petition, and if in any of the posts the commandant at the same time will state that the lands asked for are vacant and belong to the domain, and that the petitioner has obtained permission of the government to establish himself, and referring to the date of the letter or the advice they have received." *American State Papers, Public Lands,* V, 732.

dependence on the United States, for indispensable supplies. For the promotion of this object, liberal inducements were held out to those Americans who would establish themselves as Planters or Farmers in the province. I cannot conceive, that it was the intention of government to compel these People, on their arrival in the country to suspend their labours, until an order of survey could be procured from the Intendant at the distance of fifteen hundred miles. And no man I presume, would think of making expensive establishments until his limits were permanently ascertained.

The principle for which I contend, accomplishes the object contemplated in your instructions of 2d of April 1807 the 'Confirmation of all equitable claims' founded as in the instances before us, on *good faith,* less in their quantity than *800 arpens* and supported by actual *residence* and *cultivation.* It is, I think impossible that either the interests or honour of our government, should be compromitted by this *just,* and at the same time, *cautious* and *guarded* construction. On the other hand, the idea of Judge Lucas, would in its operation, be greatly injurious to those claimants, under the orders of Colo. Lassus,[182] who settled subsequently to the 6th of° Feby and before the 1st of Oct. 1800 and who did not happen to inhabit on the 20th of Decr. 1803. No provision is made for these People, in our statutes, and the Spanish Regulations will not embrace their case, if we deny to their claims a legal commencement. For no equity can be extracted from those preten-

---

[182] Charles Dehault Delassus arrived at New Orleans in 1794. In 1796 Carondelet appointed him commandant at New Madrid. In 1799 De Lemos appointed him lieutenant-governor of Upper Louisiana, a position which he held until the transfer to Stoddard in October, 1804.

sions which were *ab initio*[183] contrary to the usages of the country. *This,* confirms me in the supposition, that government has anticipated the decision of this question, and intended that there should be no discrimination between the orders of survey made *before* and *after* the promulgation of the Intendant's Regulations, unless special frauds, either proven or suggested, should cast a darker veil of suspicion over the *one* than the *other,* and thus create an accidental difference which did not exist in principle.

At the instance of Judge Lucas, and to the disappointment of the wishes of Mr. Penrose, I have consented to the postponement of these claims till the 15th of March, during which time we shall be employed on cases of unquestioned merit, and on which no difference of opinion is expected to arise. This deference I thought due to the Government, who, if we are wrong will set us right, and prevent the unpleasant business of revision.

A claim of *400* arpens[184] founded on a concession or order of survey of the Lt. Gov: has been lately confirmed. Habitation and cultivation for about nine years were proven. Judge Lucas opposed it, and protested on the minutes, — as the order contained a condition for the building of a Bridge, which condition had never been performed. It was my opinion that the Ordinances had prescribed the terms of contract between the Government and the settler and that additional obligations created by the Lt. Governor, (The Claimant indeed himself proposed this condition in his Petn. to the Lt. Gov: but it is known that these Papers were always dictated by the Govt: Agents) ought by us

[183] *Ab initio,* from the beginning.
[184] "The arpent is to the statute acre nearly in the proportion of eighty-three to one hundred." Bradbury, *Travels,* in *Early Western Travels,* V, 196.

to be disregarded, when the claim was of no greater extent than the individual might have demanded, for himself and family under the provincial policy. This is the spot, on which the town of Herculaneum, has been lately laid out, at the mouth of the Joachim.

I do not know by what authority it has been familiarly spoken of here, that the board would probably be reformed, on the model of those on the east of the Mississippi,[185] with a design to suppress that acrimony and those fervors of parliamentary debate, which have heretofore, as is alledged, retarded the public business, and contributed to keep alive the flame of former animosity. Should it be my fate to give place to some more deserving Officer, my chief mortification would arise, not, assuredly, from the loss of Office, but from the displeasure of those, whose good opinion I have been so solicitous to deserve. I have never for a moment forgotten, that my country pays a high price for my services, and that those services should be faithfully rendered to her, — or rather that she confides in my honour and that I have no right to disappoint her.

Thomas F. Riddick the Clerk of the Board has more than justified that favorable opinion, which was at first entertained of him. He is a man of business and continues to give new proofs of his capacity. His friends mistaking my standing at Washington, have pressed me to recommend him as Receiver of Public Monies when that

---

[185] For Indiana Territory an act of congress of March 26, 1804 established three land offices, one at Detroit, one at Vincennes, and one at Kaskaskia. For each office a register and receiver of public monies was to be appointed. For each district the register and receiver were to be commissioners for examination of claims based upon French and British grants. The various boards were to meet in their districts on or before January 1, 1805 to hear claims. U. S., *Statutes at Large*, II, 277-278.

Office should be created. To these solicitations I have replied that I well know the worth of Mr. Riddick; his qualifications for the Office and his attachment to the government; but that I had no influence and that the Secretary of the Treasury, to whom alone, I could write, did not expect to hear from me on such subjects.

GALLATIN TO THE SPEAKER OF THE HOUSE OF REPRESENTATIVES[186]

TREASURY DEPARTMENT
January 5th 1809

SIR,

I have the honor to enclose the copy of a letter from the Commissioners appointed to settle the land claims in Louisiana; from which it appears that they cannot complete the business within the time fixed by law, and apply for a continuation of compensation. Their case is similar to that of the Commissioners West of Pearl river in the Mississippi Territory who acted several months after the time during which they were entitled by law to compensation had expired. The Register of that district still urges the justice of the claim; & so far as relates to himself, no officer is better entitled to an allowance for the time abovementioned, if the principle shall be admitted in any one case.

JOHN W. HONEY TO BATES

ARKANSAS 12th Jany. 1809

DEAR SIR

His Excellency Meriwether Lewis having done me the honor of entrusting me with several offices of trust in this

[186] Original in the Treasury Department, Mail "E," 3455.

District, Considering myself at present a Citizen of the same, I consider it my duty to 'make known the several inconveniences which the Citizens of this District labour under at present and also those which they have laboured under (and which I am afraid are not entirely removed) at least such as has come to my knowledge, And having a more particular personal acquaintance with yourself than with his Excellency, and doubting whether he is at present in St. Louis I take the liberty of addressing you on the Subject. In the first place I shall endeavour to give you an account of Mr. James Mc Farlane who was sent on here by the Governor on a special Mission to regulate the trade and Intercourse the several tribes of Indians in this quarter.

Having engaged a passage with Mr. Mc Farlane from St. Louis to Arkansas he was very particular before leaving St. Louis in requesting that I would not mention to any person whatever, the cause of his Mission or to what place he was bound thinking that perhaps his business might be of a secret Nature But in reality not knowing the cause of his Mission I was particular in not mentioning it to any person untill after we had left St. Louis. In few day however finding that he did not keep the secret himself But told it and braged of his importance to every person we met with, I no longer considered myself bound to keep my tongue tied any longer But mentioned to several persons here the oppinion I had of Mr. Mc Farlane and the cause of his Missions which I heard him repeat more than once in descending the Mississippi —

I accompanied Mr. Mc Farlane as far as the river St. Francois where having hired two men and Bought a small Canoe I came on immediately to this place and he ascended

the St. Francois where having remained for some Days at
the risk of his life he returned down the St. Francois and
came to Arkansas. Finding Mr. Mc Farlane to be rather
illiterate and knowing that he boasted of more authority
than he really was clothed with I was suspicious that during his Stay up the St. Francois he had Committed some
unlawfull act which would be a disgrace to himself and
perhaps prejudice some people against the good and amiable man who sent him among us, impressed with this idea
I took the Liberty of enquiring how he succeeded among
the Cherokees and obtained the following account from
himself in presence of several respectable Gentlemen in this
place among whom was Capt. George Armistead.

Mr. Mc Farlane ascended the St. Francois without any
thing particular occuring, But on his arrival at the Cher-
okee Village he found that a Certain Mr. Jones of Vincennes had sent a Considerable quantity of Merchandise
to their Village among which was about six Barrells of
Whiskey which he found in the hands of their Chief Named
Connatoo, he immediately attached them in the Name of
the United States as Goods belonging to an illicit trader,
but thinking that he might take them away as well another
time this mighty man of reason left them in the hands of
the identical Man from whom he took them and in the hands
of a man that was interested in the sale of them and who
had been selling whiskey to the rest of the Indians ever
since he first received them in so much that all the Indians
were drunk on Mr. Mc Farlanes arrival among them and
continued so untill his departure.

But his Career among the Indians does not cease here he
found among them a white man who the Indians informed
him had been marking out several tracts of land and had

told them that the land did not belong to them — meaning the Cherochee But that it belonged to their great father the president of the United States who gave him leave to mark out the land and reside among them as he had done. Mc Farlane instead of taking that man and bringing him to a Court of Justice where he might have a fair and just trial he took him without any process whatever and I say without Justice (for it all ways has been a principal among Americans that a man is entirely inocent let him be accused of what Crime whatsoever untill he is found guilty by his Country) and having disarmed him of his Gun and Cut a whip Mc Farlane drew his dirk approached the man & ordered him not to move upon pain of instant Death when he gave him as he observed about forty stripes well laid on.

Mr. Mc Farlane left the Cherochee nation and descended the St. Francois on his arrival at the little prairree at the mouth of that river this Enlightened Stateman in endeavouring to inforce the Laws of his Country as he thought, tho in too rough a manner got himself into another Scrape I will not attempt to discribe it to you for I dare say he will make it known himself at St. Louis and you will have a better oppor. of knowing more concerning his Conduct.

He arrived here in Arkansas about the 23d — 24th or 25th of November last where he has produced universal terror, a few day after his arrival here he demanded thirty men from Capt. Armistead the then Commanding Officer at this poste and gave out that he should go with those men together with the Militia and Indians reconnoitour the woods and Drive every hunter home, that if they made the least resistance he would tie them and whip at the first tree he should find, a Messenger was sent to the hunters by some of the Inhabitants as I have understood to inform them of the intentions of Mr. Mc Farlane the hunters hearing this and that all their property was to be Confiscated many of them returned to Arkansas terrified almost to Death expecting that otherwise they would have been sent home in Chains. —

He threatened to take our sheriff, and our judges away with him in order to bring down these hunters and as to myself he threatened to put me, (I having taken the liberty of telling him I would not obey his Commands) into Prison if I did not —

Some time before he left this which was on the 15th of December a Party of the Ossage Indians consisting of about ten men came to this place in order to hold a Counsel with Mr. Treat. Mr. Treat in his Counsel advised them to go to St. Louis with Mr. Mc Farlane the Indians said that they were afraid of the Cherochees and other nations with whom they were at war, But Mc Farlane having assured them that while he was with them no person dare lay hands upon them! they Consented and left this place with him, and got as far as the Cherochee village on the St. Francois river where (as I understood by a Gentlemen immediately from there) the Osage Indians were detained by the Cherochees who said that the whites had been triing a long time to make peace between the red skins But had never succeeded and as they had the Osages then there they would keep them untill they could assemble the Shawnees, Delawares, Chicasaws and Choctaws to trie to make a peace among themselves and the Osages say as Mc Farlane has brought them into trouble they will keep him untill he take them out so that there is an embargo laid on him he has his foot in the fire and I doubt very much whether he knows how to get it out, the Indians call him a liar and say that he is sent on here by Choutcau who they believe is the cause of their being Declared out of the protection of the United States. —

Of Mr. Mc Farlane I'll say no more the subject is so mysterious and there is so many instances of his absurd Conduct that I do not know where to begin or end But was I with you I could tell you more about him than you can possibly imagine —

Mr. Fooy[187] excepted his Commissions, I administered to him the oaths of office and came on here as quick as possible But can assure that my passage was not very short, I arrived here on the 15th of November last and on the Day after my arrival here I waited on Mr. Charles Refeld for whom I was the bearer of a Commission appointing him a Judge of the Court of Common pleas of this District But he immediately refused acceptance though not without expressing his Gratitude in the highest term and with many Gestures to the Governor for the honor which he done him in placing so much Confidence his Integrity and abilities, Mr. Vaugine and Stillwell[188] excepted But knowing them not to be (tho very good men) very well acquainted with the proceeding in Courts I was particular in making enquirees for a suitable person to recommend to the Governor in place of Mr. Refeld, Mr. Daniel Mooney has been frequently mentioned to me and I am Confident that there is not an other who would please the Citizens of this District more to see on the Bench of Justice, Neither do I believe there is one more worthy of the trust, Mr. Vaugine

---

[187] Benjamin Fooy, a surveyor then located at Esperanza, modern Hopefield, Arkansas.

[188] Probably Harold Stillwell, a lieutenant in the New Madrid regiment in 1812.

and Stillwell will write by this opportunity and they being better acquainted with Mr. Mooney than myself will give you a better account of him

The Governor having neglected to give me Commissions for Commissioners of rates and Levies and not having had an opportunity of obtaining a Copy of the Law regulating the same no property has been assessed and no taxes collected Mr. Vaugine will recommend some persons in his letter as Commissioners and Mr Bates will greatly oblige the District if he will send on Commissions by the first favourable opportunity together with the Law regulating rates and levies —

The papers with which you entrusted me I delivered to Mr. Treat and took up your receipt which I send enclosed.

By a Gentleman from Oautchitau I learn (tho from what source he derives his information I know not) that war has been declared between the U S. and France that George III of Great Britain is Dead and that George IV has ascended the throne.

I am sorry that I have no news very interesting. . . .

P. S. enclosed I send you a piece of poetry[189] composed by a Gentleman of this place which I presume you will understand without any remark I forgot to observe that we have no seals for this District —

LEASE OF SALTPETRE CAVES TO WILLIAM MATHERS

This Contract made and entered into at Saint Louis the 23d day of February one thousand, eight hundred and

[189] The poem is missing.

nine, between His Excellency Meriwether Lewis, Governor
of the territory of Louisiana, on the one part, and William
Mathers Esquire of the other part, witnesseth, that for and
in consideration of the stipulations herein after mentioned
the Governor on his part engages that the said William
Mathers shall, for the term of twelve months from the date
hereof, have, hold, use, occupy, possess and enjoy four
lots of ground of twenty acres each, all of which are above
the mouth of the little Meramec, and lie on both sides of
the main river of that name — and embrace, *each,* as said
Mathers alledges, a Salt-Petre-Cave, the property of the
United States: — And the Governor engages that the said
Mathers shall, during the said term, be permitted to make
use of as much of the timber and fire wood of the United
States, to be found on their adjacent lands, as may be sufficient for the establishments, which he said Mathers, shall
make, at the several caves above mentioned.

And the said William Mathers, on his part, engages, and
binds himself, his Heirs, Executors and administrators, in
consideration of the above Lease, to pay to Meriwether
Lewis Governor as aforesaid, or to his successors in office,
the sum of Five hundred dollars, money of the United
States, — With these conditions, nevertheless, that if the
said William Mathers, shall manufacture the Salt Petre
of the said Caves, in conformity with such regulations, as
the Government of the United States, may think proper
to establish; if he shall furnish to the United States all the
Salt-Petre, which he shall make or cause to be made at the
said Caves, at such prices as government may determine
on, not less than seventeen cents per pound; if he shall
not dispose of any of the Salt Petre to any person, until
the pleasure of government shall be known; and, if he shall

(in the event of government's declining to take the Salt Petre, at the rate of seventeen cents per pound or the gun powder manufactured therefrom, at the rate of fifty — cents per pound, which they stipulate for the privilege of doing) give to the Governor, quarterly, a just and true account of the quantity of the Salt Petre manufactured at the said Caves, and pay to him, for the use of the United States, at the town of St. Genevieve or St. Louis to such agent as said Lewis shall appoint to receive the same, five per cent of the Salt Petre so manufactured, *then,* to wit, on a compliance with these several conditions, the obligation which the said William Mathers has herein before taken upon himself, to be void, else to remain in force.

It is moreover stipulated between the parties that if it should appear that those lots or either of them is or are the private property of any person or persons or claimed as such before the Board of Commissioners, this lease is to be thenceforth void as to such lot or lots. It is also to be void on the forfeiture of any of the conditions of the foregoing obligation. —

In witness whereof, the parties have set their hands to duplicates hereof, at St. Louis, the day and year first above written.

Sealed and delivered   Meriwether Lewis (Seal)
    in presence of   Wm Mathers (Seal)
    Wm Clark
F. Bates as to
Wm. Mathers

TO ABRAM MUSICK[190]

Sir,   St. Louis April 1. 1809

I send herein enclosed, the Certificate of the Commissioner confirming to you 400 arpents of Land on Bon Homme.

If you are desirous of conveying this Land to Mr. Lewis, as I think you mentioned to me, you have only to execute the deed with reference to the Certificate of confirmation; — acknowledge the same before a Justice of the Peace, and deliver all the Papers to Mr. Lewis. — He will then, at his leisure present them to me in exchange for a Patent Certificate.

TO CAPTAIN JAMES HOUSE, BELLEFONTAINE

Secretary's Office
Sir,   St. Louis April 13. 1809.

By order of Gov Lewis, I take the liberty to enclose you a Commission for Mr. Pryor as a Justice of the Peace for the township of Cuivre,[191] district of St. Charles. Also, a Dedimus by which you are empowered to administer his oaths of Office. —

I also take the liberty, at the instance of the Governor, to transmit you two letters, which it is said have relation to a Deposition, which Mr. Kingsley is expected to give in an affair at law, in the Indiana. —

190 Abram or Abraham Musick was from Albemarle County, Virginia. During the Revolutionary War he served as a spy on the North Carolina frontier. In 1797 he was living in the Bon Homme district.
191 Now in Audrain County, Missouri.

I hope you will have the goodness to attend to this business. If certificate of the qualification of Mr. Pryor be forwarded to me, together with the Deposition I shall be enabled to give assurances to the Court, in which the suit is depending, that the forms have been complied with —

EXTRACT FROM A LETTER TO RICHARD BATES

DEAR RICHARD: April 15, 1809

I have spoken my wrongs with an extreme freedom to the Governor. — It *was* my intention to have appealed to *his* superiors and *mine;* but the altercation was brought about by a circumstance which aroused my indignation, and the overflowings of a heated resentment, burst the barriers which Prudence and Principle had prescribed. We now understand each other much better. We differ in every thing; but we will be honest and frank in our intercourse.

I lament the unpopularity of the Governor; but he has brought it on himself by harsh and mistaken measures. He is inflexible in error, and the irresistable Fiat of the People, has, I am fearful, already sealed his condemnation. Burn this, and do not speak of it.

TO JAMES ABBOTT

DEAR SIR,   ST. LOUIS Ap 20. 1809

.   .   .   .

I am happy to hear of the smoothness & exemption from difficulty with wch. you are about to complete the Land-Business. Ours cannot be finished in less than 18 mos. —

Our personal quarrels retard the adjustment. We have a mighty stir & bustle about Indian War; but those who are best acquainted with Indian matters, say, there is no danger — There certainly is none except in the event of a British War. Accept my best wishes for your prosperity & happiness.

JOHN COBURN TO BATES

Dear Sir,   St Genevieve May 2d 1809

By the time you receive this line, you will have seen Doct Farrar[192] who will inform you of the unpleasant trip we have had on his return home.

I return my sincere thanks to you for the use of your horse; and regret that he should not be in better order. The continued rains and the badness of the roads will reduce any thing formed of flesh. I assure you my best exertions have been used to treat him well.

The Gen. Court met on Monday, and determined to adjourn; my impression is, that by continuing the Court open, we should have embarrased the inhabitants of the Territory; between their business as Suitors, Witnesses & Jurors, and their Services as Militia Men. —

I am induced to believe we should have been instrumental in defeating the projected expedition; and have performed

[192] Dr. Bernard G. Farrar was born in Goochland, Virginia, in 1785. The Farrar family moved to Kentucky. After studying medicine in Philadelphia, Dr. Farrar located at Frankfort, Kentucky. Judge Coburn, his brother-in-law, was appointed a judge of the Territory of Louisiana, and this caused Farrar to locate at St. Louis in 1807. In 1810 he fought a duel with James A. Graham, a young lawyer. Graham's injuries eventually proved fatal. In 1812 Farrar was elected to the territorial assembly. In 1815 he helped to found the *Western Journal.* In 1817 he served as surgeon at the first Benton-Lucas duel.

very little business in Court, provided we had not adjourned.

Under this conviction I was averse to placing obstacles in the way of the orders of the Executive. How far the safety of the Territory is endangered by the movements of the Indians, I am unable to say; But I am convinced the cautionary steps taken in the defense of the Territory are highly proper. It would afford me pleasure to have seen you, but I shall return to Kentucky without delay. —

TO ROBERT SMITH, SECRETARY OF STATE

Secretary's Office

Sir,   St. Louis May 20. 1809

I have the honor to transmit for the information of the President the copies required by the 2d Sec of the 'Act further providing for the government of the district of Louisiana.'

The Report should have been made on the 1st day of April last — I pray you to pardon the delay.

The Executive proceedings of the six months preceding that day were so inconsiderable as to be made up in a few moments; but I thought it best not to transmit them, unaccompanied by the Laws.[193] These latter were in press and I had weekly assurances of being supplied with a copy. Some accidental derangement in the business of the Printer delayed the completion of the work, much longer than was expected.

[193] Fifteen acts were passed between October 1, 1808 and April 1, 1809. See *Mo. Territorial Laws*, I, 195-236.

The General Orders and other military arrangements, are not deposited for record in my Office.

TO GEORGE HOFFMAN, COLLECTOR, MACKINAC

D<small>R</small> S<small>IR</small>,   S<small>T</small>. L<small>OUIS</small> May 25. 1809

Mr. Cheney will hand you this letter. He is a gentleman of very respectable standing in our town and merits on his own account, rather than on my recommendation, every civility which you can show him.

I had the pleasure to receive by last Post, yours of the 7th March, from Detroit. The restoration of our commercial relations with G. Britain, which takes place the 10th of next month, will fix you permanently at Mackinac.

I have a two fold pleasure in congratulating you on this desirable event, the prosperity of our country and the promotion of your individual interests.

I will give some account of Louisiana very soon — Ill health and a pressure of business now prevent me.

TO RICHARD BATES

S<small>T</small>. L<small>OUIS</small> July 14, 1809. —

When yr. Friend Stuart[194] arrived in town he called at the Land Board before the usual hour of the meeting of the commissioners & left yr. letter with the clerk. I waited

---

[194] Alexander Stuart was a Virginian. He practiced law at Kaskaskia as early as 1806. He was an intimate friend of Governor Lewis and was one of the three executors of his estate.

on him in the afternoon of that day & on the following morning, pressed him to call on me and in fact tendered to him all those civilities which were due to yr. request and to his merits. Notwithstanding which I was not favored with a visit until yesterday. We live indeed in different parts of the town & at considerable distance from each other. Besides which I have attached myself to the French circles into which he appears to avoid an introduction. The Seat of the Illinois Government (Kaskaskia) is no more than 60 miles from this place, on the other bank of the river. The Judge has procured apartments in our town, and appears to be permanently settled among us. — He will get office here as soon as he can.

Gov Lewis leaves this in a few days for Phila. Washingn &c. He has fallen from the Public esteem & almost into the public contempt. He is well aware of my increasing popularity (for one scale sinks as the other rises, without an increase of gravity except comparative) and has for some time feared that I was at the head of a Party whose object it would be to denounce him to the President and procure his dismission. The Gov: is greatly mistaken in these suspicions; and I have accordingly employed every frank & open explanation which might have a tendency to remove that veil with which a few worthless fellows have endeavoured to exclude from him the sunshine. He called at my Office & personally demanded this explanation. It was made with that independence which I am determined shall mark my conduct on all occasions; and accompanied with an assurance that the path of life, which I had long since prescribed to myself did not admit of prevarication. As a Citizen, I told him I entertained opinions very different from his, on the subject of civil government, and that those opinions had, on various occasions been expressed with emphasis; but that they had been unmixed with personal malice or hostility. I made him sensible that it would be the extreme of folly in me to aspire above my present standing: that in point of *Honor,* my present Offices were nearly equal to the government and greatly superior in *emolument* — And that the latter could not, from any motives of prudence be accepted by me, if offered by the President. 'Well' said he 'do not suffer yourself to be separated from me in the public opinion; When we meet in public, let us, at least address each other with cordiality.' My very humanity, yielded a prompt assent to this Request, and for this I am resolved to take every opportunity of convincing the People that however I may have disapproved & continue to disapprove the measures of the *Governor,* that as a *man,* I entertain good opinions of him. He used me badly, but as Pope says 'Twas when he knew no better' — In one particular case when he had determined to go to Washington (tho' he did not go) he left certain Executive Business to be performed by *Genl. Clark;* tho' the Laws have expressly provided for his absence. I waited on His Excellency & demanded that the General should be called in. The Gentlemen were then told that I would suffer no interferences &c. &c. &c. — How unfortunate for this man that he resigned his commission in the army: His habits are altogether military & he never can I think succeed in any other profession —

When I sat down to write this letter, I intended that it should have been a very short one; but since I have gone so far into a relation of my misunderstandings with the Governor, I will briefly state to you those contests which for the last 11 months I have been obliged to maintain with my colleague Judge Lucas.[195] You have heard of this man: He was formerly a member of Congress from Pittsburgh & a Judge of one of the circuit courts of Pennsylvania. He was never my friend, since I began to gain a little credit at Washington; and commenced his attacks (in business I mean & shielded by his official character) on my return from the lower districts, last year. It was imagined by the whole country that I had done my duty faithfully — & this *good word* was sufficient to excite all the angry malignity of the Judge. He attacked my Report which was contained in three quires of Paper, & which was no doubt, in many respects defective with so much precipitance, as not to discover its vulnerable points, and it had the good fortune to triumph, at length, over all his censures. Foiled in this object he commenced a system of poignant pleasantry at *some times,* and of sarcasm at *others* by which he has frequently raised a storm from which he has been willing enough to retreat. A winter campaign was carried on with vigilance & activity on both sides — but at length the People so unanimously took part with me as to reduce the Judge to silence, except at long intervals. — He is indeed a man of superior order, but so completely the child of passion the creature of impulse, as to run every hour into the grossest & most palpable inconsistencies. He has absolutely no attachments & his animosities are immortal. He is capable of the darkest & most desperate intrigues, yet a skilful antagonist may, at all times develope his machinations & draw him from his ambitions by playing on those passions which have of late become too strong for his Control.

195 About three thousand claims were decided by the commissioners. For these decisions and the votes of the commissioners, see *American State Papers, Public Lands*, **II**, 388-603.

C. B. Penrose, the other Commissioner, as he has been always accustomed to lean on some body, rests for the present on Lucas, from whom he fears to differ in opinion, on any question of moment. P. is, indeed a man of sense, but too weak minded & versatile to be entrusted with the transaction of important business. When Lucas & myself quarrel, as we had the indecorum to do last winter, before crowded Audiences of Claimants, Penrose had the good sense to hold his tongue. He is however a willing Dupe & shares with Lucas the public execrations. These two men have treated the People with so much harshness & travelled out of their own sphere with so little dignity, that the most respectable individuals of the country have been on the point of compelling them to cross the Mississippi. Their insolence of Office is boundless; their usurpation of power unparalelled. The U. States have counsel at the Board a Lawyer by profession and in all respects worthy of the trust reposed in him: Yet they take the business out of his hands; they plead the cause & pronounce the doom of affluence or poverty afterwards. They voted the necessity of the commissioners personally making a survey when the U. States have surveyors[196] (very intelligent ones too) regularly appointed for that object: But on my refusal to accompany them, they shrunk from the ridicule of such wanton and illegal interference and rescinded the order. —

[196] By act of congress of February 28, 1806 the surveyor general was given authority to have surveys made of the United States lands in the Territory of Louisiana to which Indian title had been or might be extinguished. It was his duty to appoint skilled surveyors as his deputies, one of whom was to be designated as the principal deputy. The principal deputy was to reside in and keep an office in the territory, and under the general superintendence of the surveyor general, was to cause surveys authorized by law, as might be directed by the commissioners, to be made. U. S., *Statutes at Large*, II, 352-353.

Lucas is a man of the finest fancy & most brilliant imagination with whom I was ever acquainted, and when he chuses to be pleasant, his conversations are obsolutely fascinating. But (as I think) he wants judgment, he wants principle & will one day become, in the opinions of all a designing old Ruffian. I am myself astonished at the success with which I have repelled the protean like attacks of this crafty old Cerberus.[197] I was once on the brink of despair, but animated by a consciousness of right & by the popular support, I have at length obliged him to grind his teeth in silence. A circumstance, besides has lately transpired, as much *for* me, as *against* my Colleagues, and I really feel so triumphant on the occasion that I cannot forbear mentioning it to you. The People had appointed a committee of correspondence on the subject of their claims to Lands depending before the commissioners. A part of the business of this committee was to procure, if possible an amelioration of those principles by which the Board have been heretofore governed; & for this purpose the gentlemen addressed themselves to certain members of the Senate who replied that 'the opinions of Mr. B if in favour, would have great weight in inducing government to grant the Petition,' — I had, indeed, no doubt, that those liberal & concilitory constructions which I had placed

[197] Proteus was the prophetic old man of the sea. He was placed by Homer on the Island of Pharos; by Virgil on the Island of Carpathos. At mid-day Proteus rose from the sea and slept on the shore with seamonsters about him. Those wishing to learn the future from him must seize him at that time. As soon as seized, he assumed various shapes to escape prophesying. If he saw that his efforts were of no avail, he resumed his usual form and told the truth.

Cerberus was the dog stationed at the entrance of Hades. Hesiod gave him fifty heads, but Sophocles and most of the Latin poets described him as triple headed.

on the Law would be acceptable to government; but such a direct reference to myself, in exclusion of my Colleagues was somewhat more than I had counted on. It places me however in the most dangerous & delicate of all imaginable situations, to conduct myself in which with prudence & exempt from imputation will require all the wariness & circumspection of which I am master. . . .

TO ALBERT GALLATIN

Sir,   St. Louis July 16. 1809.

I have the honor, in compliance with the earnest wishes of Gov: Lewis, to state, that previously to his making a contract for the printing of the Laws of this territory, he conversed with me on the subject, and appeared to entertain an opinion that the work should be paid for, by me, from the contingent fund in my hands. —

The Governor was informed that the fund was too inconsiderable for such an object; and indeed barely sufficient, (as I then conceived it) for Office rent, Stationery and printing (occasional) as mentioned in your instructions.

I stated to the Governor also, that before and after his arrival in Louisiana, I had, with him felt the necessity of a promulgation of the Laws; and believing that the labour of manuscript copies was not properly chargeable on my Office, I had, notwithstanding employed a young man, for a considerable length of time in that work, for which I neither had nor intended to make an account, as there had been no appropriation.

This was in relation to the Laws of the Territory: But when the Governor has desired me to supply him with copies, of any of the United States' Statutes, such as the Indian intercourse Law, I have thought that I might employ a young man for the occasion (not my own clerk) and make it a public charge.

I have vouchers for disbursements of this kind, but am yet to learn, whether or not they will be admitted. — I beg you to excuse this liberty which I have very hastily taken at the instance of Governor Lewis —

MERIWETHER LEWIS TO NINIAN EDWARDS[198]

Sir,   St. Louis July 20. 1809

I have the honor to enclose an authenticated copy of an Indictment, found by the Grand Jury at the last court of quarter Sessions for the district of St. Louis against Simon Vannorsdale for obstructing the execution of Process and beating a Constable in the regular discharge of his duties.

Information has been given me of his escape and flight to the Territory of Illinois. I have therefore to request, by authority of an Act of Congress, concerning Fugitives from Justice, passed the 12th Feby 1793,[199] that your Excellency will cause said Simon Vannorsdale to be apprehended and secured, and that notice of his arrest be given me as soon thereafter as circumstances will permit, in order that the purposes of said Law, respecting Fugitives, may be fully accomplished. —

198. For his career, see Ninian W. Edwards, *History of Illinois and Life of Ninian Edwards*, and *The Edwards Papers*, Chicago Historical Society, *Collections*, III.

199 U. S., *Statutes at Large*, I, 302-305.

TO JAMES ABBOTT

DEAR SIR,   ST. LOUIS July 25th. 1809

.   .   .   .

Our Gov. Lewis, with the best intentions in the world, is, I am fearful, losing ground. His late preparations for Indian War[200] have not been popular. *He acted for the best.* But it is the fate of great men to be judged by the results of their measures. He has talked for these 12 Mos. of leaving the country — Every body thinks now that he will positively go, in a few weeks.

TO ALBERT GALLATIN

Recorder's Office
SIR,   ST. LOUIS Augt. 12. 1809.

I have this day taken the liberty to draw on you in favor of Edw. Hempstead Esquire for the sum of one hundred & forty dollars fifty four cents the amt. of the contingent expenses of the Board of commissioners for ascertaining and adjusting the titles and claims to lands in this territory from 1st day of January till 30th of June last

I also transmit herewith the acct. & receipts.

---

200 Throughout the fall of 1808 and the winter of 1808-1809 the settlers were disturbed by insistent rumors of an Indian uprising along the northern frontiers. By order of November 28, 1808 Governor Lewis called out a special force. A second call was issued in the spring, five companies being asked to rendezvous on May 4. A detachment under Captain Pratte was sent to reinforce Fort Madison. On June 5 Captain Pratte returned to St. Louis and reported that the border was quiet. On July 6 Lewis issued a general order saying that, as the immediate dangers on the frontier had subsided, the troops especially assembled by order of November 28 were to be discharged and again enrolled in ordinary with the general militia. *Missouri Gazette*, July 26, 1808; December 7, 1808; April 26, 1809; June 7, 1809; July 26, 1809.

MERIWETHER LEWIS TO NATHANIEL POPE,[201]
SECRETARY EXERCISING THE GOVERNMENT
OF THE TERRITORY OF ILLINOIS

Sir,   St. Louis Augt. 16th. 1809.

I was favored some few days ago with your letter of
the 1st inst [?] and regret that the Record The United
States versus Simon Vannorsdale[202] should not have been
authenticated in such manner, as in your opinion the Act of
Congress requires. I take the liberty to enclose a second
Copy of that record authenticated in more ample form.

Simon Vannorsdale after committing the misdemeanor
set forth in the indictment, fled from the justice of this
government, and as my informations state, has taken
refuge in the territory of Illinois: I have therefore to
request that you will be pleased to cause the said Simon
Vannorsdale to be arrested and secured and that notice
may be given me as soon thereafter as convenient to you.
You justly remark that the proximity of the two territories
greatly facilitates the escape of offenders from the one to
the other, and I beg you to be assured, that I shall feel an

201 Nathaniel Pope was born at Louisville, Kentucky, January 5, 1784.
He was educated at Transylvania University. He moved to Illinois Territory and in 1809 became secretary. In 1817 he was elected congressional
delegate. When Illinois became a state, he was appointed judge of the
United States district court, an office which he held until his death in
1850.

202 The following notice appeared in the *Missouri Gazette*, February
1, 1809: "THE PUBLIC are cautioned against purchasing a certain note
of hand, given by me to Wm. Morison of the Point of the Missouri, of
the purport following to wit. 'That I was to pay him Four Hundred
Dollars upon condition that I should not deliver to him this day at
Camp Belle Fontaine a certain bay stud horse that I traded to said
Morison and dated the 26th instant.' I am determined not to pay said
note, as the horse was in the first instance obtained from me under false
pretences and by fraud, and the note under duress of imprisonment.
St. Louis, Jan. 27, 1809.   Simon Vannorsdel."

equal promptitude with yourself in bringing them to justice — *and* in such manner as the Laws of our Country
appear to have provided.

TO MICHAEL AMOUREUX

Secretary's Office

SIR,   ST. LOUIS Augt. 19. 1809

Your letters to the Governor of the 1st & to myself of
the 11th inst. were, this morning, delivered by your son.

I am instructed by His Excellency to say, that no charges
of any kind, either specific or general have been exhibited
agt. you. Should the propriety of your conduct be hereafter called in question, in relation to those offices holden
at the pleasure of the Executive, he desires me to add, that
the most ample opportunities of defence shall be afforded
to you.

Your letters appear rather intended as a vindication of
yourself, than as an accusation of others. Whenever
charges are specifically exhibited against the individuals
alluded to, an inquiry into their conduct shall be, instituted,
if the alledged violation of duty be of sufficient moment to
permit the attention of the government.

MOSES AUSTIN TO BATES

DEAR SIR,   MINE A BURTON Aug. 27th 1809

I have thought many times that I would not put pen to
paper again on any subject whatever except such as immediately concerned myself. Whether in the present case, I
shall receive thanks, or be considered as a troublesome
meddler I cannot tell, but so it is that when I see and know

of plans maturing to wound the reputation of those for whome I profess friendship, I cannot forbear doing unto them as I could wish them to do unto me. Whether what I shall communicate to you be of moment, or not you will judge, be that as it may. I have to tell you that you are to consider & receive what I write as given in strict confidence. I this day had a conversation with one of the members of the Grand Committee. The substance of that conversation I shall communicate, he said. the Drafting a memorial to Congress was postponed because it was found to be all important to examine the Coms. Books & to take such extracts as would answer the intentions of the party. They are to be taken from time to time and in such a way as not to give alarm to the Comrs. it was also hinted that if the extracts could not be obtained in any other way, a friend in Court would furnish them. I will not say who this friend is, but the board you know has three members, and a Clerk. I have the . . . to believe that *B. C. L.* esq. . . . [203] are the men against whom the Extracts are intended to operate. *B. C. L.*[204] esq is more particularly pointed out. how far the board of Comsrs. are bound to suffer a mutilated Statement to be taken from the Books is not for me to say, nor do I know what authority the member with whom I conversed has for supposing a friend in Court will furnish the Extract. It may be on his part supposition, the drawing the memorial is suspended untill Octb 2 next. The object of the Enemies of Judge Lucas are not only to displace him as Comsr. but as Judge or in other words to prevent him beeing appointed again, as I have reason to believe that an attempt to obtain extracts from the Coms Books will

[203] The manuscript is mutilated where the dots are inserted.
[204] John B. C. Lucas.

be made immediately & that such Extracts are not intended to make a friendly or favourable impression on the Government of the *U S*. & knowing as I do that first impressions are not only dangerous but hard to remove, I felt it a duty incumbent on me to apprize both yourself and Judge Lucas of the plans preparing to stab your reputation with the Government. You have liberty to make known to Judge Lucas as much of this letter as you think proper but you will remember and bear in mind the conditions. I need not tell you how much I have suffered by this same party. You know what I should suffer was it known that I made a communication to either of you. I therefore pray you, as you value my safety and the peace of my family who have been already sufficiently oppressed, not to . . . seen or spoken of. . . .

NB nothing I have said will induce you to doubt Mr Thoms. T Riddicks friendship —

TO JOHN BURKE TREAT

Secretary's Office
Sᴛ. Lᴏᴜɪs Septr. 2d. 1809.

Sɪʀ,

By order of His Excellency the Governor, I have the honor to acquaint you that the accustomed trade, with the Indians of the Arkansas-River and its waters may be again opened. You have been already supplied with Blanks for this object. On the application for Licences it is his Excellency's instruction, that you take a Bond in the usual manner; administer or cause to be administered the Oath, receive the Schedule of the merchandize intended to be traded, and transmit the whole to this Office.

FRANÇOIS V. BOUIS TO BATES

DEAR SIR,   POINTE COUPEE September 3d. 09

Five weeks after my arrival at this place, 1 had the pleasure of writing to you, and have not yet had the honor of an answer. — I cannot Dear Sir give you a favorable account of my journey to this Country, having been sick with the Fever & aigue from the time I wrote you (which is about three months) till few days past.

A great Discord, Cabal & desorder, exist here among the Inhabitants, occasioned by intrigues, which has set, half of the Country against the others; this will not (very probably) end without effusion of Blood — The Negroes which are in great number here, have already showed disobedience & ill disposition. — The Heads of Militia, civil & clergy of this Country "wishing one another destituted from office" are the cause of intrigues, and in fact intrigants themselves whom carry all before them. — Nothing more worth mentioning can be said of this place.

My Brother P. V. Bouis, present you his respects and repent of having neglected to write you, according to his promess, when he left St. Louis, he assure you, that it is not for want of friendship for your person. — Remember me (if you please) to Mr. Riddick & Brother, also to any of my Friends.   .   .   .

N. B. — Should there be (to your knowledge) any vacant office, which would worth my attention, I would desire you, (if you do me the honor to write to me) to advise me of it.

PART IV
The Second Acting-Governorship

THE SECOND ACTING-GOVERNORSHIP

TO ROBERT BRENT,[1] WASHINGTON CITY

SIR,   ST. LOUIS Sept. 20. 1809.

Soon after the receipt of your letter of 23d of Novr last
enclosing a draft of 1503 06/100 dollars for the payment
of Capt. Wherry's detachment,[2] I had the honor to inform
you that the men were so dispersed in the Indian country
and elsewhere, as to render it very uncertain when the
returns could be made to you. But few of the men now remain unpaid. Every possible attention has been bestowed,
and the receipts shall be transmitted as soon as circumstances will permit. —

TO HORATIO STARK,[3] FORT MADISON

                                          Secretary's Office
SIR,   ST. LOUIS Sept. 26. 1809.

I have the honor to acknowledge the receipt of your
letter of the 15th to Gov Lewis, in whose absence from the

[1] Robert Brent was from Maryland. He was appointed paymaster of
the United States Army on July 1, 1808, and became paymaster-general
on April 24, 1816.

[2] Dr. Mackay Wherry came to Louisiana during the Spanish régime.
In 1805 he was sheriff of St. Charles District. In 1807 he commanded
a troop of horse in that district. When General Clark was negotiating
with the Osages in the summer of 1808, Captain Wherry's troop accompanied him. Houck, *History of Missouri*, II, 55, 60, 96, 384, 409; *Missouri
Gazette*, July 26, 1808, February 22, 1809.

[3] Horatio Stark was a Virginian. He entered the army in 1799 and
attained the rank of captain on May 3, 1808. At the time of this letter
he was in command at Fort Madison in modern Iowa.

territory, the Executive business is transacted at my Office. The Medal and Papers of the Ioway chief were also received. The Ioway-Fugitives the subjects of your mis-understanding with Hard Heart were tried by our courts last year; and after the Jury had found them guilty, the court sustained a Plea to its own jurisdiction. They could not then be punished by our Laws, and it ever appeared to me that their escape was fortunate, both for themselves and for us.[4] It saved them, the vexations of a further im-prisonment, and *us* the mortification of manifesting our own inability to punish — For our's is a government of *Laws,* and those whom the courts *absolve* or *fail to punish* cannot be punished by the Superintendent.

After the trial, the dispositions of the Bench were well known: they would have restored those People to their liberty by the writ of Habeas Corpus if their counsel had not been deterred from that course, by a fear of incurring the displeasure of the Governor. —

I cannot account for the new demand which has been made for these unfortunate yet guilty People. We can do nothing with them, and in such cases the transgression ought to be forgotten as silently as possible.

Hard Heart has acted with too much haste and passion and I believe him to be a man of native viciousness of tem-per; Yet we know that the Indian manners are greatly

---

[4] On July 23, 1808, two Iowa Indians were tried for the murder of Joseph Tibbeau (Thibault). During the trial "the streets of St. Louis teemed with Indian warriors," who incessantly harassed the governor and General Clark beseeching pardon for the offenders. The accused men were convicted but were granted a new trial, which was held on August 3. They were found guilty and put in jail until the advice of the Presi-dent could be obtained. They were held in the jail for nearly a year when they made their escape. *Missouri Gazette*, July 26, August 2, August 10, August 17, 1808; *ibid.*, July 26, 1809.

different from ours. They inherit from a long, uncounted List of Ancestors not the *chartered* but the *prescriptive* and *traditionary* rights of the forest, and are themselves born and brought up amidst the ruggid scenes of nature. Much licence ought then, to be expected from them in their public talks — Even a common idea is uttered by them with rude abruptness, and an intrepid Chief when representing his nation in council, has decorums no doubt, of a particular kind, but which cannot always be measured by our standards. —

It is the express expectation of the President that the Indians will not be treated with the harshness of military coercion, but with a conciliatory justice enforced or rather recommended by the manifestation of a paternal solicitude for their welfare. This man Hard Heart was made a Chief by the President himself, and I doubt our power to degrade him. At the instance of the respectable part of the nation our emblems of distinction might indeed be conferred on others but it is my first impression that a deprivation of Honors *already* bestowed is an Act exclusively of his own People. We furnish them with Insignia of power or preeminence in their nation or tribe, and these supplies should not be made unless with the *consent* at *least* of the Elders. — The subject, at any rate, requires more consideration than I have now time to bestow upon it; but will write you by Mr. Julien[5] who will leave this [place] in 10 days. —

I am much surprized at the suspension by Gov Lewis, of the trade with the Ioways. The first informations which I had on the subject were from your letters. No record of the transaction has been deposited in the Offices — And as

[5] Probably Julien Dubuque.

the measure is supported by no principle of Law, Justice, or Policy that I know of I beg that those traders who have regular licences may suffer no interruptions.

I regret that I was not in town when you ascended the River. It would have given me much pleasure to renew that acquaintance wch. I once had with you in Detroit.

[NOTATION] The Medal & Papers given to Mr. Blondeau[6] to be redelivered to the Chief.
12. July '10.

TO WILLIAM EUSTIS, SECRETARY OF WAR

SIR,   ST. LOUIS Sept. 28. 1809.

I have the honor to advise, that Gov Lewis, left this place for Washington on the 4th instant.[7] In his absence the superintendance of Indian Affairs devolves on this office.

There is a policy subordinate to, and in execution of the Law which the President may doubtless institute for the regulation of Indian Intercourse. But as the Governor has never confided to me the wishes of administration on

---

[6] The Blondeau family were early settlers of Mackinac. About 1798 several of the family migrated to Missouri and obtained Spanish grants. The best known member of the family was Maurice, a Fox half-breed. He was trading with the tribe as early as 1801. Pike encountered him on the Mississippi in 1805. During the War of 1812 he was taken prisoner by the Sacs and his goods were confiscated. He was later made sub-agent of the Sacs and was employed as an interpreter in the treaty making of 1815. In 1818 he entered the employment of the American Fur Company. *Wisconsin Historical Collections*, **XX**, 356, 357.

[7] This was the journey on which Governor Lewis met his untimely end.

this, or indeed on any other subjects (except on one special occasion) and as he has left me neither records of his own acts, nor any of his official correspondence, I have nothing but the statute as my guide.

Genl. Clark also departed for Virga. a few days ago by the shutting up of whose office, I am totally deprived of every species of information on Indian Affairs. No list of Sub Agents or Interpreters has been left with me and I do not know, even accidentally, their situations & duties. The press of business on this department is almost incessant, and deprived of all the requisite information, it is impossible that it should be transacted with intelligence and dispatch.

My judgments will compel me to abandon the paths heretofore trodden. The merchants complain of restrictions beyond the Provisions of the Law; of arbitrary regulations established without a motive and relinquished without a reason and of various other irregularities by which their commerce has suffered a damage, during the last twelve months to the amount of forty thousand dollars, at least. I should not be the Herald of these censures, if I esteemed them empty and frivolous. — I would not be the organ of the complaints of the People, unless for the purpose of justifying that liberal course which I conceive it my indispensable duty, in future, to pursue.

It is not my province to arraign the conduct of Gov. Lewis, and it is surely as distant from my inclination as it is from official decorum: yet in speaking of the present situation of territorial business it is scarcely possible to forbear a retrospect into the past. —

It has appeared to me that the *right* to *trade* is a right which the Citizen derives from the Laws, and that it is susceptible of very little modification, beyond what the laws themselves have established. The *privilege* of *hunting* is probably resumable at the will of government, and on this subject I must confess that I feel very considerable embarrassments. I have imbibed the opinion that it was the wish of the President that the hunting of white persons should be discountenanced. The cultivation of the soil affords more certain subsistence, contributes to the population of the country, and is a pursuit, in all respects more congenial to the habits (generally) of the People of Louisiana, than the *chase;* Yet there will always be found on the frontier a class of People, who will starve if deprived of the latter privilege.

The Governor, previously to his departure insisted that hunting Licences should not be granted. I took the liberty of enquiring why they should now be refused, since he had been in the practice of granting them almost without limitation? He replied that the indulgence would create disorder in the Indian Country. The Blank which I have the honor to enclose will show you the wide range and liberal encouragement which has been heretofore given to People of this description: And I have not known any rule of right, by which privileges of this kind can be conceded to particular persons and withholden from others. I beg that you will have the kindness to instruct me in my duties. When possessed of your views on these subjects as on all others incidental to Indian intercourse, they shall be inflexibly pursued. —

When at the settlements of the Arkansas last year, as a commissioner for the adjustment of Land Title, I saw the instructions of Mr. Treat the Agent, by which he was empowered to grant trading Licences. Gov Lewis, notwithstanding, continued still to grant them for that river and its neighbourhood, and was desirous that I should do so, in his absence. I declined, believing that, as Mr. Treat corresponded directly with the War Department, on the business of that remote and sequestered part of the country, the interposition of the Superintendent could produce only derangement and confusion. —

May I be permitted to enquire whether Peter Chouteau esquire the Agent for the Osage Nations of Indians has been so unfortunate as to lose the confidence of the President? Insinuations have been made to this effect tho' I have heard nothing alledged against him, except his absence by order of the Superintendent. Mr. Chouteau must have presumed that Gov Lewis acted in this affair under the orders of the President; and surely sufficient time had elapsed after the commencement of the preparations to have obtained his sanction or his censure. Previously to his acceptance of the command of the Mandan Escort,[8] the Osage business had from time to time and under various pretexts been almost entirely taken out of his hands, and I am very certain, (being in habits of daily intimacy) that his principal inducement in undertaking this distant charge, was, to escape from the official degradation into which he had fallen. It is greatly to be feared that the character of Mr. Chouteau has not been entirely understood at Washington. I do not fear to hazard the assertion that he possesses a respectability and weight in this country, beyond

[8] Early in 1809 the Missouri Fur Company agreed to convey Shahaka, the Mandan chief, to his nation. Pierre Chouteau commanded the escort. The expedition left St. Louis June 16 and reached the Mandan village on September 24. Some of the party remained in the North to trade. Chouteau arrived at St. Louis November 20. *Missouri Gazette,* March 8, September 27, November 16, November 23, 1809.

any other person employed in the transaction of Indian business. — And this reputation, together with the influence of an extensive family connection, has, on all proper occasions, been thrown into the Amercan Scale, when the policy of our government has been in collision with the prejudices of former times.

There was a time when the public mind was impressed somewhat differently with respect to this Gentleman; but he has outlived the malice of that day; not by entering into useless vindications; but by treading a high and open path, exposed to the view of his fellow laborers in the public service and of Society. —

His son,[9] an active, intelligent and very worthy young man has the entire conduct of his fathers private business, and with the tacit approbation of the Superintendent has also discharged that portion of his public duties which had not been wrested from him previously to his ascending the Missouri. By him some of the expences of the Osage department have been defrayed, and his accounts of disbursements approved by the Superintendent. It was expected by Mr. Chouteau jr that I would have drawn bills for this money; but I have thought that a draft by himself will be a less exceptionable mode. He will have the honor of enclosing you in his letter of advice, one set of his vouchers.

[9] This probably refers to Pierre Chouteau, Jr. He was born January 19, 1789. In 1804 he became a clerk for his uncle, Auguste Chouteau, Sr. In 1806 he accompanied Julien Dubuque to the lead mines. He remained there as a clerk until 1808 when he returned to St. Louis. He accompanied his father to the Mandan country in 1809. In 1813 he married Emilie Anne Gratiot, a daughter of Charles Gratiot. In his later years he engaged in many large business enterprises, and was one of the most influential citizens of St. Lonis. J. T. Scharf, *History of St. Louis City and County,* I, 182-184.

I take the liberty of enclosing copies of a correspondence with Capt. Horatio Stark Comg. Fort Madison.

Several Salt Petre caves[10] on the Gasconade and the Meramack Rivers were, some time ago, leased by Gov Lewis. The contracts contained a stipulation by which the Lessees were bound to sell their Petre to Government, provided you were desirous of taking it at the rate of 17 cts Per Pound at St. Louis, and restraining them from making any other disposal of it until the pleasure of government should be known. As we have no orders on this subject I have permitted one of these contractors to make sale of his Petre or to manufacture it into gun powder for domestic supply.

The Delaware & Shawanoe Indians who sought an asylum in this country after their defeat by Genl. Wayne claim a very valuable tract of Land by grant from the Spanish Government. It is bounded by the Mississippi on the East; by Apple Creek on the North; by Cape St. Comb's Creek on the South and by the ridge separating the waters of the Mississippi & St. Francis River on the West.[11] This claim lies in the District of Cape Girardeau and is so nearly surrounded by our white settlements as to make these Indians desirous of exchanging it for lands farther westward on the Meramack. This is a wish long since expressed and repeated to me two days ago, by some of their People who were at St. Louis for the purpose of procuring the

[10] For a description of Ashley's Cave, which was located on Cave Creek in modern Texas County, about eighty miles southwest of Potosi, see Henry R. Schoolcraft, *Journal of a Tour into the Interior of Missouri and Arkansas*, 11-12.

[11] The Delawares abandoned the tract in 1815, but the Shawanee did not formally relinquish their claim until November 7, 1825. Charles C. Royce, *Indian Land Cessions in the United States*, Bureau of American Ethnology, *18th Rpt.*, Part II, 715.

surrender of twelve of their Horses, which the whites had stolen.

The Pay Master General long since remitted to me 1503 06/100 dollars for the payment of Capt. Wherry's detachment while in public service at the fire Praire. . This payment has been made many months ago, except to six or eight men who are yet absent. The delay in making the returns has not been attributable to my negligence.

TO ALBERT GALLATIN

SIR,   ST. LOUIS Sept 29. 1809

I beg leave to mention that Thomas F. Riddick the Clerk of the Board of Commissioners has resigned his office for the purpose of attending to some private business in Kentucky. The Commissioners, unwilling to lose his services have appointed his half brother John W. Honey to supply his place, with an understanding that Mr. Riddick shall be restored on his return.

It is not in expectation of obtaining a reply; but for the purpose of shielding my conduct from that misconception to which it is liable, at the distance of a thousand miles, that I beg permission to state to you the grounds of an opinion which I lately gave, in relation to a tract of land said to contain a *Coal-Mine.*

All the conditions of the Spanish Usages had been complied with, and the question was, whether it should be confirmed *with* or *without* the reservation of the *coal.* The Lieut. Governor in his order of survey had stated, that the Coal should remain for public use, until the General Government at Orleans made another disposal of it. My

Colleagues voted that the reservation ought to be *permanently* made. I was of an opposite opinion because I conceived it an individual assumption and exercise of power, on the part of the Lieut. Governor which the usages of the country had not delegated to him. The established usages of the late Government to which we are referred in the 4th Sec of the Law,[12] did not, that I know of, make reservations of *Coal-Mines.* ˙These usages prescribe the terms upon which the cultivator shall acquire the right of property in the soil, and the Public agent who is but an organ of the law could superadd nothing to those conditions. Besides the order of survey was but an incipient process, and not a title made and completed by competent and superior authority — *all* was referred to this superior authority; as well the *coal* as the title to the *land* itself. —

This first step is an evidence merely of the Party's being put into possession in a regular manner — And his rights must now be ascertained, not, I should think, by the capricious expressions of his order of survey but, by the known and established laws of the Spanish Government. —

I had the honor of writing you on the 28th of August

[12] Section 4 of an act respecting claims to land in the territories of Orleans and Louisiana, passed March 3, 1807, read: *"And be it further enacted,* That the commissioners appointed for the purpose of ascertaining the rights of persons claiming land in the territories of Orleans and Louisiana, shall have full powers to decide according to the laws and established usages and customs of the French and Spanish governments, upon all claims to lands within their respective districts, when the claim is made by any´ person or persons, or the legal representative of any person or persons, who were on the twentieth of December, one thousand eight hundred and three, inhabitants of Louisiana, and for ·a tract not exceeding the quantity of acres contained in a league square, and which does not include either a lead mine or salt spring, which decision of the commissioners when in favour of the claimant shall be final, against the United States, any act of Congress to the contrary notwithstanding." U. S., *Statutes at Large,* II, 441.

last year, that Governor Lewis had assumed the whole management of the lead-mine-business. Your orders, if executed, would, eventually, and with very little excitement, have reinstated the government in its rights; but those orders as I have every reason to believe, have been entirely disregarded. The Governor did indeed, from time to time, speak of plans and systems of his own; but nothing, that I know of, was ever done. Even the tenants of government were left unsupported, and those very men, with whom I made contracts, afterwards approved by the President, have been driven from their leases by private adventurers and are now bankrupts.

When I was instructed to lease the Mines, I conceived that it was a special Agency, which you had thought proper to vest in the Recorder's Office; and not an appendage of the Executive Power, which I exercised at that time by mere casualty: But his Excellency on his arrival thought otherwise.

Duty, of whatever kind, was never performed by me with reluctance; but the management of this particular Affair has occasioned me so much embarrassing contest, that it was surrendered with great cheerfulness to the man, who acted as if he had brought with him all the views of administration, in his Port Folio. I beg leave to remark that the public indignation which was once loudly manifested against the rapacious speculations of certain individuals, begins to subside; and every succeeding day will render it more difficult to correct the mischief.

Those People, far from remaining on the defensive (for indeed they suffer no molestation) have become the assailants, and men in whom the government reposes its confidence are marked out as their future victims.

If, however I should be honored with your further orders on these subjects, my best efforts shall be exerted,. for their execution: and if protected from obtrusive interruptions will accomplish your wishes or assign you reasons why I have been unable to do so.

TO JOHN B. C. LUCAS AND CLEMENT B. PENROSE

GENTLEMEN, SATURDAY MORNING Sept. 30. 1809.

I was not, yesterday morning prepared to deliver an opinion, on the maximum of quantity, if any, limited by the established usages and customs of the French & Spanish Governments. I am not yet ready. — I view this question as surpassing in its magnitude and consequences, any one which has yet been decided by us — And as new ideas have arisen in my mind, on this subject, as well spontaneously, as on the suggestion of those with whom I have conversed, I feel myself impelled, however reluctantly, to ask further delay until monday morning. — I will then meet at as early an hour as you may think proper.

TO MICHAEL AMOUREUX

SIR, ST. LOUIS Oct 1. 1809. —

I take the liberty of enclosing an Indian Trading Licence for Mr. Louis Coignard,[13] which you will oblige me by delivering to him, on his executing and leaving with you the accompanying bond.

---

[13] Louis Coignard was a native of Chatillon, France. He came to St. Louis during the Spanish régime. In 1796, after the visit of General Collot to St. Louis, he organized a "Sans Coulottes" society. In 1800 he bought property in New Madrid and engaged in business there as a merchant.

I must ask the favor of your giving date to the Licence, correspondent with the date of the bond, which latter may be sent to me by some private conveyance when convenient.

Mr. Coignard wished that he might be permitted to trade at the Arkansas. Will you have the goodness to inform him that the Agent at that place is charged with the local affairs of that river, and that to him the application must be made.

TO ROBERT SMITH

Sir,   Octo. 1. 1809. —

In obedience to the 2d Sec of the 'Act further providing for the government of the district of Louisiana' I have the honor to transmit for the information of the President, copies of all the legislative and executive acts, which have been deposited in my office for record and preservation from the 1st day of April till 30th day of September —

Also a table of the territorial and district officers in commission at this time.[14] I beg leave to remark, that the General orders to the Militia, have not been filed in this office. Neither have I been desired by the Governor to procure the printing of them.

TO PIERRE ANTOINE LA FORGE, NEW MADRID

Secretary's Office

Sir,   St. Louis Oct 4. 1809.

Your letter of 23d of last mo. was delivered by Capt. Le Sieur.[15] It gives me much pleasure to observe the rapid progress which you make in the acquirement of the

---

[14] The list is missing.
[15] François Le Sieur of Little Prairie.

English language. I *read* French with some facility, but have not yet familiarized its pronunciation and much habit will be necessary before I either write or speak it with correctness. —

I do not know how it has happened that under the American administration, your talents have not been heretofore employed in the public service. It is high time that they should be employed and I request your acceptance of the two offices of Judge of the Courts and Auditor of the Public Accounts — The latter of these offices has become vacant by the resignation of Mr. Amoureux. I enclose the Commissions.

I have for some months past, heard much of the collisions between the District officers of N. Madrid. It is not proper that I should enter into these private disputes and I have consequently been silent with respect to them. It is hoped and expected that you will exert some activity & zeal in the discharge of your new duties & that you will endeavour to give facility to the operations of the Laws. Shall be glad to hear from you frequently. Apply, if you please at the Clerk's Office for a copy of the Laws. Mr. Humphreys[16] will supply you.

A PROCLAMATION

By FREDERICK BATES,

Secretary of the Territory of Louisiana and Exercising the Government thereof

Whereas a general court martial held in the town of St. Louis, on the 9th day of June last, and of which Lieut. Colo. Auguste Chouteau was President, did, with laudable zeal for the promotion of the public service, impose certain

[16] Joshua Humphreys.

fines on the individuals herein after mentioned, for their not having obeyed the general order of the 10th day of April last, to wit, on Sergeant Wm. Long[17] to the amount of two months' pay; and on the following Privates to wit, Jos: Wells 2 Mos. pay; Bart Honory one months pay, Jos Lardoise & Jno. Latresse 2 Mos. pay each, Benj Stedman 2½ Mos. pay, Benj Quick, three months pay, Saml. Rogers 2 Mos. pay, Jas. Burnsides 2 Mos. pay, Jno. Sullins 2½ Mos. pay, Jno. Nichols 2 Mos. pay, George Sesep 1½ Mos. pay, Nathl. Warren, 3½ Mos. pay, Jas. Baggs 3½ Mos. pay, John Wilson four months' pay, George Simpson six months' pay, John Manly six mos. pay, Jno. Keller 2 Mos. pay, William Wells 3 Mos pay, Joseph Martineau six mos. pay, Stephen Malboeuf six mos. pay, Danl. Moore, four mos. pay. —

Now therefore, be it known, that in consideration of the praiseworthy alacrity, with which the Militia of Louisiana, have, on all proper occasions, obeyed the calls of the constituted authorities of their country; and by virtue of the powers vested in the Governor by the 1st Section of the 'act further providing for the government of the district of Louisiana' I do hereby pardon the several offences for which the said fines were imposed, and require that all sheriffs govern themselves accordingly.

In testimony whereof I have hereunto affixed the seal of the territory. Given under my hand at Saint Seal Louis, the tenth day of October, one thousand, eight hundred and nine, and of the Independence of the United States of America, the thirty fourth.

Frederick Bates

[17] William L. Long was a Revolutionary War veteran from Virginia. In 1804 he was interested in a grist mill at Carondelet. In 1812 he was an ensign in the St. Louis regiment.

TO CLEMENT B. PENROSE

Sir,   St. Louis Oct. 20. 1809

In our conversations this morning I charged you with having said, in the presence of certain gentlemen, that the motives of my misunderstandings with Governor Lewis, were, the hopes of acquiring the Executive Office on his removal; and not an honest difference in opinion, in the transaction of the territorial business — This, I think you denied — And indeed, if you have common sense or a very ordinary portion of consistency, you *must* deny it, since you have, on very many occasions, been quite as noisy on the imputed irregularities of the Governor, as any other person. —

I have spoken with the gentlemen — and understand from them, that they may, possibly, have made some *inferences* from your remarks on these subjects and that they cannot recollect the precise words in which your ideas were conveyed. Here, then, I drop this part of the subject. — But you still say, that I *have been,* and *am* the enemy of the Governor, — and that I would be very willing to fill that office myself. — I told you this morning that it was *false* — and I repeat that it is an impudent stupidity in you to persist in the assertion. How is it possible that you should know my *wishes,* except from my declarations or my conduct? — And what declaration of mine, or what part of my conduct justifies you, in the repetition of *falsehoods* like these?

In return, for the personal allusions with which you have honored me, I tender to you, my most hearty contempt.

TO JOHN SCOTT[18]

DEAR SIR,   ST. LOUIS Oct 24. 1809

Your letter of the 22d was handed me this morning by Mr. Watson. In reply to your recommendation of Henry King esq for the Recorder's Office of N. Madrid in the event of Judge Amoureux' resignation, I can only say, that I have not yet heard of a vacancy; but that your assurances of Mr. King's fitness shall not be forgotten, if I should hereafter have it in my power to serve him.

In the discharge of those arduous duties which have lately devolved on the Secyship, I can have no other object than the promotion of the Public good, and knowing your acquaintance with the Affairs of the lower districts, any intimations with which you may think proper to favor me will be very acceptable.

TO NATHANIEL POPE

SIR,   ST. LOUIS Oct 24. 1809

It is with unaffected diffidence that I take the liberty of addressing you on a subject, in which in all probability you feel but little interest.

The term of Gov: Lewis' services, will expire I understand, in Feby or March next. He has been too unfortunate

18 John Scott was a Virginian. After graduating at Princeton he moved to Vincennes where he studied law. In 1805 he moved to Ste. Genevieve, being the first lawyer to settle there permanently. In 1807 he was attorney-general of the territory. In 1817 he was elected delegate to congress from Missouri Territory, and later was the first representative in congress from the State of Missouri. His support of John Quincy Adams led to his retirement from political life in 1828. Scott County is named after him.

to expect a second nomination — such, at least is the prevailing opinion: whether well founded or not a very general solicitude is felt, that some worthy man of talent and experience may be selected to succeed him in the Executive Office.

Judge Coburn has a growing reputation: His manners as you know, are plain, yet conciliatory, and no doubt sufficiently dignified; his discharge of public duty prompt intelligent and exempt from imputation. In a word, I believe he would, more nearly than any other man, unite the public suffrage. For myself, I have not concealed my ardent wishes that the Judge might be appointed our Governor. A popular address to the President might be very readily obtained; but such Papers have not of late been esteemed conclusive evidence of merit: Besides which all feeling minds are, in different degrees, affected by the unhappy situation of Governor Lewis, and would feel a painful reluctance in contributing to his mortifications. The name of Judge Coburn will however be mentioned to the President by private friends of some influence and sanguine hopes are entertained of the success of their application.

If you could feel yourself at liberty to lend us your aid in this affair you would add new confidence to these hopes, at the same time that you convince us of your willingness to promote the welfare of the People of Louisiana. You have indeed determined to gather your laurels in a sister territory; yet I cannot suppose that you have so soon forgotten a people, who are proud to have ranked you among their fellow citizens.

The weather has of late been so remarkably pleasant, that I hope, by this time, I may congratulate you on your entire recovery.

A PROCLAMATION

By Frederick Bates

Secretary of the Territory of Louisiana and Exercising
the Government thereof

Whereas His Excellency Governor Lewis, did, by proclamation, bearing date of the 22d day of June last, offer a reward of six hundred dollars, for the apprehension and delivery of Meranante and Mashkakaki two Indians of the Ioway Tribe, charged with the murder of Joseph Tebeau;[19] or half that sum for the apprehension and delivery of either of them: — And whereas, in addition to the supposed illegality of detaining those Fugitives, in the event of their commitment much doubt may be reasonably entertained with respect to the fund, on which this disbursement could be legally chargeable:

Now, therefore, be it known, that after mature consideration of the Premises I have, and do hereby revoke the said Proclamation, so far as it may be considered as an assurance of reward for the apprehension of both or either of the said Indians. In testimony whereof I have hereunto affixed the seal of the territory of Louisiana. Given under my hand at Saint Louis the 30th day of October, 1809 — and of the Independence of the United States of America the 34th.

Frederick Bates

[19] The name was variously spelled. It appears at Thebalt, Tebo, Tibbeau, Tebeau, Thiebeau. He was an old French trader who, for many years, made his headquarters at Beloit, Wisconsin. *Wisconsin Historical Collections*, VI, 423, 424. The proper spelling was Thibault. See Kaskaskia Church Register, II, 198, the original of which is owned by St. Louis University. The Missouri Historical Society has a copy. The murder was reported in the *Missouri Gazette*, August 2, 1808.

JOHN BURKE TREAT TO BATES

My Dear Friend Washington City October 31st 1809

This moment the Secretary at War has mentioned to me his having by this days Mail received an account of the extraordinary death of Governor Lewis: for which no one here undertakes to account for — & certainly the short acquaintance I had with him at St. Louis in June last wholly precludes my having any reason to offer for his committing an act so very extraordinary & unexpected.

It is already ask'd here who will become Gov. of the Territory: Some say one, others another — but those acquainted with the present Secry. of the Territory point him out as the most suitable and proper person: he certainly possessing more local knowledge of that part of the Country than perhaps any other person who might be selected as possessing talents adequate thereto — on the other hand, there are those who assert that if offered he would not accept it — as it might be necessary he should in that case relinquish the place of Commissioner, Register &c &c however of this you will undoubtedly be best able to determine —

Here we are all tranquil and have not any foreign News more than the Gazettes of the day will probably communicate to you — though — should any thing occur, which may be either interesting or amusing to you it shall by the earliest opportunity be communicated by [me].

TO NICHOLAS BOILVIN, SUB-AGENT OF INDIAN AFFAIRS, PRAIRIE DU CHIEN

Sir, St. Louis Nov 2d. 1809

Mr. Pope, the acting Governor of the territory of Illinois has complained to me that you have licensed persons to trade within his territory — and demanded that this practice should be discontinued. It is a proceeding with which I have been totally unacquainted, and must confess myself altogether at a loss to conceive your object.

The Orders of the Superintendent of Indian Affairs for Louisiana can have no operation East of the Mississippi — And no Licences in Gov Lewis' name ought to have been issued at Prairie du Chien or for any other part of the Illinois. — It appears to me that you ought to correspond on these subjects with Mr. Pope. Gov Lewis is no more. He died in Tennessee about 20 days ago.[20] —

TO JOHN COBURN

Sir,   St. Louis Nov 2d. 1809.

I have been somewhat too sanguine in my expectation of the popular address which we spoke of — Not, that the People would be better satisfied with any other appointment; but a reluctance of which I have not been able to discover the true cause, has heretofore thrown a damp on my exertions. Until the news of Gov Lewis' death, the fear of incurring his displeasure was the ostensible motive — & now, the impropriety of dictating to the President will serve as a pretext for their backwardness. I did not myself sign the Peto. as I conceived that the wishes of the *People* & not the Secy's wishes should be expressed in it.

I send you the copy of a letter which I wrote last week to Mr. Pope. He has not answered me — The communica-

[20] Governor Lewis met his death on October 11, 1809.

tion of which I spoke, has not yet been made to Government — It will go by next week's mail. If the proper efforts are made at the city I shall not dispair of your success.

TO JACQUES PORLIER[21] AND JOHN BLEAKLEY,[22] MERCHANTS OF THE BRITISH MACK-INAC COMPANY

GENTLEMEN,   ST. LOUIS Nov 3. 1809. —

The statement which you yesterday did me the favor to submit, in relation to your conduct among the Sacs, Foxes and others Indians of the Mississippi, has been read and reflected upon with all that candour and attention which it certainly merits.

The charges[23] were indeed such as to create much prejudice in the public mind, and some alarm for our defenceless

[21] Jacques Porlier was born in Montreal in 1765. In 1783 he made his first trip to Mackinac. In 1791 he went to Green Bay where he engaged as clerk with the fur trader Pierre Grignon, Sr. For a year Porlier worked at the Green Bay store and then was sent by Grignon to his trading post on the St. Croix. The following year he became an independent trader and spent many years on the upper Mississippi and its tributaries. In 1798 he formed a partnership with Noel Rocheblave. The firm was dissolved in 1810. *Wisconsin Historical Collections*, III, 244-245; VII, 247; XVIII, 462.

[22] In 1783 Bleakley was storekeeper and clerk at Mackinac. For many years he was operating on the upper Mississippi, being engaged in trade as late as 1814. *Wisconsin Historical Collections*, XIX, 275-276, 323-324.

[23] In April, 1809, Nicholas Jarrot of Cahokia, who was on his way to Prairie du Chien, met Porlier and Bleakley, who had been trading among the Sacs. Jarrot reported that Porlier complained bitterly of conditions in the Indian trade, claiming that the Indians forced the traders to sell goods at the prices charged at the government factories, the result being a loss to the traders. Jarrot then visited Ed. Lagotrie, another trader, who confirmed Porlier's statement. Jarrot claimed that the traders informed him that the Indians had two plans to get rid of the

frontier. It gives me pleasure to be convinced, that the prejudice was unmerited and the alarm without foundation.

You were advised, Gentlemen, that, as the acting Governor of Louisiana, I had no power to institute an enquiry in this mode. An investigation at my office was known to be extra judicial: Yet the earnestness with which you have insisted, together with the trouble which you have given yourselves of a personal attendance at Saint Louis, determined me to adopt that course, as the only one which the circumstances of the Affair, placed within our reach. — Your development of facts, has demonstrated the rectitude of your motives and conduct — and I am truly happy to find, that your characters, heretofore known for their individual worth, have, in no wise, deserved reproach or imputation, during the late transactions in the neighbourhood of Fort Madison. I believe that Garrison never was in danger. —

The honorable frankness with which you avow your allegiance and political attachment to the Crown of Great Britain is the best guarantee of your decent submission to our laws, as long as you voluntarily live under their protection.

TO NICHOLAS BOILVIN

DEAR SIR,   ST. LOUIS Nov 4. 1809.

I wrote you on the 2d & again address you at the pressing instances of Madame Boilvin. You will hear from other quarters of the melancholy circumstances of Gov Lewis's

---

white men: one was to get into Fort Madison with knives and stab the soldiers; if that did not succeed, they would watch the men and kill them and their cattle. *Missouri Gazette*, June 23, 1809.

death. — You have lost a Friend. — There are many expectations of change in the Indian Department. — Heaven only can foresee the future. — Genl. Clark is in the City of Washington — I suppose you are now acting under his instructions.

My dear Sir, I pray you to be extremely circumspect in every thing you do. Particularly grant no licences, enter into no arrangements in Illinois unless under the directions of the Governor of that territory. You will count confidently on my friendship whenever it may be in my power to serve you.

TO WILLIAM HENRY HARRISON

Sir,   St. Louis Nov 9. 1809.

I had the honor to receive by yesterday's mail, your letter of the 31st ulto. and avail myself of the return Post to give you all the information which I possess, of the seizure of certain goods, on the St. Francis, the property as alledged of Mr. Thomas Jones.[24]

Gov Lewis issued his warrant for this seizure on the 31st of March last, founded on the oath of James McFarlane, 'That these goods were offered for sale to the Indians by Wm Webber & Jno. Connature, supposed Agents of Thos. Jones, *without License'.*

I am advised by our Atty. General Mr Hempstead, that as process has been instituted for the condemnation of this merchandize, my interference would be irregular.

The goods themselves, might, no doubt, be obtained, under Writ of Replevin, a process which will not affect

---

[24] Thomas Jones was an early American settler on the Meramec.

the main enquiry, *whether or not they were offered for sale in violation of the Law of intercourse.*

We had been lately told that this merchandize was not indeed the property of Mr. Jones; but that it had been fairly sold and transferred by him to those Indians in whose hands it was found. Had this really been the fact, the propriety of the seizure, would have been in my mind, much more questionable.

This cause will probably be tried on the 4th Monday of this month in the district court of New Madrid.

TO RICHARD BATES

Sᴛ. Lᴏᴜɪs Nov 9. 1809.

You have heard no doubt, of the premature and tragical death of Gov: Lewis. Indeed I had no personal regard for him and a great deal of political contempt; Yet I cannot but lament, that after all his toils and dangers he should die in *such a manner.*[25]

At the *first,* in *Washington* he made to me so many friendly assurances, that I then imagined our mutual friendship would plant itself on rocky foundations. But a very short acquaintance with the man was sufficient to undeceive me. He had been spoiled by the elegant praises of Mitchell[26] & Barlow,[27] and over whelmed by so many flattering caresses of the *high & mighty,* that, like an over-

[25] For the circumstances connected with the death of Lewis, see Coues, *History of the Expedition under the Command of Lewis and Clark,* I, 43 *et seq.* See also the *Missouri Gazette,* November 2, 1809.

[26] Probably Samuel Latham Mitchill, one of the best known American scientists of the period.

[27] Probably a reference to Joel Barlow's *Columbiad.*

grown baby, he began to think that everybody about the House must regulate their conduct by his caprices.

'*De mortuis nil nisi bonum*'[28] is a good old maxim; but my character has been assailed, as respects our late Governor, and I owe to those I love some little account of myself.

I never saw, after his arrival in this country, anything in his conduct towards me, but alienation and unmerited distrust. I had acquired and shall retain a good portion of the public confidence, and he had not generosity of soul to forgive me for it. I was scarcely myself conscious of my good fortune; for the still voice of approbation with which I was favored by the People, was, as yet drowned in the clamours of my enemies. As soon as I was seen in conflict with my associates in business, my friends came forward with a generous and unexpected support. — I bore in silence the supercilious air of the Governor for a long time; until, last summer he took it into his head to disavow certain statements which I had made, *by his order* from the Secretary's Office. This was too much — I waited on him, — told him my wrongs — that I could not bear to be treated in such a manner — that he *had* given me the orders, & as truth is always eloquent, the Public *would believe* it on my assurances. He told me to take my own course — I shall, Sir, said I, and I shall come, in future to the Executive Office when I have *business* at it.

Some time after this, there was a ball in St. Louis, I attended early, and was seated in conversation with some Gentlemen when the Governor entered. He drew his chair close to mine — There was a pause in the conversation — I availed myself of it — arose and walked to the opposite

[28] Of the dead nothing but good.

side of the room. The dances were now commencing. — *He* also rose — evidently in passion, retired into an adjoining room and sent a servant for General Clark, who refused to ask me out as he foresaw that a Battle must have been the consequence of our meeting. He complained to the general that I had treated him with contempt & insult in the Ball-Room and that he could not suffer it to pass. He knew my resolutions not to speak to him except on business and he ought not to have thrust himself in my way. The thing *did pass* nevertheless for some weeks when General Clark waited on me for the purpose of inducing me to make some advances. I replied to him '*NO*, the Governor has told me to take my own course and I shall step a *high* and a *proud* Path. He has *injured* me, and he must *undo* that injury or I shall succeed in fixing the stigma where it *ought* to *rest*. You come' added I 'as *my* friend, but I cannot separate you from Gov Lewis — You have trodden the *Ups* & the *Downs* of life with him and it appears to me that these proposals are made solely for *his* convenience.'

At last, I had business at the Executive Office — He pressed me to be seated and made very handsome explanations. I told him that they *sounded* well; but that I could not accept them unless with the approbation of my friend Wm. C. Carr — *He,* with some other Gentlemen were then called in, & *this* particular misunderstanding adjusted to the entire satisfaction of Carr and myself.

Oh Lewis, how from my Love, I pity thee!
'Those who stand high, have many winds to shake them
And if they fall, they dash themselves to pieces'

I should not speak of these things now, but for the purpose of explaining what followed. Gov. Lewis, on his way

to Washington became *insane.* On the arrival of this unhappy news and before we heard of his death, an Honble.
Gentleman of this place, a Colleague of mine at the Land-
Board, commenced a regular and systematic traduction of
my character — He asserted in several respectable companies that the mental derangement of the Governor ought
not to be imputed to his political miscarriages; but rather
to the *barbarous conduct* of *the Secretary.* That Mr Bates
had been determined to tear down Gov Lewis, at all events,
with the hope of supplanting him in the Executive Office'
with a great deal of scandal equally false and malicious.
The persons who listened most attentively to these accusations, happened to be my very intimate friends Judge
Coburn and Doct Farrar.

I deliberated with myself 24 hours in what manner I
ought to proceed. Clement B. Penrose was worthy of my
resentment, as being nearly connected with the 'illustrious
House of Wilkinson' as well as on many other accounts.
But he has a *Wife* and *family.* A defiance ought not then,
if it could be avoided, to come from me. The second day
after I had heard these slanders I met him in public, at
the Board of Commissioners, after we had adjourned. I
charged him with the falsehoods which he had propagated
in concise and angry terms. He denied them and explained
'I have said that you were the enemy of Gov Lewis and
would willingly be the Governor yourself.' 'You have
gone farther than this Sir' said I 'and I will prove it upon
you. *I will not submit to your malicious impertinence Mr.
Penrose — I will chastise you for it — for two years past,
you have been in the habit of gossiping your scandals with
respect to me, and I pledge my word of Honor, that if you
ever again bark at my heels, I will spurn you like a Puppy*

from my Path' These reproaches made no impression upon him — he was only apprehensive of another kind of attack. He had denied the charge and I thought him too worthless for further notice. I satisfied myself with obtaining from Judge Coburn a Certificate of what I had alledged and with sending Aid Major McNair with a letter to Mr. Penrose, expressive of my hearty and everlasting Contempt for him. His reply to the Major was, that he would have me indicted for an Assault.

Richard, this is a strange world, in which we live! I had thought that my habits were pacific; yet I have had acrimonious differences with almost every person with whom I have been associated in public business. I have called myself to a very rigid account on this head, and before God, I cannot acknowledge that I have been blamable in any one instance. My passions blind me I suppose.

It is certain, nevertheless, that I float on a flowing tide of popular favor, without a diminution of credit that I know of at the City. 9/10ths of the People are ready to push me into the government, as much I presume, against the determinations of the President as contrary to my own inclinations.

The Recorder's Office united with the Secretaryship are *better, safer,* more *permanent,* more congenial with my habits, and offer me duties with the discharge of which I am intimately familiar. In the Government, I might have a three years' greatness and sink into oblivion. I could not hope to 'escape from the world's great snare uncaught.' My efforts are making for Judge Coburn; but *my* friends are not hearty in *his* support. I greatly fear that we shall miscarry.

I love you with unbounded confidence. Adieu.

JAMES ABBOTT TO BATES

DEAR SIR,   DETROIT, 9th November, 1809.

.   .   .   .

The troubles of Louisiana Territory are somewhat analogous to those of Michigan. — Governor H and the J[udges, th]at is, Woodward & Griffin are at open War, and have become so violent against each other, as to materially affect the prosperity of the Territory. — I am of opinion that the General Government will take notice of them; and it is the General opinion that one side must fall, to give peace. — The cry is no longer the People *vs.* the Governor & Judges   It is now the Heads of our Local Government against each other.

I am sorry to hear that your Governor Lewis is losing ground — I have always considered him as a worthy character, but as you say "Great men are generally judged by the results of their measures," and not by their intentions.

Mr. Hoffman requests me to tender to you his best respects and to inform you that he is in anxious expectation of the Letter you promised him in the note which Mr. Chené delivered to him at Mackinac last summer.

TO NATHANIEL POPE

SIR,   ST. LOUIS Nov 10th 1809

Assuredly, If I were in your situation, I should not recommend Judge Coburn, and it is as certain that if I had been acquainted with the personal causes of alienation which subsisted between you I never should have made the request.

TO WILLIAM O. ALLEN[29]

DEAR SIR,   SAINT LOUIS Nov 10. 1809.

Your friend Scott and myself conversed lately, on the subject of Judge Shrader's intended resignation. *You* were mentioned as his successor. Such an event, I have no doubt, would be pleasing to the country. Would not your friends in Virginia, mention you to the President? Those men of respectability and influence with whom you have correspondence in Williamsburg and Richmond, would, I should think without hesitation, give the proper assurances of your qualifications.

I take the liberty of writing to you, in-this business, with the openness of friendly regard. Your establishment in our country would give me particular pleasure; and could I be instrumental in your advancement, my aid should be contributed with the utmost alacrity.

But Sir, neither the President nor the Heads of Departments expect information of this kind from me. The standing of a territorial officer is generally precarious, and the scope of his influence, most commonly, I believe, limited to the sphere of his duties.

TO SAMUEL TREAT, ACTING FOR JOHN B. TREAT AS AGENT FOR INDIAN AFFAIRS AT THE ARKANSAS

SIR,   ST. LOUIS Nov 11. 1809

Capt Harvey delivered your letter of the 12th ulto. since which I have scarcely had a moment to answer it. An

[29] William O. Allen was a Virginian by birth. He enlisted in the regular army in 1812 and became a captain of infantry.

unusual press of unpleasant business of various kinds, has, for the last three weeks, afforded me but little respite.

The Letter *opening* the trade with the Indians, was written as you will observe by order of Governor Lewis — It was my private opinion that it should never have been *shut* and while I remain in the exercise of the government, the right of the citizen, which he derives from the Law of intercourse will not be suspended, unless in the event of war, *actual* or *impending.* — On the subject of Licences — John B. Treat Esq. has been authorized, by the late Secty of War to issue them — To prevent any disappointments which the absence of your brother might occasion, I enclose half a dozen blanks — With respect to the intrusions and depredations of the Cherokees, I think you ought to represent them to the War-Department. I shall also take the liberty of transmitting an extract of your letter. —

We cannot yet send you, your original Papers from the Recorder's Office. They are at this time before the commissioners, and in the keeping of their clerk. My young friend Mr. Honey who now acts in that capacity on behalf of his Brother has not had leisure to prepare the copies. —

TO THE JUDGES OF THE DISTRICT OF ARKANSAS

GENTLEMEN,   ST. LOUIS Nov 16. 1809

On the eve of Mr. Harvey's intended departure he called on me and resigned the several offices which he lately held in your district.

I send you blank commissions, and ask, that you will employ your best efforts in filling them worthily. On your success in this attempt will probably depend the existence of your Settlements as a *Separate District.*[30]

TO WILLIAM HENRY HARRISON

Secretary's Office
St. Louis Nov 16. 1809

SIR,

A question has lately arisen, which cannot be determined by the records of my Office, with respect to the District boundaries between Saint Louis and St. Genevieve. I am compelled to solicit information from you.

On relieving my Predecessor Dr. Browne, no record of the Executive acts of your Excellency, during your government of this country, was delivered to me. If the Secretary's Office of Indiana can supply any information as to the establishment of our Districts I take the liberty of requesting that you will have the goodness to cause it to be certified. Your attention to this request will confer on me a singular favor.

TO JEREMIAH CONNOR, SHERIFF OF THE DISTRICT OF ST. LOUIS

St. Louis 29 Nov 1809

SIR,

I expect you, as Jailor of the District of St. Louis to furnish my office with information as to the subsistence

---

[30] The previous year Governor Lewis issued a proclamation dividing the District of New Madrid. All that portion lying between the 33d parallel and the Second Chickasaw Bluff, and running indefinitely westward, was made into the District of Arkansas. Houck, *History of Missouri*, II, 412.

of persons in your custody under prosecution of the United States. In an especial manner I require you to report the manner in which a Sac Indian,[31] in your custody, has been provided with Fuel, if any, and provisions, from his commitment till the present time.

The manner in which you have thought proper to neglect my verbal request on the latter subject obliges me to inform you that I hope for an immediate compliance.

TO JEREMIAH CONNOR

SIR,

ST. LOUIS Nov 30. 1809.

I have received your letter of this day — It is a strange one, and such as I do hope no person exercising the government of this country will ever again receive from the Sheriff of the District of Saint Louis.

You are ignorant 'whether the Sac Indian has been furnished with 20 or 90 meals per month'!

Sir, that Indian, altho' guilty and condemned by the Laws is not to perish with hunger. If you have not a [reliable] Deputy Gaoler on whose honesty and diligence [you are able to depend] either provide one or per[mit me to appoint one. I do] not like the expressions of your

[31] The Sac Indian referred to killed a white man at Portage des Sioux. He was tried on July 27, 1808, found guilty, and sentenced to be executed, but was reprieved by the governor to avoid the appearance of partiality to the two Iowas who were tried about the same time. In October, 1809, a deputation of Sac and Fox chiefs visited St. Louis, one of their purposes being to ascertain the fate of the prisoner who had been held in jail for many months. Quasquami, a Sac chief, delivered an empassioned speech before Governor Lewis and General Clark. *Missouri Gazette*, July 26; August 2, 1808; and October 4, 1809.

letter. You are not to prescribe times for the adjustment of the public accounts. The application was *mine,* rather than *Anderson's.* — I do not choose to admit the certificates of Anderson as vouchers for his own accounts. The man is unknown to me. If his word is all sufficient, why not make it the basis of your certificate (since he is your Agent) rather than expect me to take it as a voucher for the payment of the public money?

I desire your attention to the 4th Section of an act of the 9th of November 1808 Page 342 of the territorial Laws.[32] Your duties are there ver, clearly prescribed as to persons prosecuted criminally under the laws of the territory: And I expect your promise, *unreservedly* and in *writing* and divested too of all reasoning which does not belong to the subject, that you will, in future, conform yourself to the provisions of that section, in all cases of criminal prosecution under the United States' Statutes.

TO JEREMIAH CONNOR

St. Louis Decr. 3d 1809. —

SIR,

You have satisfied but one branch of my demand — For the *future* we have made an adequate provision — Your promise is deemed most amply sufficient: But as to the *past* you have obstinately, and as I think, somewhat rudely, refused to account. — I *had* determined that you should be indulged in this; and were it reconcilable with my duty and

[32] Section 4 of the act of November 9, 1808, providing for compensations to deputy-jailors may be found in *Missouri Territorial Laws,* I, 224-225. Bates' reference is to the first edition of the laws.

with the regular transaction of the public business, I should have no objection to forget your late wanderings in expectation of an amendment: But certain intimations lately received, oblige me, to reiterate my original enquiry, made personally at your office, with no other alteration than a limitation of time How has the Sac Indian in your custody, been subsisted, from 4th Sept. till 30th Nov last?

If you suspect that your Deputy Gaoler has been negligent in supplying him with provisions, why not say so? If he has been faithful in the discharge of those trusts which *you* and not the government have reposed in him, let the account be settled. I have a right to know the truth and I will know it — And am determined that no private quarrels between you and your deputy, shall deprive me of that information, which you ought, on the first application to have promptly given.

Into whose custody was this criminal delivered on his condemnation? Sir, into *Your's* — and from *You* alone will I expect an account of him.

There are other charges which you will be obliged to answer in their proper order. *This* is the subject, however, on which I intend to establish my right of enquiring into your conduct. You appear, by no means satisfied that the Laws have established in *my* office, a censorship over *your's*. I shall proceed slowly and deliberately to convince you of this truth. One glaring neglect of duty has awakened accusations which might otherwise have slept. I had rocked the cradle of their repose.

Your contempt of my authority shall not provoke me to do you an injustice. I shall take care to be well assured of facts before I act upon them.

TO WILLIAM CHRISTY

SIR,   ST. LOUIS Dec 14. 1809

When I last spoke with you on the subject of Mr. Connor's intended removal, you expressed a desire that some arrangement might be made, by which he might be enabled to close certain business already commenced. — It was my first impression that I could not be a party to such arrangements, — and nothing which has since occurred, has in any wise contributed to change this opinion. — I write you this note in compliance with the promise which I made you.

TO ALEXANDER McNAIR

Secretary's Office
ST. LOUIS Dec 14. 1809.

SIR,

Desirous of availing the public of your services, I take the liberty to enclose you a commission as sheriff of the District of Saint Louis.

Jeremiah Connor esq has been removed from this office — and as the duties are pressing and incessant, it is much to be wished that you should immediately commence them. The Laws have made it the duty of your Predecessor to deliver to you the Papers appertaining to the office.

TO JEREMIAH CONNOR

SAINT LOUIS Dec 14. 1809.

SIR,

I received, this afternoon, your letter desiring a statement of the reasons or the facts, on which my late determinations with respect to your removal, were founded.

Without entering into a discussion of the principles on
which you have thought proper to make the demand, I have
no hesitation in giving you the statement. I promised you
this, a few days ago, in the conversations which we had
on these subjects; and the performance of this promise
was only *delayed,* not *forgotten.* It was desirable that there
should not be a vacancy, until a successor was provided.

The reasons inducing the removal grow out of the following facts

1st   Irregularity and remissness in discharge of the
Sheriff's duties

2nd   A mode deemed oppressive and unknown to the Laws,
in the collecting of taxes

3d   Repeated failures, for years past, to settle your accounts with the district

4th   The charge of Fees not provided for by Law.

Entirely convinced of the truth of these facts, it is my
unpleasant duty to inform you, that your commission as
sheriff of the District of St. Louis, has been, this day,
revoked.[33]

[33] The following statement appeared in the *Louisiana Gazette,* January 18, 1810:

To the Public.

I had indulged the hope that the uneasiness naturally occassioned
by a removal from Office, would not in my case, be aggravated by a misrepresentation of the causes assigned or conjectured, which produced it.
A short excursion into the country have convinced me how fallacious
my expectations have been. What these misrepresentations are, I deem
it unnecessary *at present* to state, they have served, however to awaken
a solicitude for my *reputation,* which I had trusted have remained un-
assailed: and nothing but the imperious necessity which such a consideration imposes, would have induced me, thus to trespass on the public
attention.

The anxiety naturally felt, and, I hope, correctly indulged, leads me
to request a temporary suspension of the opinion of the Public, and of

Alexr. Mc Nair esq has been appointed your Successor. He will receive from you such Papers, keys of the Jail & other appurtenances of the Office as the Law requires to be delivered.

TO WILLIAM EUSTIS

St. Louis Jany. 12th. 1810

Sir,

On the return of Major Chouteau from the Mandans it was his intention to have visited the City, in order to explain those parts of his conduct, which had not, as he feared, been sufficiently understood. I heard this determination with the more regret, as I had always been of opinion that an honest and frank account, by letter, would dissipate all distrusts and be entirely satisfactory. I prevailed with him therefore, to suspend, for the present, all anxiety on a subject with respect to which I entertained no doubt, that his conduct would be ultimately approved. The truth was, that the business of the Indian Department could not be transacted without him and the occurrences of every day rendered it indispensable that his weight and authority should supply the absences of others. This was seen and felt by us both; and altho' I did not think myself

my Friends, relative to my dismissal; and I feel a becoming confidence, that whatever impressions may have been made on the mind of the acting Executive, either from his own knowledge of my Conduct, or misrepresentations thereof by others, I shall be able when a proper opportunity offers, to present to them such testimonials as shall convince them, that no conduct of mine has been such as to incur the forfeiture of their esteem for me as a Man, or Confidence in me as an Officer

Jeremiah Connor

Late Sheriff, of the District of St. Louis.
St. Louis, Jan. 18, 1810.

authorized, absolutely, to prohibit his departure, yet, he acquiesced with cheerfulness in the propriety of my suggestions.

I have thought it advisable that the department generally, should be paid by Major Chouteau for the last quarter, and in the hope of your approbation have ventured to give an order to that effect. The Interpreters have been accustomed to this regularity and suffer much embarrassment from delay. These disbursements amount to the sum of $985. .44 cts the vouchers in support of which are believed to be correct and regular. The contingent part of this account was incurred with my previous approbation.

TO EDWARD HEMPSTEAD

St. Louis Jan: 20. 1810

Sir,

Major Christy has just delivered me your note of yesterday. I owe you no explanations. It is a plain case. Your conduct[34] has extorted from me certain accusations, the truth of which is sustained by the most imposing facts. It is in vain that you unite yourself with other persons. I shall know how to separate you. The gentlemen of this town have an unquestionable and permit me to say an *unquestioned* right to entertain and to express their opinions of individual character: But *you* — You have committed yourself.

Men of worth and honor heard our conversation and will not fail to stamp this transaction with its true character.

[34] Hempstead signed a certificate of good conduct of Connor, the sheriff who was removed from office. This was the cause of Bates' anger.

TO THOMAS F. RIDDICK AND WILLIAM O. ALLEN

St. Louis Jany 20. 1810.

Gentlemen

The conversation, a few evenings past, between Mr. Hempstead the Atty. General & myself in the office of Mr. Riddick was of too unpleasant a nature to have been altogether forgotten by you.

An incident of this morning has rendered it very desirable that I should obtain a written statement of the affair.

You were the only gentlemen present; and surely there are none on whose accurate recollection, or on whose love of truth I would sooner repose myself than on yours'.

I take the liberty then of requesting that you will have the goodness to state the *subject* of conversation, the *manner* and the *circumstances,* in such detail, as to exhibit to others a true account of the misunderstanding and to prevent facts from future misrepresentation.

Note. This letter was answered by a circumstantial & satisfactory detail wch. I have filed.   F. B.

TO EDWARD HEMPSTEAD[35]

St. Louis Jany. 22d. 1810. —

Sir,

In discharge of the executive duties it will be incumbant upon me to inform the President of your having been counsel for this office, in the removal of the sheriff of the District of Saint Louis; and of your having afterwards signed a certificate of that officer's good conduct.

[35] This letter was marked "not sent."

You are no longer Attorney General of the territory of Louisiana. Consider this as your dismission.

TO EDWARD HEMPSTEAD

SIR,

St. Louis ·January 22d. 1810

We have been long acquaintances, and altho' nothing like *friendship* entered into our intercourse, I nevertheless feel some little desire to assist you in forming a just estimate of yourself. — Hempstead! I charge you fling away ambition. Forbear all hasty and blustering pretensions to the rank of a gentleman: The doors are closed upon you by memorable *faux pas* of former times: Be satisfied with that course which the Fates have marked out for you, and do not aspire beyond the reputation of *instrumentality,* and a *pettyfogging readiness* in business, for which alone you are valued. Transfuse a little of that close arrangement for which you are so remarkable in ordinary business into your moral oeconomy, and regain by modesty and repentance the forfeited regards of the Public. — Do not mistake me; — this is not intended, either as injury or insult. Your reputation languishes; and nothing but health-restoring medicines ought to be administered. Be honest — O cease to be treacherous, and some hopes may be entertained of you. — If you are wise enough to receive this advice with the same candour in which it is given, you may possibly live to thank me for it. But if, on the contrary your usual cunning should forsake you, and you should be stupid enough to take it as an affront, recollect that I am not to be answerable for the consequences. — O well remembered! Have you forgotten your unworthy suggestions about Judge Stuart? This enquiry is not foreign,—it is closely connected with the subject of the present difference. — Hempstead! retrace your wandering footsteps — You see that between ourselves I can substantiate everything against you. Do not impose upon me the unpleasant task of publishing you to the world. You know the perseverance of my temper and I am ready, however reluctantly, to give you new specimens.

[Note.] The foregoing was to have been sent with a statement of Messrs. Riddick & Allen but suppressed in consequence of E. H's having recalled a saucy Letter wch. he wrote me in reply to mine of the 20th instant.

F. Bates.

TO EDWARD HEMPSTEAD

St. Louis Jan 30: 1810.

Sir,

Mr Riddick has this moment delivered me yr. letter of yesterday. The circumstances to which there has been much painful reference, warranted the construction which I put upon your conduct, and, as I then believed, justified my resentments. I do now regret the whole affair.

And since you state, that in signing the certificate you did not intend to certify any thing contrary to the conversation which you had with me previously to the removal of Mr. Connor, nor as censuring me for his removal, which you have always thought was proper, I think I ought to say that I never should have taken offence at *that* or any other act of your's, if known to have been unaccompanied by intention — I do freely declare that any asperity of expression made use of by me arose, solely, out of the circumstances.

A PARDON

FREDERICK BATES

Secretary of the Territory of Louisiana and Exercising the Government

to all whom it may concern

Whereas the Court of Quarter Sessions for the District of New Madrid, did, at July term last, impose on William Ordway two several fines, the One of $30 for selling spiritous liquors to Indians; the other of $20 for trading with a slave in violation of the Laws[36] of this territory: And Whereas the said William Ordway, after the imposition of the said fines, departed this life, leaving a Wife and numerous family of infant, female children in indigent circumstances. Now therefore, be it known that I do hereby pardon the offences for which the said fines were imposed & require that all sheriffs or other collecting officers take one notice hereof. In testimony whereof I have hereunto affixed the Seal of the Territory of Louisiana. Given under my hand at St. Louis the 15th day of February, in the year of our Lord, one thousand eight hundred & ten & of the Independence of the United States of America the thirty fourth.

Frederick Bates.

[36] Trading with a slave, without the consent of the master, owner, or overseer of such slave, was prohibited by sections 11 and 18 of a law of October 1, 1804. *Missouri Territorial Laws*, I, 27-33.

WILSON P. HUNT TO BATES

NEW YORK March 8. 1810

DEAR SIR

I had this pleasure some days ago at Washington, and should have repeated it during my short stay there but was so hurried, in leaving that place a few days sooner than I contemplated I defered it for more leisure.

Every thing relative to our territory stood as when I last wrote you — the Government seemed to be determined to proceed in the appointments, at least slowly, if not judiciously, but from what I could learn I had great hopes of Coburn for Governor. As to the discontinuance of Judge Lucas I could scarcely form a conjecture (my wishes lead me to hope a great deal) and I had considerable encouragement from a number of Senators that they would oppose him — but he having written to a number of his old acquaintances I suspect they will have sufficient interest with the President to procure his nomination, and I fear to contest the confirmation.

. I made such interest with the Federalists as to secure their unanimous votes against him, and Mr Bayard[37] promised to *oppose* his confirmation.

Judge Griffin[38] being at York in Virginia, and knowing he wished to be transferred to Louisiana I wrote to him to come to Washington, which I presume he has done. Col. Meigs[39] was much in favor of him — and Bradford prom-

[37] James Asheton Bayard, United States senator from Delaware. He was one of the commissioners who signed the Treaty of Ghent. For his *Papers*, see American Historical Association, *Annual Report, 1913*, II.

[38] Cyrus Griffin, judge of the United States district court for Virginia from 1789 until his death on December 14, 1810.

[39] Probably Return J. Meigs, Jr., United States senator from Ohio.

ised Smith[40] he would try to bring about the transfer, and I should very much like to see it, for I think Griffin would suit us better than a stranger — I am sure he would please the people generally —

Gen. Clark returned from Washington with the same situation he held when he came, and I believe there is no doubt of the government having been offered to him — I admire his prudence in refusing it very much.

I believe I mentioned having seen Mr Gallatin at his own house, but had not any conversation with him of consequence — I met him a few evenings before I left Washington at Mr Madison's where we had a little chat that was very pleasing to me, and I presume will not be ungrateful to you. Speaking of the Commissioners, generally, and particularly, he said little of Lucas — Penrose was a good man, but a very weak one — and as to you to use his own words "we had wished to make him Governor, but in the land business we have always considered him a kind of Umpire without whom we should not know how to proceed — we might get as good a man but he is now so well acquainted with the business (and something about the confidence we have in him) we consider him as indispensable" —

I mentioned to this gentleman and the Secretary of War your having allowed Bleakley &c to come on our side the Mississippi, and explained the thing — why you did it — thinking it best they should have correct information, and fearing it might be represented differently — they both seemed to understand it, and are alike your friends

[40] Probably John Smith, a congressman from Virginia. At that time there were three other Smiths in congress: Senator John Smith of Ohio, Senator John Smith of New York, and Senator Samuel Smith of Maryland.

You will see from the papers that there appears to be no apprehension of war between us & England, and that our commerce is likely to resume its former liberty —

JAMES ABBOTT TO BATES

DETROIT, 15th March, 1810.

DEAR SIR:

I wrote you on the 9th November 1809 (a duplicate of the same is enclosed) since which I have not had the pleasure of any of your favors.

You will perhaps be surprised to hear of the Death of George Hoffman, Esq.: he died on the 2nd instant after an illness of five days. The *bottle* I believe was the cause of his exit at such an early period of his life. From all accounts he drank very hard. After his death two wills appeared; one of which was executed in April 1809 and the other in February 1810. By the first he disinherits the child which his wife was then pregnant with; leaving her one third of his personal property, and the remainder together with his real estate he bequeaths to his family connections at Chillicothe. In his last will he does not even mention his wife nor child, but bequeaths the whole of his property real and personal to his parents. What could be the cause of such conduct is almost incomprehensible. I have read of children being disinherited for dishonesty, libertinism and disobedience to their parents, but a child yet in the mother's womb to be disinherited I have never heard of, and there is something in such an act horrid beyond expression. You can judge of the feelings of Mr. Audrain in this case.

·JOHN RICE JONES[41] TO BATES

SIR,

KASKASKIA 23d March 1810

Shall I beg the favor of you to deliver Mr Robert Morrison, who does me the honor to be the bearer hereof, a Copy, certified by you as Recorder, of the Claim and all the Papers laid in by the heirs of Renaut to lands in the District of Louisiana — These papers I have immediate need of, so that I hope you will forward them by Mr Morrison[42] — who will pay office fees —

TO JOHN DONNOHUE[43]

SIR,

ST. LOUIS Mar 30. 1810

I had the honor some time ago to receive your letter of the 9th Inst. The Commissions therein recommended will be handed you by Adjt. Genl Delaunay, except that of Pay Master: The 24th Sec of the Militia-Law[44] having provided the manner in which that Officer shall be nominated, I must

[41] John Rice Jones was a prominent lawyer of Kaskaskia.

[42] Robert Morrison was an extensive land claimant in Illinois. He was violently opposed to Harrison and was one of the leaders for the separation of Illinois from Indiana Territory. In 1810 he was clerk of the general court.

[43] Major of the 1st battalion of the Ste. Genevieve regiment.

[44] The 24th section of the militia law of July 6, 1807 was as follows: "A majority of the field officers of each regiment with the commandant, shall nominate fit persons within their bounds to the governor of the territory, the one as paymaster, the other as judge advocate of the regiment. And the governor shall, if he thinks the said persons, respectively qualified, appoint and commission them for these several duties. It shall be especially the duty of the judge advocate, to prosecute in behalf of the United States, and also perform such other services as are by this act prescribed." *Missouri Territorial Laws*, I, 157.

trouble you to mention the subject to Colo. Cook,[45]   Mr. Mc Arthur[46] is no doubt, a very proper person; but as the nomination is vested by law in the Field Officers, we ought not, for a little delay, for a slight neglect of theirs, to forget their rights.   In the commissions which I send you, I have left blanks for the No. of the company.   Will you have the goodness to fill them up[?]

TO ROBERT SMITH

Sr. Louis April 1st. 1810

Sir,

I have the honor to transmit herewith copies of the Executive Acts for the last six months.   During this period there has been no meeting of the Legislature.

I have never been favored with any intimations of the manner in which these Reports should be made.   Perhaps they are too much compressed; and it is possible that they may be deemed defective in some other respects.   Should they not meet the expectations of the President in their present form, my letter Book together with the Files of the Office will enable me to amplify them.

TO ALBERT GALLATIN

Sr. Louis April 1st. 1810

Sir,

I have the honor to enclose accounts of the contingent expences of the Secretary's office for ye. two years pre-

[45] Nathaniel Cook.
[46] Probably John McArthur, who, in 1812, became a lieutenant in the Ste. Genevieve regiment.

ceding the present day; together with the receipts vouching the expenditure. The errors in former accounts are corrected in these & I hope no new ones committed. I beg permission to draw for the amount.

TO NINIAN EDWARDS

Sir,
St. Louis April 24. 1810

I beg leave to introduce to your acquaintance Mr. Morehead of the house of Messrs. Henry M. Shreves & Co.[47] — He is lately from Philadelphia, and has established himself, as a resident merchant in our town.

Mr. M. did me the favor to present Letters from General Neville of Pittsburgh in which he is mentioned by that Gentleman in the most handsome terms. His connections are very highly respectable. His Lady is the daughter of the late General Shreves, who bled in the revolutionary cause; and I will venture to assure you that Mr. M. is himself worthy of those attentions which I take the liberty of soliciting in his behalf. — He will probably have business at the Executive Office. — Should security be necessary in granting him, a Licence for Indian Trade, I am willing, if accepted, to join him in the bond: Or if my non residence should be an objection, I will engage, as these Gentlemen are Strangers, whose business would suffer by delay, that satisfactory Security shall be supplied in one month.

[47] Henry M. Shreve and Company ran a general store in St. Louis.

A PROCLAMATION

By Frederick Bates

Secretary of the Territory of Louisiana and Exercising
the Government thereof

Whereas the extended limits of the township of Bon Homme
in the district of [St.] Louis, render the distribution of
justice inconvenient and burthensome to the Western Settlements of the said township:

In remedy whereof and in discharge of those duties
imposed on the Executive by the 'Act further providing
for the government of the district of Louisiana' I do hereby
declare that the Settlements of the present district of Bon
Homme lying westward of a line to be drawn due south
from the mouth of Tavern Creek on the Missouri to the
Merimac shall, from and after the 15th day of the present
month form a new township to be known and denominated
the township of Labbadie.   And those civil officers appointed heretofore for the township of Bon Homme,
and who reside within the limits, herein designated, of
the new township of Labbadie, shall, from and after
the said 15th day of the present month, be considered
as Officers of the latter township.   In testimony whereof
I have hereunto affixed the Seal of the Territory of Louisiana.   Given under my hand at the town of St. Louis the
fourth day of May in the year of our Lord, one thousand
eight hundred & ten & of the Independence of the United
States of America, the thirty fourth.

(Seal)   Frederick Bates

TO ALBERT GALLATIN

SIR,

ST. LOUIS May 8. 1810

Thomas F. Riddick esq the Clerk of the Board, resigned his office on the 4th inst. compelled by the urgency of his private business in Virginia. His half brother Mr. Jno. W. Honey was on the same day, unanimously elected to supply his place.

If Mr. Riddick should visit the City on his way to Nansemond he will be desirous of paying his respects to you & if your leisure permit will have the honor of handing you this. I beg permission to say that his representations with respect to the business in which he was lately employed, may be relied upon. By an unwearied and intelligent discharge of his duties he acquired and preserved the entire confidence of every individual of the Board.

TO JAMES ABBOTT

SIR,

ST. LOUIS May 9. 1810

.   .   .   .

As to domestic news, we are told that Benj. Howard[48] of Kentucky, has been appointed Governor of Louisiana. Judge Lucas has been reappointed, contrary to the expectation of a host of enemies,[49] but very much to my satisfaction. I was at one time fearful that Government would

[48] In 1800 Howard was elected to the Kentucky legislature. In 1807 he was elected a member of congress from Clay's district, a position which he resigned to become governor of Louisiana Territory.

[49] For attacks upon Judge Lucas, see the *Missouri Gazette*, October 12, 1809; *Louisiana Gazette*, January 11 and March 8, 1810.

listen to the clamours which had been so industriously raised and supported by ignorance and prejudice. Our old acquaintance Mr. Griswold[50] is certainly appointed a Judge of the Illinois territory. . . .

TO RICHARD FLETCHER, NEW MADRID

ST. LOUIS May 16. '10

SIR,

Yr letter of the 1st inst. was recd. yesterday. You mistake my powers. I neither make sales nor give permissions to settle. The Settlement of Congress-Lands is, at this time, punished with much severity — There has been much forbearance in the execution of the Laws, but I should betray my trust and violate my duty by giving the least encouragement — Until an office is opened for the sale of Lands there are in Louisiana, no means by which they can be procured, except by purchase from individuals.

TO JAMES ABBOTT

ST. LOUIS May 23. 1810

DEAR SIR,

I send the power of Attorney, so long expected, and so unnecessarily delayed since last year. — No news — Our Governor has not arrived — Under his administration I do greatly hope that party animosities of former times will be forever forgotten. — The People petitioned Congress

---

[50] Illinois Territory was proclaimed April 28, 1809. Stanley Griswold soon replaced Obediah Jones as one of the three judges. Alvord, *The Illinois Country, 1673-1818,* p. 430.

last year for the 2d grade.[51] It has for the present been refused them, but in such terms of encouragement as will probably induce them to renew the application at next Session. My private convictions are that it is inexpedient *now,* and for some years to come; yet as our population is most aboundantly sufficient, and as I could have nothing but arguments drawn from an abstract reasoning to alledge, I have thought it most prudent not to partake in the discussion.

TO GEORGE RUDDELL AND OTHERS

GENTLEMEN

St. Louis May 31. 1810

Mr Galliher this moment presented your application for a district organization, the seat of justice for which to be at the Little Prairie —[52]

Considerations of various kinds induce me to believe that the establishment of such a district is at present inexpedient. Yet, altho' I cannot feel myself at liberty to hazard an experiment, which would, in operation I am persuaded, disappoint the hopes of its advocates, I will, notwithstanding submit your Papers to the Governor, on his arrival, who will probably act on them uninfluenced by any opinions of mine.

[51] The petition was presented to congress on January 6, 1810. *Annals of Congress*, 11 Cong., 1 and 2 Sess., 1809-1810, Pt. I, 1157, 1253. For the text of the petition, see Shoemaker, *Missouri's Struggle for Statehood*, 27. A bill further to provide for the government of the Territory of Louisiana was presented by Rhea of Tennessee on January 6, 1810, but it died in committee.

[52] The trading post at Little Prairie was established in 1794. A settlement grew up about it and prospered until the earthquake of 1811.

JOSEPH N. AMOUREUX[53] TO BATES

HONORED SIR   NEW MADRID June 6th 1810 —

Your kind reception of me when at St Louis makes me feel a Confidence in adressing you at this time. A wish to make myself useful to Government makes me desirous of having the appointment of an assistant to take the Census of The Inhabitants of this District; I hope that from the knowledge I have of the Country & Speaking both Languages I will be able to be Correct and expeditious. —

TO ALBERT GALLATIN

SIR,   ST. LOUIS June 13th 1810.

I had the honor to receive by this week's mail your letter of the 5th ulto. and submitted it without loss of time to the commissioners. They have not instructed me to make to you, any assurances of their future diligence in the adjustment of the Land-Claims. They know however that it would be my duty to reply to your letter by the first Post, and trusted, no doubt, that my knowledge of their industry heretofore, together with much general conversation which we had on the subject, would enable me to satisfy your inquiries.

The Commissioners, I am very sure, are truly sensible of the importance of a speedy and final adjustment of the claims. They regret indeed that the pressure, in Congress,

---

53 Joseph Amoureux, a native of Boucheville, Canada, was a blacksmith at Vincennes as early as 1769, and moved to New Madrid in 1793. The writer of the above letter was probably his son, an ensign in the Ste. Genevieve regiment during the War of 1812.

of other business, should have caused them to be neglected; but at the same time are not conscious that that neglect has occasioned any relaxation on their part. I am entirely convinced that every effort will be made to transmit the report during next session. — The want of compensation has been embarrassing to the clerk of the Board, of whose resignation, some time since, I had the honor to advise you. The business, nevertheless has suffered no interruption on that account — as John W. Honey the half brother of Mr. Riddick, and formed to business by his precepts and example has accepted the Office — the duties of which he discharges now as on a former occasion, to the entire satisfaction of the commissioners. — We were informed, indirectly, that the Bill reported for our compensation, provided *fees* on the final disposal of every claim. May I be permitted to say, that such a mode would have been less acceptable to a *majority of the Board* than the entire silence of Congress with respect to us.

TO JOSEPH N. AMOUREUX, NEW MADRID

SIR,   ST. LOUIS June 26. 1810.

Your letter of the 6th was received, some short time ago — but as the instructions of the Secretary of State had not then come to hand, I resolved to wait their arrival, that I might answer you with the more certainty. —

I have now recd those instructions, and have much pleasure in naming you as the Assistant to take the Census of the Inhabiants of New Madrid.

In order that there may be an entire conformity in the returns from the several states and territories the Secretary of State has transmitted blank forms; but as the Packet must be of considerable bulk it has not yet come forward. As soon as it arrives I shall lose no time in sending you all the necessary informations.

I enclose you the Oath which you will take as well as subscribe, and return to this office.

The enumeration is expected positively to commence on the first Monday of August. . . .

P. S. I send you herewith the three Acts passed at the last session on the subject of the census — Mr Gallatin has as yet given no orders on the subject of manufactures —

TO HENRY DODGE, SHERIFF OF THE DISTRICT OF STE. GENEVIEVE

St. Louis June 26. 1810.

Sir,

Under the several Acts of Congress which you have probably seen, on the subject of the Census I have been instructed by the Secretary of State to appoint Assistants for the several civil divisions of the territory and to cause the enumeration to commence on the 1st day of August next.

I take the liberty of enquiring whether it will be agreeable to you to act as Asst. Secretary in this business for the district of St. Genevieve? —

I know that the emoluments are scarcely worth your acceptance; but in the discharge of your duties of Sheriff it may perhaps be in your power to take the census with less additional trouble than others would experience.

There are pressing applications for this appointment by persons in whom neither the Public nor myself have much confidence. — You will oblige me by writing as soon as convenient.

TO ROBERT SMITH

Sᴛ. Lᴏᴜɪs June 26. 1810.

Sɪʀ,

I had the honor to receive by yesterday's mail, your letter of 17 ulto. with its several accompaniments on the subject of the Census to wit

1 copy of the Letter of Instructions
1 do. of the Acts
4 do. of the Oaths of Assistants
2 copies of the Oaths of the Secretary
1 do. of Returns of Assistants
2 do. of do. of Secretary

The next mail will probably bring a second Packet, containing the other Papers which you have mentioned.

TO JAMES GREEN,[54] ST. CHARLES

Sᴛ. Lᴏᴜɪs June 29. '10

Sɪʀ,

Since I had the pleasure of conversing with you I have recd. instructions from the Secy. of State on the subject of the Census. In these instructions I am directed to select as Assistants those persons who are presumed to be best acquainted with the several settlements within their respective limits.

This injunction induces me to ask the aid of the Sheriffs, unless in cases where special reasons decide the preference

---

[54] James Green came to Louisiana in the winter of 1797-1798.

in favor of others. *Besides,* the necessity of this course appears to be dictated by the selection which the law makes of the Marshals in the States. I regret that these considerations should have prevented the arrangement of which we spoke. The views of Govt. are better accomplished by the appointment of an individual already in the discharge of ministerial duties.

TO JOSEPH N. AMOUREUX

SIR,   ST. LOUIS July 24. 1810

I wrote you on the 26th ulto. accepting your offers of service as an Assistant for taking the Census . . . within the district of New Madrid.

I send you the Papers as noted below from which you will gather all the instruction which can be necessary for an intelligent discharge of your duties.

You will observe from the manner in which you are to be paid that service must precede compensation — Your Returns must be made to this Office by the first Monday in January next But counting as I think I reasonably may on your diligence I entertain the hope that it will be as convenient for you to transmit them in Decr. as Jany. Be pleased to acknowledge the receipt of this letter & its accompanyments.

TO BENJAMIN FOOY

SIR,   ST. LOUIS July 24. 1810

I make so free as to appoint you an Assistant for taking the Census of the People of Hope Field, and of the settlements near the mouth of the river St. Francis.

You must not decline this Office; for I am solicitous to shew Government that I am aided in the discharge of my duties by men of worth and character.

The accompanying Papers will give you every necessary information. Should it not be in your power to execute this trust, I shall be very thankful if you will procure some fit person whose fidelity may be depended upon. Let him take the Oaths and go on with the business without waiting for a regular appointment from me.

You have given me so many friendly instances of your disposition to render me service that I take the farther liberty to enclose to your care a Packet for Danl. Mooney esq. Asst. within the settlements of the Arkansas. I know that you will be so friendly as to give it the most expeditious conveyance. The Returns are required to be made by the first Monday in January next. Yet I shall esteem it a favor if you will let me have them much earlier than that time. Oblige me by sending duplicates by different conveyances for fear of a miscarriage.

TO DANIEL MOONEY, SHERIFF OF THE DISTRICT OF ARKANSAS

SECRETARY'S OFFICE July 24 1810

SIR, .

I appoint you Assistant for taking the Census of the People for the district of the Arkansas except those in the settlements of Hope Field, and at the mouth of the river St. Francis, which latter places have been allotted to Judge Fooy. This Office is not expected, as you will remark from the law, to be a profiitable one, yet it is one, which it appears to me no good Citizen will decline unless altogether incompatible with his other pursuits.

I send you all the necessary information viz The Laws, the Circulars of the Secy. of State, — Assistants' oaths, a blank return as a model and which you can enlarge by sewing in additional sheets: Also two heads of Returns, which will be pasted on a quire, ½ quire or other proper quantity of Paper, ruling afterwards from the indications in the heading. Should sickness or other unavoidable accident prevent your undertaking this business, I hope you will without farther reference to myself (as the distance will not permit it) cause the Oaths to be taken and the enumeration made by some other discreet person. —

You will observe that your Returns are to be made to this office by the 1st Monday in January 1811 But in consideration of the delays and even frequent miscarriages between Arkensas and St. Louis, I must request that you will, with all possible diligence make the enumeration, and transmit duplicate returns by different conveyances as soon as circumstances will allow.

TO HENRY DODGE

                                    St. Louis July 25. 1810
SIR,

I recd. your letter of the 3d inst. and was gratified by your acceptance of a troublesome and profitless office. I now send you 2 Circulars of Secy of State — The Census Laws — 2 Assistants Oaths — 1 blank Return as a model & 4 Schedules or heads of Returns. —

Your Returns must be made to this office by the 1st Monday in January next. I should be much obliged if they could be made before that time.

TO JAMES CALLAWAY[55]

Secretary's Office
SIR, ST. LOUIS July 25th 1810.

I had the pleasure to receive, in due time, your letter of the 26th ulto. and do hereby appoint you Secretary's Assistant for taking Census of the People within the district of St. Charles.

I should have written you sooner, but for the miscarriage of certain dispatches from the Department of State. It has been necessary to cause the printing to be done here — and it has required time.

I now transmit you 2 circulars of the Secretary of State — 2 copies of the Census laws, 2 Assistant's Oaths, 2 blank Returns — and four heads of Returns — These latter, as you may have occasion for them, are to be pasted on a quire, or other proper quantity of Paper in the manner of the Model. The Paper, after being sewed, at the usual fold of the quire, will be ruled with very little trouble, from the indications in the heading. I am sorry that your lameness deprived me of the pleasure of seeing you. I am persuaded that the informations which these Papers contain are all which you will require on the subject.

---

[55] James Callaway was a grandson of Daniel Boone. He eventually settled in what is now Howard County. In August, 1813, he served under Nathan Boone who conducted a reconnoitring expedition into Illinois. Early in 1814 he was in command of a party of rangers who were attacked by Indians near the confluence of the Prairie Forks of Loutre Creek. Callaway and four others were killed. The Callaway Papers belong to the Missouri Historical Society.

TO WILLIAM GARNER

Secretary's Office
ST. LOUIS July 25. 1910.

SIR,

I do hereby appoint you Secretary's Assistant for taking the Census of the People within the district of Cape Girardeau. The accompanying Papers will give you every information which can be necessary in the discharge of your duties viz 2 copies of the Census Laws, 2 circulars of the Secy. of State, 2 Assistants Oaths, 1 blank Return as a model, and which if you please can be enlarged by sewing a number of sheets of Paper in the middle, at the usual fold & ruling them by the indications in the heading: also 4 Schedules as heads of Returns, which may [be] pasted by yourself, on quires of Paper, in the same manner as I have done for you, in the model.

I beg that you will read the Laws and the circular instructions of the Secy. of State with much care. I count much on your attention and diligence in this business. Your returns must be made at this office by 1st Monday in January next — and should be much pleased to have them sooner.

TO JOHN HAYS,[56] SHERIFF OF THE DISTRICT OF CAPE GIRARDEAU

SIR,   ST. LOUIS July 26. 1810.

I take the liberty of enquiring whether it will be agreeable to you to act as Secretary's Assistant in taking the

---

[56] John Hays was commissioned by Governor Harrison as the first sheriff of the Cape Girardeau District.

Census of the Dt. of Cape Girardeau? If inconvenient to
yourself, you will greatly oblige me by naming some person in whom that trust may be reposed, and will be willing
to accept it. As the arrangements must be immediately
made, I beg that you will answer this letter without delay.
In the event of your acceptance, the forms, and every necessary information will be transmitted to you.

TO JOHN B. C. LUCAS

SIR,   ST. LOUIS July 29. 1810.

I think it my duty to inform you that Mr. Penrose is mistaking the sphere of his usefulness & discharging the trust
lately confided to him very contrary to, and much beyond
my constructions of the Resolution of the Board. He is
not only entering the whole business (as I am told) in the
rough minutes; but also filling up the Registry with rejected cases, and noting by anticipation, *future* confirmations, with a conjectural date too, on the margins of the
books.

This appears to me to be departure from his duty both
wide & wanton; and it is probable that he will proceed in
the same course tomorrow, unless he be told that no such
power either has been or could have been committed to him.

TO ROBERT SMITH

SIR,   ST. LOUIS July 31. 1810

In addition to the papers on the subject of the Census,
the receipt of which I had the honor to acknowledge in a

letter to you of the 26th ulto. I yesterday received a 2d packet, containing 7 Cops. of Instructions 7 Cops. of the Census Laws, 14 Copies of Assistants Oaths & 7 Cops. of Assistants Returns.

I beg leave to observe that I had so many and just reasons to apprehend a miscarriage of this latter packet, that I caused the necessary printing to be done at this place. The receipt of the first packet was fortunate, as it enabled me to ascertain your views, and, in due time, to make the preliminary arrangements in conformity with them. Some days previously to the arrival of this second packet, the allotment had been all completed and every necessary paper transmitted to the several Assistants. Duplicates were sent to the distant settlements of the Arkensas, by private conveyance, lest the packets by mail should suffer delay or miscarriage.

It is probable that the accounting Officers of the Treasury will admit this little charge of extra printing, in the contingent expenses of my Office.

TO BENJAMIN FOOY

Sir,   St. Louis Augt. 1. 1810

I wrote you on the 24th July appointing you Secretary's Assistant for taking the Census of the People within the Settlements of Hope-Field, and of those near the mouth of St. Francis' River.

As this [is] a business on which government is anxious to be accurately informed I take the liberty of repeating, by private conveyance, my most earnest hope that you will not refuse me your assistance. Accompanying this, you will receive 2 circulars of the Secy. of State — The Census Laws — 2 Assistants Oaths, 1 Blank Return and 4 heads of Schedules. By Post, together with your own packet, you will receive one for Mr. Daniel Mooney Asst. for the settlements of the Arkansas.

TO DANIEL MOONEY

SIR,
St. Louis Augt. 1st. 1810.

Apprehending miscarriage, or at any rate, delay of my letter to you by Post, of 24th of last month, I avail myself of a private conveyance to inform you, that I have appointed you Secy's Assistant for taking the Census of the People of the district of the Arkansas, except those at Hope Field and near the mouth of the St. Francis, which have been allotted to Judge Fooy. Enclosed herewith you will find the Census Laws, 2 Circulars of the Secy. of State, 2 Assistants Oaths, 1 Blank Return and 4 Schedules or heads of Returns. If, from any unforeseen, or unavoidable circumstances, it should be out of your power to attend to this business, I beg that you will cause it to be done by some intelligent and discreet person, as the distance & difficulty of communication will not allow me time to make a second appointment. An Answer is requested containing a receipt for the pàpers.

TO NINIAN EDWARDS

SIR,
St. Louis Augt. 2d. 1810

I take the liberty to enclose you a Petition of Charles Relle and Baptise & Francis Piqueur. The application was improperly made to me, as the Kickapoos by whom the property is alledged to have been stolen, reside within your government. —

I avail myself of this occasion to say that the Illinois Indians make frequent visits to this place under the pretext of talk with the public Agents, and not unfrequently commit some violence or other, immediately before their departure. The appointment by yourself of an Agent resident in this neighbourhood, would contribute very much to the suppression of these practices. Altho' the duty would be somewhat burthensome, I have no doubt, that Mr. Peter Chouteau would, at your request, very cheerfully undertake it.

CIRCULARS ADDRESSED TO HENRY DODGE, WILLIAM GARNER, AND JOSEPH N. AMOUREUX

Sir,   St. Louis 8 Aug '10.

In addition to the Papers accompanying your appointment as Secy's Assistant for taking the Census within the district of ———— some time since transmitted, I now enclose duplicates of the Schedule, the instructions the Laws and the Oaths, lest the first should have miscarried. Be pleased to acknowledge the receipt of the whole without delay —

JOSEPH N. AMOUREUX TO BATES

Sir,   New Madrid 15th August 1810 —

I have the honor to acknowledge the receipt of your official favors of the 26th of June and of the 24th of July last; the first naming me an assistant for taking the Census of the Inhabitants of this District, for which please to accept my sincere gratitude, the second inclosing the printed, Laws, Instructions etc. agreeable to the note thereto annexed —

I have begun to take the Census on the day appointed by Law, and shall endeavour to conform myself in every Instance to yours and the other general directions: I shall particularly attend to your desire of having the returns made to you as soon as possible: for that purpose I shall take the opportunity of the good season to go to those scattered places, to which at rainy times the access is almost impracticable; so that I am in hopes that after having complied with all the requisites I will be able to send my returns in the course of November, by some good safe opportunity, unless you would think best to prevail on some gentleman of the bar, returning from the November Districts Courts, to take a particular charge of those returns, upon which I shall await your further Instructions. —

I send here inclosed the oath taken by me before a Judge of the Court of Common Pleas.

TO WILLIAM C. CARR, LEXINGTON, KENTUCKY

DEAR SIR,   ST. LOUIS Aug 18. 1810

I owe you my best thanks, for your unexpected favor of 25th ulto. Your informations were very acceptable. Of Gov: Howard, we had heard nothing which could be relied upon — And indeed apprehensions began to be entertained, that he would altogether decline the discharge of a trust, which in the opinions of all, had been so worthily reposed.

I rather think there must be some misconception in the idea that Mr. Gallatin was authorized to pay the salaries of the commissioners &c. It is not possible that he would have withholden the money, except for the best of reasons.

Your bad health gives much concern to your friends. Even your rivals in practice would regret the circumstance which should protract your stay in Kentucky. I sincerely hope that your confidence in the good effects of the medicinal waters of your parent state may not be disappointed, and that with new recruits of health and alacrity, we may soon welcome your arrival among us. In society as in business, I am persuaded your absence occasions a void which would not be immediately [filled] by another. Of your family, you say nothing — I hope they enjoy health. —

I can very readily enter into those feelings of pleasure and of surprize which you must have experienced on your return to Kentucky from the astonishing increase of wealth, population and manufactures. We shall, in our turn, I have no doubt, enjoy these blessings: and the overflowings of national prosperity elsewhere will find easy channels, and a capacious reservoir for their reception in Louisiana. From every internal symptom, as well as from every indication from abroad, I am led to conclude that those of you who have made early purchases of lands will, at no very distant day, find your account in it. Taking up my opinions from those who are well informed on the subject, I have no doubt that our soil is perfectly well suited to the growth of Hemp.[57] Our friend Riddick has not arrived.

[57] Hemp was produced in Upper Louisiana by Laclede as early as 1775. Two years later he was instructed by the Spanish authorities to encourage hemp and flax culture. Laclede advised that slaves be sent if the business were to develop. Galvez replied that the king had decided

I am impatient to see him. In his absence and yours I have not a friend to whom I can unbosom myself in any delicate emergency. I did not take up your paper in the hands of Mr. Chouteau, for the reason that he settled my note with Mr. Philipson[58] who had money of mine some time previously to the 1st of July and without my knowledge. It can still be done, if you desire it.

TO WILLIAM GARNER

SIR,   ST. LOUIS Aug 22. 1810

I received by last post, your letter of the 10th. Some general account of manufactures will be acceptable. The Secretary of the Treasury has not thought it worth while to extend the Law as respects them to this country, — And indeed, in the infancy of our Settlements we have very little to boast of on that score. The Proclamation of 20th April 1808, to which you allude is of no authority as respects boundaries. The Governor had no power extending to objects of that kind. Boundaries between the Whites and Indians must be established either by the general government or by treaties —

to make provision for supplying the needed labor. Houck, *History of Missouri*, I, 305.

In the American period, as the settlements developed along the Missouri River, hemp became the great staple, and it was in the hemp country that slavery got its strongest hold. H. A. Trexler, *Slavery in Missouri, 1804-1865*, in Johns Hopkins University, *Studies in Historical and Political Science*, XXXII, No. 3, pp. 23-26.

[58] In 1808 Jacob Philipson came from Philadelphia and opened a store in St. Louis. His advertisement appeared in the *Missouri Gazette*, December 14, 1808.

TO JOHN MICHIE, GOOCHLAND COURT HOUSE, VIRGINIA

D<small>R</small>. S<small>IR</small>,   S<small>T</small>. L<small>OUIS</small> Aug 22. '10

I very much approve your determination to visit Louisiana rather than rely on the informations of others. With the best intentions I might mislead you into error: And indeed your enquiries of 26th June embrace so wide a field that I am very sure it would not be in my power, satisfactorily to answer them. A residence of three years in this country has impressed upon my mind the most lasting prepossessions in its favor and induced me to give it the preference to all other parts of the U States which I have visited. But my pursuits, it must be confessed have been of too special a nature to enable me to decide with respect to its agricultural advantages. For the present, I merely send you notes of my momentary recollections — Hereafter, if you desire it, I will forward the results of my conversations with those, who are better informed than I can pretend to be —

'Price of Slaves?' variously from $300 to $500 'Hire?' $8. & $10 Per Mo. — 'Crop?' Corn, Wheat, Oats and other small grains — Hemp at some future day will probably be the Staple. 'Price of the Crop?' — very fluctuating — consumed at home — and the demand depends on the number and ability to purchase, of the new comers. Emigration however numerous and constant, nothwithstanding the supposed insecurity in the land titles. — Corn has sold for 25cts. — sometimes 75cts. per bushel — Whiskey 50cts. Peach Brandy 100cts. Per Gal: Beef $3 Per Cwt. — Pork $3 — Cwt. Bacon $4 to $8 Per Cwt. — 'Money?' Silver and Kentucky-Bank Bills. — a deficit of these as a medium

of exchange induces the practice of making contracts, for
specific articles of that kind of property which has been
found most negociable, such as Lead, Beaver, Peltry.
'Land?' On this subject I will give you the opinions of
Judge Lucas who has been a practical farmer for the last
20 years. He says that 2d rate *here,* produces better than
1st in *Pennsylvania* The soil is light, and attention rather
than labour is necessary in cultivating it. There is no
doubt a great *diversity,* from the rocky barrens to the
unexhaustable low grounds of the Missouri & the Mississippi. The man of business can never be deceived in the
titles, altho' the adjustment is not yet completed. 'Price
of Lands?' You know the habits of a frontier People —
They are fond of hunting and they are averse to Laws.
As soon as the Settlements approach them they sell out —
Sometimes good Plantations, with Vacant Cabbins, orchards &c. have been sold for 50cts. Per Acre — And if the
Sheriff has the disposal of them, they bring much less.
Lands of the very first rate are sold, by those who are not
thus strongly induced to make sacrifices at $3 Per Acre.
The Lands produce, of Corn 50 Bushels and of Wheat 30
Bushels Per Acre. The soil is well suited to the growth
of Tobo. tho' very little is cultivated. The quantity of
its produce Per Acre, has never, that I know of, been
fairly ascertained. 'Water?' Very excellent in its quality,
but not very abundant. The river water is drunk in our
village in preference to all others. Tho' in its natural
state, it has a muddy, and almost an abhorrent aspect, yet
after it has deposited its sediment in large Jars of 80 &
100 Gals. it becomes pure as the clearest spring water.
'Air?' Somewhat changeable — Sudden transitions from
heat to cold, but extremes in neither — However, on this

subject as well as with respect to 'Health?' and 'Prevailing diseases?' I cannot adventure any thing very positively, until I talk with our philosophical People. I am satisfied however that we have more comparative Health here than you have in Virginia. 'Society?' is as you might conjecture it to be, in a new country — somewhat promiscuous. — 'The business of a Lawyer?' Those who have been *qualified* to succeed have succeeded.

I shall be very glad to see you in St. Louis It is here only that you can form correct judgments on the Affairs of the country. — Lead $5 & $6 Per Cwt. . . .

[P. S.] Since writing the above have been told that Negro men hire at the mines from $10 to $15. —

PART V

The Administration of Governor Howard

THE ADMINISTRATION OF GOVERNOR HOWARD

JOHN G. HEATH[1] TO BATES

. Dear Sir.   Saint Charles 23d Aug 1810

When last I had the pleasure to see you I requested permission to hunt beaver in the Osage country the ensueing winter. You generously took upon you to mention the thing to Majr Choteau their agent. I am now fully equiped to make the tour & most earnestly entreat you to assist me to procure permission if it does not at this time belong to you officially. I hear that a Govr. has arrived. I am not satisfied whether it appertains to his office or not. The thing is of the utmost concern to me as my fortune good or bad depends upon it. Therefore your kind interference will oblige me in the Greatest posible point for which my feelings will always be greatful — favour me with an answer if you please — I have hard times. Men whom I have sweated by night and day to save from the devil have turned upon me & try to force me to cut my own throat for a few cents — poverty & troublesome Enemes at the same time are difficult things I can assure you. Adieu.

---

[1] Heath and William Christy established the first salt works in Cooper County (1808). Heath was admitted to the bar at St. Charles in 1808 and in 1814 represented St. Charles County in the territorial assembly. In 1816 he was circuit attorney of Howard County, and in 1820 represented Franklin County in the constitutional convention.

(159)

JAMES ABBOTT TO BATES

DEAR SIR,   DETROIT, 28 August 1810.

I have the pleasure to acknowledge the receipt of your letters of the 12th January, 9th & 23d May; the former advising of your having drawn on me in favor of the Hon: A. Chouteau for three hundred and eighty one dollars and seventy four cents, which has been duly honored; the latter covering a Special Power of Attorney for conveying a certain donation lot; which has not yet been done, but, as all the Judges of the Territory are now present, I am in hopes of obtaining a Deed for the same in the course of a few days, when the business will be attended to.

Very little news — Our Territory continues to be torn to pieces by party animosities, so much so, that the people are in a great measure determined on petitioning the General Government to be attached to the State of Ohio. I have thought it prudent not to interfere.

I have the pleasure to inform you that my Brother Samuel has been appointed Collector and Inspector for the District of Michilimackinac: His commissions are dated 3rd May, which you will please recollect, was after the adjournment of Congress, consequently, his appointment will have to be laid before the Senate, at their next meeting, for their approbation. Permit me my Dear Sir to solicit your interest with the members of that Honorable Body and the Treasury Department in his behalf. If you consider it agreeable so to do, it would be advisable that your letters on the subject should reach Washington City a few days before the next session of Congress.

TO ROBERT SMITH

SIR,   SECRETARY'S OFFICE Oct 1. 1810.

I have the honor to enclose herewith copies of the Executive Proceedings in this territory during the half year, commencing 1st April and ending 30 September. The Legislature did not convene in this term.

TO BENJAMIN HOWARD

SIR,   Oct 22d. 1810

In execution of your Orders of this morning I have the honor to enclose the only papers in the files of this Office which appear to have a material relation to the fiscal concerns of the territory, they are, 1st The letter & statement of Geo Henderson late Treasurer of the district of Cape Girardeau of 26th of March 1809

2dly The statements of Michael Amoureux late Auditor of the Public Accts. for the district of New Madrid

3rdly The letter & statement of Joshua Humphreys clerk of the courts of the district of New Madrid dated 8 Sep 1810

4thly The Returns of the late commissioners of Rates & Levies of the divisions of their respective districts into townships with statements of the taxable inhabitants

The provision in the 6th Sec of this Act establishing courts of justice and regulating judicial proceedings P. 88 of the Laws,[2] has not, as far as relates to returns to be made to the Governor been very strictly observed.

[2] The reference is to an early edition of the *Laws*. The original act of July 3, 1807 is in *Missouri Territorial Laws*, I, 105-125. It was amended October 20, 1807 (*ibid.*, I, 183-184), and again amended November 7, 1808 (*ibid.*, I, 223-224).

ALBERT GALLATIN TO BATES[3]

Treasury Department

SIR,   5th Novemr 1810.

The Surveyor General writes that Mr Bent[4] is required by the Commissioners to execute surveys at the distance of 500 or 1000 Miles, which it is impossible for him to do without incurring considerable expence for travelling.

If there is a number of Surveys to be executed in the same quarter, I should suppose that a deputy might be appointed for the purpose.

But if there are insulated claims at that distance, and no danger of interference, might not the confirmation by the Commissioners be made without a previous survey, and in such manner as to direct the manner in which the Survey should be hereafter executed?

That mode was very, perhaps indeed too generally adopted by the Commissioners in the Mississippi Territory.

Upon the whole I have no doubt that the Commissioners will try to arrange that difficulty and have no disposition to require from the principle Surveyor services which, though within the letter of the Law, he cannot reasonably be expected to perform. The discretion in that respect is theirs, and I am sure that it will be properly exercised.

TO ROBERT SMITH

SIR,   ST. LOUIS 9 Nov 1810

I had the honor to receive by this week's mail, your letter of the 1st ulto.

[3] Original in the Treasury Department, Mail, "N-O," 3466.
[4] Silas Bent.

We have been diligent in the business of the census. On the appointment of the Assistants I entreated them to furnish their enumeration as such earlier than the prescribed periods, as a careful and regular discharge of their duties would permit.

Returns have been already received from the districts of St. Charles & St. Genevieve and from part of the district of the Arkansas. As soon as all the returns shall have been made, but little time will be required to make the general statement.

TO JOHN COBURN[5]

Sir,

St. Louis, Nov 14. 1810.

It was stated to me this morning, that you had written a letter to Governor Howard containing some strictures on the removal of the late Sheriff of the district of St. Louis.

I waited on the Governor to learn particulars: He declines as I had foreseen to say any thing on the subject. The correctness of his determinations in this respect cannot be doubted. You will therefore do me a favour, and probably the last I shall ever ask of you, by stating explicitly whether or not these strictures were made, and if affirmatively what they substantially amounted to. I am not so unreasonable as to expect that you will enter into a laboured argumentation on the subject. I entreat *facts* and facts alone; for from these I am very desirous of drawing my own conclusions.

[5] This letter was suppressed at the suggestion of Governor Howard. See Bates to Coburn, May 1, 1811.

If you should be disposed to make the mental enquiry of yourself 'For what purpose can these informations be wanted?' *Simply* Sir, at my leisure moments to amuse myself with *contrasts,* to complete my collection of the epistolary writings of The Honorable Judge Coburn!—

Were you not in Kentucky, at the time of this transaction? And could you have known the circumstances, except from the partial relations of interested People? Why not let them tell their own story? How *durst* you decide on that evidence which you imagined the Governor was about to weigh? Why obtrude your advices on that excellent man, who, at the same time that he throws around you the veil of silence appears, from his profound neglect of the subject, to disregard, with the *truly* honorable feelings of a Gentleman, your malicious and intermeddling insinuations?

You have professed *friendship* for me too; and you do know Sir, that I had deserved something more at your hands, than empty *professions!* —

It was the saying of a celebrated Roman of Antiquity, who even caused it to be inscribed on his tomb, that he had repaid, as well the injuries of enemies, as the good offices of friends with ample interest. There was a ferocious justice in *this* but pardon me the liberty of saying, that I cannot fathom the morals of that man, who, like the Bear of the Satirist, embraces only to destroy.

TO JAMES MADISON

SIR,   ST. LOUIS Nov 28. 1810

I cannot suffer the term of my Secretaryship to expire without expressing to you my grateful sense of the confidence heretofore reposed. It has been my uniform endeavour to prove myself not altogether unworthy of it. The exercise of the Executive Office which has twice, for long periods, devolved on me, presented duties, with which indeed I was not familiar, but from the discharge of which I did not shrink. — Errors, most probably have been committed; — yet I take the liberty to assure you that I am not sensible of them. *'Mens sibi conscia recti'*[6] is my general defence, rather than a claim to indulgence: for I believe myself prepared to submit the entire series of my conduct to the most rigid investigation.

With respect to re appointment I have foreborne solicitation, in the ordinary forms, determined to ask it only of you Your favorable opinion would be greatly flattering to me, at all times; but particularly gratifying under existing circumstances.

TO ALBERT GALLATIN

Sir, St. Louis 5th Decr. 1810

I have to acknowledge my forgetfulness heretofore of that part of your instructions of 2d April 1807 which relates to the monthly return of Patent Certificates. The Report in progressive numbers from 1 to 101 and up to the last of November is herewith transmitted For the time to come I hope to avoid your censure in this respect.

When last I had the honor to address you in reply to your enquiries as to the probable progress of the adjustment of the Land-Claims, I entertained the belief that the

---

[6] The mind conscious of right.

Report might be made during the present Session of Congress. It is not now possible.

The 'hatons nous lentement' so necessary in the discharge of complex and important business is a faculty which we never shall acquire. The Commissioners are incessantly disappointed in their own calculations, for the obvious reason that the order of business is forever changing: They hazard statements which you have not required, and they decline to answer your direct enquiries, because the *Recorder* had been chosen as the medium of correspondence.

I enclose a duplicate of mine of 13th June last Much remains to be done, and for causes which it would be presumptious in me to assign, some degree of uncertainty will continue to exist, as to the time which will be necessary to complete it.

TO JOSEPH CHARLESS, SR.

Mr Charless,[7]   St. Louis Dec 10. 1810.

As I have observed that you sometimes fill your columns with scraps of Indian Eloquence, I make so free as to submit to your criticism, and for publication, if you think proper, a talk of the Big Soldier[8] delivered May 1807 in a council held with the Osages by Major Peter Chouteau.

It may perhaps be said that there is nothing great or Chieftain like, in these persuasive supplications. Where the Indian character is known this will not be objected. At

----

[7] Editor of the *Louisiana Gazette.*

[8] Big Soldier was known to the French as Grand Soldat and to the Indians as Peno-we-gouna. He was a Menominee chief. *Wisconsin Historical Collections*, X, 110; XI, 278; XII, 193, 197, 198, 200, 277. The speech appeared in the *Louisiana Gazette*, December 12, 1810.

any rate, I do not know that he is less of a hero, on account of the extreme sensibility of his domestic attachments. If Priam without derogation could descend to humiliating entreaty, in order to obtain the dead body of his son,[9] it appears to me that the Osage may be excused when both his Hecuba and his Hector, from whom alone he expected his earthly consolations, were in the hands of his enemies.

No embellishment of this speech has been attempted: On the contrary, many of its native beauties as I am told disappear under its foreign drapery —

WILLIAM GARNER TO BATES

Sir,   CAPE GIRARDEAU 17th Decm. 1810

I Received Your letter of the 8th August — enclosed in a Packet containing duplicates of the Schedule the Instructions the laws and the Oaths all of which came safe to hand — I now send you by the bearer hereof Mr. Andrews a Schedule containing the number of Persons within the district of Cape Girardeau the division alotted to me, I have been particular in setting the Townships Separate and Giving the agregate number in each Township; I did not consider the Town of Cape Girardeau as forming any district or Civil division of the district, I have not therefore Separated it from the Township of Cape Girardeau, nevertheless I have certified the agregate number residing within the Town at the end of the Schedule; I have also at the end of the Schedule made a return of the manufac-

[9]Hector, the eldest son of Priam and Hecuba, was slain by Achilles. Priam went in person to the Grecian camp to ransom the body. Achilles, moved by his entreaties, permitted a truce of twelve days for the funeral of Hector.

tories, the articles, and the probable Value of the articles manufactured annually in my division in dollars & c as this chiefly consisted of Household manufactures I found it to be very troublesome — The dispersed Situation of the Inhabitants in my division and the Intervention of other business caused me to be longer in making my return than I at first expected, but Hope it will reach you in due time and the manner in which it is done will be to your Satisfaction — I wish to know if any application is necessary on my part to make for my fees; and, if any in what way I shall apply, also how much I may expect for my Services.

TO ROBERT SMITH

Sir,   St. Louis Jany 10. 1811

I have the honor to transmit, An Aggregate amount of each description of persons within the territory of Louisiana in conformity with the laws and your instructions. . . .

I enclose a copy of their [the assistants'] approbation to Mr. Gallatin, to whom I suppose the application for a settlement of the accounts will be properly made. My oath of office accompanies the schedule.

TO ALBERT GALLATIN

Sir,   St. Louis Jany. 10. 1811.

Not having been honored with your instructions under the 2d. Sec of the Act 'further to alter and amend &c.'[10] I did not make with the Assistants any arrangements on

---

[10] The original act providing for the taking of the census was amended four times. An amendment of April 12, 1810 provided that the

AGGREGATE AMOUNT OF EACH DESCRIPTION OF PERSONS WITHIN THE TERRITORY OF LOUISIANA.

NAMES OF THE RESPECTIVE DISTRICTS AND SETTLEMENTS	FREE WHITE MALES					FREE WHITE FEMALES					All other free persons, except Indians, not taxed	Slaves	Totals in each County	Total
	Under ten years of age	Of ten, and under sixteen	Of sixteen, and under twenty-six, including heads of families	Of twenty-six, and under forty-five including heads of families	Of forty-five, and upwards, including heads of families	Under ten years of age	Of ten, and under sixteen	Of sixteen, and under twenty-six including heads of families	Of twenty-six, and under forty-five including heads of families	Of forty-five, and upwards, including heads of families				
Dt of St. Charles	660	224	305	347	183	[657]	231	256	257	101	13	271	3505	
do. St. Louis	942	360	513	590	283	[866]	330	432	326	165	120	740	5667	
do. St. Genevieve	672	269	214	411	174	[578]	205	232	306	112	459	988	4620	
do. Cape Girardeau	693	258	273	380	146	625	275	275	261	105	8	589	3888	
do. New Madrid	310	150	173	193	111	338	165	164	141	66	5	287	2103	
Hope Field & St. Frances Settlemts	29	14	17	21	9	26	12	16	15	—	—	29	188	
Arkensas Settlements	132	70	73	127	61	123	47	56	63	13	2	107	874	
	3438	1345	1568	2069	967	3213	1265	1431	1369	562	607	3011	20845	Twenty thousand, eight hundred & forty five

THE number of persons within my division, consisting of the Territory of Louisiana, appears in a schedule hereto annexed, subscribed by me this 10th day of January, A. D. 1811

Frederick Bates
Secy. of Louisiana

the subject of manufactures. Two of them, however, have volunteered statements wch. I make so free as to transmit. — I enclose also a copy of the return this day made to the Secretary of State of the population of the territory, together with Mema. of the am'ts due to the several Assistants. The Judges concurred with me in opinion that the Assistants should be allowed the maximum compensation provided by the Law. A Copy of this approbation accompanies the Mema.

Mess'rs McNair & Garner have had some additional trouble in collecting their informations as to manufactures. They know that they have no direct claims; yet I have expressed to them my hopes that some extra provision would be made.

TO ROBERT SMITH

SIR,   ST. LOUIS Jany 14 1811

On the 10th I put into the office the Returns of the enumeration of the People of Louisiana. But as very little reliance can be placed in the regularity of the mails at this season of the year I have the honor to transmit herewith, by private conveyance to Nashville, a duplicate of those Returns.

enumeration should close within five months from the 1st Monday in August (U. S., *Statutes at Large*, II, 570). On May 1, 1810 the form of oath for marshals, secretaries and assistants was changed and provision was made for the gathering of information concerning manufactures *(ibid.,* II, 605). On March 2, 1811 the time for the completion of returns to marshals and secretaries was extended to the 1st Monday of June, and of marshals and secretaries to the 1st Monday of July *(ibid.,* II, 658.) On March 3, 1811 the secretary of the treasury was authorized to allow such compensation as he deemed adequate for those who collected information on manufactures, but the total sum was not to exceed $30,000 *(ibid.,* II, 661).

DAVID ROBINSON TO BATES

SIR,   KASKASKIA Jan'y 16th 1811

I have for some years past been making remarks and taking notes of the most particular things relative to the upper Louisiana indavouring to Give a true Statement of that part which lieth proxemate to the Missouri river on both Sides from its mouth to Fort Osage with a Sceth [*sic*] of the Osages Customes manners and habits with a Short Vocabulary of their dielect: but my principle object is to remove Some Objections which Some persons have entertained with respect to the Salubrity of the Country and Give a correct account of what has presented it Self to my view both by land and water without Exaggeration and the Population of the Districts of St. Charles and St. Louis. I am under the necessity of Solisiting the favour of you to Give me the Censes of those Districts to inable me to show the Migration which has taken place in a few years. Your patronage in this will meet with the merit it deserv's from your friend and Humble Servant. . . .
N. B. my work will appear in the Northern States as it is most wanted there.

TO THOMAS T. CRITTENDEN[11]

SIR,   ST. LOUIS March 12. 1811

Altho' the papers have some time since, announced my reappointment to the Sec's office, I have yet no official ad-

---

[11] Thomas T. Crittenden was a brother of Senator J. J. Crittenden of Kentucky. He was appointed deputy attorney general in 1810 by Governor Howard. On October 1, 1811 he killed Dr. Walter Fenwick in a duel on Moreau's Island, below Ste. Genevieve. Henry Dodge acted as Fenwick's second, and John Scott served in similar capacity for Crittenden.

vices on the subject. It is therefore merely as an individual[12] anxious for the welfare of the country that I take the liberty to subjoin a copy of a letter which I have just received. Accept assurances of my respects.

TO MOSES AUSTIN

St. Louis Mar 27. 1811

Sir,

Yr letter of the 19th Mar was deld. yestery. by your son.[13] I have not heard from the City, therefore cannot say any thing in an official way on the subject of lead mines in your neighbourhood. It has ever been a subject of regret and mortification to me that individuals should have been permitted, without the forms of law, or the semblance of justice to dispose of the public property, and to appropriate to themselves its emoluments. I did hope that long ere this a period would have been put to these usurpations.

It is said, altho' I have no certain information that Gov: Howard left Virga. for this place about 4th He would stay in Kentucky but a few days.

Yr letter enclosing the address for the division of the district is received. You already know my opinions on that subject.

---

[12] The absence of Governor Howard and the fact that Bates did not receive his commission of reappointment as secretary, left the territory without a functioning executive for many weeks. Bates' commission arrived May 7, 1811, and for a short time he acted as governor.

[13] Stephen Fuller Austin.

TO ALBERT GALLATIN

Sir,   Sᴛ. Louis April 1. 1811

1 have this day taken the liberty to draw on you, in favor of Edward Hempstead or order, for the sum of sixty dollars, being the amt. of the contingent expenses of the board of Coms. for ascertaining & adjustg. the titles & cls. to lands in this territory for the quartr. endg. 31 Mar last. I enclose the voucher. The board has been in most anxious expectation of advices. We have rumours of new arrangements; but the irregularity or rather the total failure of the Mail has prevented the receipt of any intelligence on wch. reliance could be placed.

ALBERT GALLATIN TO JOHN B. C. LUCAS, CLEMENT B. PENROSE AND FREDERICK BATES[14]

Gentlemen,   Treasury Department
                                   April 24th 1811.

I enclose for the use of your Board a copy of the Land Laws collected pursuant to the act of Congress of 27th April 1810; to which the Land Laws passed during the last Session of Congress have been added. Amongst these you will perceive one which provides for your compensation, and that of the Clerk and translator. So far as relates to the claims rejected it does not appear that the allowance made for these can be paid untill your report thereon shall have been received. But the allowance for claims confirmed and on which you have issued certificates may be

---

[14] Original in the Treasury Department, Mail "N-O," 3470.

paid from time to time; and each of the Commissioners as well as the Clerk, is authorized to draw on the Secretary of the Treasury for the amount respectively due on account of such confirmed claims. It will be necessary that the number of certificates for which the draft is made should be expressed on its face, that a transcript or abstract of the certificates designating the No., name of Grantee and number of acres respectively granted to each, should be previously or at the same time transmitted by the Clerk; and that the certificate of attendance as required by the act should accompany or precede the draft.

TO JOHN SMITH T, CANNON MINES[15]

Sir,   St. Louis April 29. 1811

When you were last in town we had much conversation on the subject of your misunderstandings with the Messrs. Perrys. I stated to you that Mr Perry, (meaning William, who had been in St. Louis a few days before) 'Had not obtained a *Lease* of a Lead Mine. That it was impossible he should have obtained one since his application was made after the expiration of my term of service and before I had official advices of its renewal.' '

It is true that about twelve months ago, I did ver-

---

[15] The Cannon Mines were in modern Union Township, in Washington County *(American State Papers, Public Lands,* III, 576). They were about ten miles from Mine à Burton. In a report of October 7, 1816 of Moses Austin to Return J. Meigs, commissioner of the general land office, Austin listed thirty-three mines in Washington County, the Cannon Mines being in the list *(ibid.,* III, 609-613). In Schoolcraft's list of active mines in 1819, forty-five mines were mentioned (Henry Rowe Schoolcraft, *Scenes and Adventures in the Semi-Alpine Region of the Ozark Mountains of Missouri and Arkansas,* 158-175). This is in striking contrast to conditions in 1811 when, according to Henry M. Brackenridge, there were only thirteen active mines *(Views of Louisiana,* 146-153).

bally permit Mr. Saml. Perry to search for Lead Mineral on the *Public Lands,* assuring him that if he made a discovery he should be permitted to occupy fifty acres as the Tenant at Will of the Government. *No writings were drawn.* Had this circumstance however occurred to me at the moment, I should have mentioned it to you. The transaction had escaped my memory.

He now tells me that the discovery made under this verbal permission and assurance, is the spot for which your agents and himself are contending.

We all know that it is not within my province to adjust individual differences, and I take the liberty of mentioning these things for the sole purpose of preventing the possibility of misapprehension.

TO JOHN COBURN, STE. GENEVIEVE

Sir,   St. Louis May 1st. 1811

I wrote you a few lines last fall, and had besides some little conversation with Governor Howard on your subject. His prudent intimations induced me to suppress that letter, and to await your semi annual visit to this country. In the meantime I have been sporting my railleries at your expence.

He whose public character and whose private life are exposed to exception, should not, if I might advise, make rash and blundering attacks on others. —

Let me know, in a few words, the extent of what you have attempted against me in Louisiana, and Kentucky as well as in Washington. Of this I am most anxious to be informed, that my returns of courtesy may be, as nearly as possible adjusted to the provocations which I have received.

Be brief, I pray you; for I tell you plainly that your eloquence has lost its persuasion. At any rate, *I* am no longer to be amused with the music of your periods, nor mislead by the emptiness of your rhetorical flourishes.

TO MOSES AUSTIN

Sɪʀ,   Sᴛ. Lᴏᴜɪs May 1. 1811

I do not know in what way to write on a subject with respect to which so much has been already *said* and *written.* Your letter of 27th ulto. was deld. this morning. — I do, very heartily regret the party dissensions which exist at the mines — and if I had the power, I should certainly have the disposition to put them at rest forever, by shielding the public property under the safeguard of the laws: But really, after so much abortion and ineffectual interference on the part of the Public Agents heretofore, it does appear to me ridiculous for them to talk of giving regularity and system to matters so inextricably involved.

I will never hereafter act in the business, but with decision, and as I hope, with effect.

The com[mission] has not arrived — probably lost.

TO THE SECRETARY'S ASSISTANTS FOR TAKING THE CENSUS WITHIN THE TERRITORY OF LOUISIANA[16]

May 1. 1811.

I have not been enabled by government to adjust your accounts. The delay may have arisen from the general irregularity, and entire failure of some of our mails.

[16] This notice appeared in the *Louisiana Gazette*, May 2, 1811.

The Report was made in January last, accompanied by a statement of the amount of your respective demands.

TO BENJAMIN HOWARD, LEXINGTON, KENTUCKY

Sir,

St. Louis May 2d. 1811

A young man lately from Frankfort informs that you had arrived in Lexington. Altho' probably among the *last* to congratulate you, on your marriage with an amiable and accomplished woman, I beg you to believe that I offer the usual good wishes with the utmost sincerity of heart.[17]

Nothing has transpired during the winter of a very interesting nature, and if I have been less communicative than you had a right to expect, it may be ascribed to a dearth of materials. —

It appears by the news papers that I have been re appointed to the Secretaryship. This serves me as a proof, if not of your positive regards, at least, of a friendly neutrality with respect to me — And for which I assure you, I am very grateful. The commission has not arrived, and is probably lost, as some of our mails have failed, totally. If not too troublesome, may I hope that you will write to the Secretary of State, who will no doubt, transmit a duplicate?

Some little inconvenience has arisen from the entire absence of Executive authority — chiefly as to the authentication of records, and certifying the official character of

----

[17] On March 14, 1811 Governor Howard married Miss Mary Thompson Mason, daughter of Stephen Thompson Mason, deceased. The Mason home, where the marriage ceremony was performed, was in Loudoun County, Virginia. *Louisiana Gazette*, March 21, 1811.

subordinate officers. The files being still in my hands, I have in very many instances given private certificates, which have answered every purpose, except where the parties were disposed to take legal exceptions.

When equipments have been made for the Indian Country, the trader has called at the Office, professed readiness to do whatever the law might require, obtained a writing in acknowledgment of this tender and thought himself at liberty to prosecute his voyage. The cool, deliberate and barbarous murder of Ezekiel Rogers by Moses Kinney some few weeks ago, in the township of Bon Homme, has excited the indignation of every humane bosom.[18] The son of Rogers with a copy of the Inquest, pursued the murderer to Paris in Kentucky, where he was committed to prison, as I hear, by Judge Bayley, and released in a manner which I cannot comprehend, by Judge Allen.[19] Governor Scott[20] is furnished by this day's mail with the evidence which was filed in the Clerk's office of the district,

[18] "Died on the 24th ult in Bon Homme township Ezekiel Rodgers; in consequence of boiling water poured over him while asleep and afterwards much beat and bruised. The name of the villain who committed this foul deed we are informed is Moses Kenny, of Bourbon County, Kentucky. Justice is robbed of its victim. Kenny has fled." *Louisiana Gazette*, April 11, 1811.

[19] John Allen was born in James City County, Virginia, in 1749. He rose to the rank of major during the American Revolution. In 1781 he began to practice law. In 1786 he moved to Kentucky, locating in Fayette County. Two years later he settled at Paris in Bourbon County. He was appointed judge of the Paris District court and in 1802 was appointed judge of the Kentucky circuit court. Lewis Collins, *History of Kentucky* (revised ed.), II, 80-81.

[20] Charles Scott was born in Cumberland County, Virginia, in 1733. He served under Braddock as a non-commissioned officer and during the American Revolution became a brigadier-general. In 1785 he moved to Woodford County, Kentucky. He served under St. Clair in 1791 and under Wayne in 1794. He was governor of Kentucky, 1808-1812. *Ibid.*, II, 706.

under the expectation that he would cause him to be again arrested, and delivered over as required by an Act of Congress of 12th Feby. 1793, respecting Fugitives from Justice. Every man who has heard of the murderous transaction is shocked at the bare possibility of the criminals escape.

————————

TO BENJAMIN HOWARD

Sir,   St. Louis May 8. 1811

Yr letter from Washington of 11 Jan did not arrive till last evening. The Commission also came to hand by the same Mail — And I am now sorry that I made the request for a duplicate. The trouble which you gave yourself to wait on the President with a view to my reappointment demands my warmest acknowledgments. You had given me no reason to count on your *good word* in the City — and I did not presume to ask such a favor. It shall be my study to justify your favorable opinion by the utmost circumspection in my public conduct; at the same time that I feel a pleasing weight of personal gratitude of wch. I hope to give you some better proof than mere words.

As the territorial Judges are now at St. Genevieve, I shall set out tomorrow for the purpose of taking the Oath.

The People of the Mine townships have been pressing for a separate district. I have been of opinion that their request might be granted: But as it is a matter of questionable expediency it appears to me that the Secretary ought not to hazard it, unless he get an intimation from the Governor to use his discretion. I would not designedly do any thing wch. might be displeasing to you — And as we are led by rumour to hope for your arrival very shortly it might be unnecessary to mention these things.

You intimated to me the propriety of *ascertaining* or *creating anew* the district limits between St Louis and St. Genevieve. This would have been done last fall if I had not imagined that you would prefer an ascertainment by reference to the Proclamation of Gov Harrison in the office of the Secretary of State at Washington. I took the liberty to write you to this effect last winter.

The Law for the final adjustment of Land Claims[21] has given much dissatisfaction to the People at large. The commissioners & the officers of the board are equally displeased: But their discontents are matters of very subordinate consideration. The People had indulged the hope, perhaps an unreasonable one, that Congress would have enacted more enlarged principles of confirmation. The Compensation of the Clerk is indeed much less than he had expected. If there has been unnecessary delay it is to be imputed to *us*. It is somewhat severe to make the officers of the board share in the reproof. My Colleagues Messrs Lucas & Penrose have persuaded the Translator to resign that the business may progress no farther until Government make arrangements wch. may better please him. I cannot approve an intrigue of this kind. They give assurances to the Translator that if this office again becomes profitable he shall be reinstated.

With best wishes for your happiness I have the honor to be Your Excellency's obliged and obedt Servant.

[21] The act providing for the final adjustment of land claims in the territories of Orleans and Louisiana became effective on February 15, 1811. It provided, among other things, that each of the commissioners and the clerk of each board should be paid fifty cents for each claim undecided on July 1, 1809 and on which a decision was made subsequent to that date. Five hundred dollars were to be paid to each commissioner and clerk upon completion of the reports. Translators were to be paid

TO NINIAN EDWARDS

Sir,   St. Louis June 18. 1811

I beg leave to state to yr Excy. that some time in last mo. the barn of Mr. Peter Chouteau in the neighbourhood of this town was burned by a party of Ottowa Indians, who, I am told reside within your territory. I have advised Mr Chouteau to procure written evidences of this burning and have chosen the men jointly with himself for the estimation of the amount of his loss. These Papers will be transmitted to you.

I pray yr. Excy. to bestow as early an attention on the subject as your convenience & the circumstances will permit.   .   .   .

Estimation
    Barn ....$592. .90
    17 tons Hay .... 140. .00
                                                                         ————
    Total ....′......................... 732. .90

TO ALBERT GALLATIN

Sir,   St. Louis June 20. 1811

An accidental concurrence of circumstances has enabled me to gain possession, without the employment of force, of a Lead Mine, which promises to be abundantly richer than any yet discovered in Louisiana. Reuben brother of

six hundred dollars a year until the report was completed, but were not to be paid for more than eighteen months. It provided for a land office for the Territory of Louisiana, and for a register and a receiver of public monies. U. S., *Statutes at Large*, II, 617-621.

John Smith (T) in the summer of 1808, before his departure for Mexico, located 1000 acres of the St. Vrain-Grant on these lands, presuming that they contained mineral but without having found the rich strata. Several hundred men are now employed, and Capt. Dodge tells me that one million of mineral has been already raised, altho' the discovery is so recent that furnaces for smelting have not yet been established. I lose no time, in transmitting a copy of the lease, that the pleasure of the President may be known with respect to it. The Renaut-Agents are commencing suits to *stay waste,* and for the recovery of damages against a great number of persons. From the best informations which I have been able to collect, this new discovery lies two miles at least beyond their limits: tho' I have heard a lawyer, probably retained by the Agents, assert the contrary. Of this, however I am very confident that unless *something* be done, there are individuals who will very soon possess and govern the most valuable parts of this country as Proprietary Lords. —

Smith (T), Moorhead[22] & Riddick have become purchasers under an order of the General Court of a part of the mineral tract of the late Julien Dubuque.[23] Several of

[22] Fergus Moorhead was a St. Louis business man. He had a mercantile establishment, and for a time was in partnership with James Baird in the blacksmith business, and with Alexander McNair in the buying of cattle and hides. With Baird he opened and worked a coal mine in Illinois. In 1810 Moorhead, John Smith T, and Thomas F. Riddick purchased the holdings of Dubuque for about $3000. Moorhead was also interested in the mines of Prairie du Chien. See *Louisiana Gazette,* March 7, July 18, September 19, and October 19, 1811; Bradbury, *Travels,* in *Early Western Travels,* V, 252-253.

[23] Julien Dubuque was born at the village of St. Pierre les Brecquits, Quebec, on January 10, 1762. By 1785 he had a trading house near Prairie du Chien on the west side of the Mississippi River. From the Sacs and Foxes he learned of their lead mines. In 1788 he received a

their boats have ascended the river with about 100 labourers for the purpose of extending the old establishment. Notwithstanding the extreme emptiness of these pretensions, *originally,* the affair appears to me, to be so circumstanced at this time, as to forbid the interference of the local authorities. It is possible that there may be some collisions between these People and the Fox and Sac Indians, who have already as I understand from General Clark, made complaints on the subject. I fear to take responsibilities which it might be difficult for me to answer: but I entreat you to believe that I am only anxious to know my duties that I may discharge them. Judge Lucas has asked for the original Papers for the purpose of moving for a revision of the proceedings. They are not in the office, they were delivered, by the Board, thro' their clerk, to the claimants at the time of the ascertainment. After the just censures which government has passed on that ascertainment, it appears to me that nothing farther is left for the commissioners to do with respect to it.   .

I beg permission to say a few words as to the landbusiness. Your letter of 24th April accompanied by a volume of laws &c. &c. has been received. I expected that the commissioners to whom it was addressed, would have made some acknowledgments. Resignation has been hinted at; yet I rather think that that course is not seriously con-

concession from the Indians to work the "Spanish Diggins" near modern Dubuque. In 1796 he obtained from Carondelet a grant in that region of a tract seven leagues along the river and extending three leagues back from the river. In 1808 he asked the United States to ratify the claim. The matter was not settled until 1853 when the United States supreme court decided against the claim. Dubuque died on March 24, 1810. At the time of his death he was heavily in debt to Mackinac and St. Louis traders. *Wisconsin Historical Collections*, XIX, 320; *Annals of Iowa*, 3d Series, II, 329-336.

templated. The *Translator* has resigned long since, under the assurances, as he tells me, from Messrs Lucas & Penrose, that he shall be reelected, if his office again become profitable. I expressed my surprize at such an intrigue, the effect of which must be, if not altogether to suspend the business at any rate, to embarrass its progress and retard the final adjustment. — Since we lost the services of Mr Le Duc we have been employed in the examination and signature of many hundred confirmations and grants which include Orders of survey. These Papers were made up by the Clerk, from time to time, but not signed by the board, as it was thought best to deliver them collectively to the Surveyor. I am not very thoroughly acquainted with the reasons which govern our present movements; but there appears to be an unexpressed determination to close the business as far as it has gone, that every thing may be left in intelligible order in the event of resignation.

My Assistants in taking the Census have become importunate for a settlement. I suppose the delay is attributable to myself — for Mr. Pope Secy. of Illinois informs me, that his accounts, transmitted in the form prescribed by you, have been paid. I was not so fortunate as to receive your orders; but I took the liberty to forward an ascertainment of the several sums due, in January last, and make so free as to send a similar statement herewith.

A LEASE TO WILLIAM WILSON

The undersigned Recorder of Land Titles for the territory of Louisiana, does hereby lease to William Wilson Esquire a tract of United States' land containing the quantity of two hundred acres, 'In the neighbourhood of the

Gum Spring near the road leading from Mine A Burton to Herculaneum, so as to include a dry branch that makes into the waters of the Joachim about 10 or 12 miles from the Mine A Burton' and on which tract there is a lead mine lately discovered by the said William Wilson — Under the expectation and with the express Proviso, that the said tract does not interfere with any private claims, depending before the board of Commissioners. —

And the said William Wilson does on his part promise and engage that he will pay to the said Recorder, or to the person deputed by him for that purpose, for the use of the United States, one tenth part of all the *mineral* raised on said tract, or the amount thereof in *Lead* at the option of the said Wilson.

These covenants to continue for the term of twelve months, — It being understood, nevertheless, by the parties, that they are to be submitted to the President who has reserved to himself the power to modify or altogether to annul the same — In the mean time the said Wilson shall be maintained in possession, with the Proviso above stated. —

Given under our hands and seals at St Louis the 30th day of June 1811.

Frederick Bates — Seal —
Wm. Wilson   — Seal —

TO ALBERT GALLATIN

Sir,   St. Louis July 17. 1811

On the 20th ulto. I hazarded the communication of a *fact*, without intending to exhibit a *charge*, with respect to the

intrigue which brought about the resignation of the Translator. That Officer finding that the business was neither
suspended, nor, in any great degree retarded by his absence
lately assured me that it was always his intention to have
accompanied the investigation thro' all its progress had
it not been for those incidents which I have already had
the honor to relate.

Struck with the absurdity and the injustice of our decid-
ing on claims, the evidences of which are frequently in a
language which no one of the commissioners pretends to
understand, I this day moved for the election of a Translator — And named M. P. Le Duc He has been chosen —
Judge Lucas dissenting. —

Trusting to present appearances, I should believe that
the judicial part of our business would be finished in eight
or ten weeks.

TO JOHN MICHIE, GOOCHLAND COURT HOUSE, VIRGINIA

Sir, St. Louis July 23d. 1811

I never shall be able to satisfy a mind so wary, so circumspect and so prudent as yours. All your letters have
been received; but to answer them satisfactorily is a task
beyond my leisure and above my capacity. Nothing short
of a whole lifetime would suffice for the accumulation of
such a vast fund of topographical, agricultural, mechanical
and commercial knowledge as you appear to expect from
me. You say that you must trust to the eyes of your
friends. Mine are none of the best, I do assure you, and
scarcely discharge their natural offices in the guidance of
their owner. The offspring of necessity, the creature of

circumstances, I have been so often thrown about the world, that a prudent regard to my own peace of mind has never failed, in a short time, to reconcile me to the place where my interests may have placed me. *You* are not in this situation. *You* are *wealthy*. *You* may choose your own residence. The whole *world* is before *you*. *I* with *sweat* and *toil* and *drudgery* have thought myself sufficiently fortunate in gaining a snug retreat in the most sequestered *corner* of it. I am partial to Louisiana, because I have determined to live and die here, and will not be such a fool as to quarrel with my destiny. But at the same time, if I had *Lands* and *Slaves* and *Cattle* and *Money* it is not altogether impossible, but that I might pitch my tents on other shores. —

You might not like the land which I should *'price'* for you — We have such variety — *Hill & bottom* Woods & Prairie — *high* near the town — *cheap* in the country — Suitable for *hemp here,* for *Tobo. there,* for small grains in *another place* — perhaps — or, at any rate, you might think so. — Mills might be established on *this stream,* the springs of water are delicious in another neighbourhood — but then it is uncertain whether the current of emigration will have that tendency — besides it is too far from the courts of justice — And, after all is said, perhaps *that* little neglected spot, where *nobody* thinks it worth while to build a cabbin, will hereafter *get a name* and become the flourishing market of the neighbouring country.

Small considerations decide questions of vast moment sometimes, but, then, these must be motives of *our own* and not the whimsical cogitations of other People. It follows very conclusively, from all this argumentation that you will have to choose a tract of land for yourself — but

I would advise you, by all means, to bring your books along with you — They are not to be procured here — At least a man of letters cannot complete a library. All kinds of Household furniture & farming utensils may be left *be-hind* — And I suppose we have as good gardens and orchards as you have in Virga. Yet as garden seeds are light carriage, you had better bring them, for you may chance to have particular vegitables which are not found in this country — And particular fruit trees too, if the season of the year permit their transportation.

Robt. Wash²⁴ esq is a young man of good promise — I read a part of your letter to him — He will probably write you.

TO ALBERT GALLATIN

Sir,   St. Louis Aug 30. 1811

I had the honor to address you by last weeks mail in reply to your letter of 14th March, which had just then come to hand — And in obedience to the orders which that letter contained, I enclosed you the original concurrence of the Judges as to the compensation of my Assistants in taking the Census. By this week's mail I have been honored with your letter of 31st ulto. repeating your commands of 14th March, and covering a duplicate of that

²⁴ Robert Wash was born in Louisa County, Virginia, in 1790. He graduated from William and Mary College in 1808. In Louisiana Territory he rose rapidly, becoming attorney general, and during the War of 1812 being attached to the staff of General Howard. In 1815 he was one of the backers of the *Western Journal*, and in 1818 represented St. Louis in the legislature of Missouri Territory. In 1824 he was appointed a judge of the supreme court of Missouri, a position which he resigned in 1837.

letter together with other useless papers, with which I am sorry to have troubled you. Your circular Instructions of 17th May 1810 never have been received.

TO ALBERT GALLATIN

Sir,   ST. Louis Sept 4. 1811. —

I have had the honor to receive your letter of the 6th ulto. & to present it to Governor Howard with whom it remains. — The Lease to Henry Dodge, approved by the President, will certainly be productive, if I am permitted to make those arrangements for the regular receipt and disposal of the Lead, which the circumstances of the case appear to require I should have adventured this, without express sanction, if the Governor had not been of opinion that a previous intimation of the Presidents views might be necessary, or that it might be prudent to wait for it.

If I should be so fortunate as to have the President's confidence in the affair, I pledge myself for the success with which it will be conducted: But whether the trust be confided to me or to another, I beg leave, with much deference to express the opinion, that one undivided agency and responsibility will be greatly for the public interest.

My letter of the 17th July informed you of the re election of a translator to the board of commissioners. The business, now, suffers no delay but that which is indispensable in bringing up the Records, neglected by my Predecessor, and in supplying, in some few instances, my own omissions. These neglects and these occasional omissions have been only discovered on a critical examination, when the claims were about to be finally disposed of.

Since the death of Mrs Lucas, Mr. Penrose and myself have been alone. Whenever we have been of a different opinion, the case has been postponed in hopes of the Judge's attendance before the final close.

The Report will be very voluminous. The manner of transmitting it to the City has not yet been talked of. I am not even able to say, what time Mr. Riddick will require to complete it He is himself in weak health and has already, as I believe, exhausted his funds in the employment of Assistants. —

TO JAMES MONROE

SIR,   ST. LOUIS Oct 1. 1811

I have the honor to enclose a report of the legislative & Executive Proceedings of the territory of Louisiana from 1st day of October 1810 till 30th Sepr. 1811

The half yearly report was not made on the 1st of April last, as the renewal of my Commission as Secy. of the territory had not then reached me.

LIST OF THE CIVIL AND MILITIA APPOINTMENTS IN THE TERRITORY OF LOUISIANA, OCTOBER 1, 1810—SEPTEMBER 30, 1811[25]

1810

Oct 5. Joseph Perkins 2d Lieut. of the St. Genevieve Troop of Cavalry vice Robert Terry resigned. —

[25] Original in Department of State, B. R. L., 3476.

14th   Elijah Collard Captain — Compy. 1st Battn. 3d Regiment

James Lewis Lieut. Compy. 1st Battn. 3d Regiment

Nov 5th   Thomas T. Crittenden Attorney General of the territory vice Edward Hempstead resigned

William Christy Register of Boatmen for the district of St. Louis

9th   Robert Simpson[26] a Justice of the Peace for the township of Upper Cuivre, district of St. Charles

11th   David Wade,[27] a Justice of the Peace for the township of Cape Girardeau, district of Cape Girardeau

John Scott and Sylvestre Labbadie Aids de camp to the commander in chief, with the rank of Majors.

16   William Clark Inspector General of the Militia

Governor Howard left Louisiana.

Decr 29.   M. A. Rocque resigns as Justice of the Peace for the township of St. Chs., district of St. Chs. & apptd. for township & district of St. Louis.

1811

Jany. 5.   Silas Bent,[28] Auditor of territorial accounts. —

24   Thomas Oliver, a Justice of the Peace for the township of St. Genevieve, district of St. Genevieve.

[26] Robert Simpson was from Redbanks, Kentucky. In 1794 he settled at Little Prairie.

[27] Wade was a carpenter and dealer in lumber.

[28] Silas Bent was born in Massachusetts in 1768. Twenty years later he moved to Ohio, and in 1806 came to St. Louis, having been appointed deputy-surveyor for the Territory of Louisiana. In 1807 he was appointed judge of the St. Louis court of common pleas and quarter sessions.

May 17   John W. Honey, Coroner of the district of St.
Louis. —

June 4.   Benjamin Emmons,[29] Justice of the Peace for the
township of lower Cuivre, district of St. Charles.
Abiel Farrensworth, Justice of the Peace for the
township of Dardenne, district of St. Charles. —

June 28.   Samuel Hammond, a Judge of the Courts of
Common Pleas & Quarter Sessions for the District of
St. Louis. —

29   William O. Allen Captain of 'The Infantry Blues' a
volunteer Company, attached to the 1st Regiment
Robert Wash 1st Lieut. Benja. Butterfield 2d Lieut.
Hubert Guion Ensign of the Infantry Blues.
Governor Howard returned 3d July. —

July 6th   John Brownson a Justice of the Peace township
of Labbadie Dt. St. Louis.

11   Stephen Callaway Lieut. 2d Comy. 1st Battn. 3d Regt.
Henry Steel Ensign   do.   do.   do.
Wm. Cragg[30] Capt 3 Compy. 1 Battn. 3 Regt.
Rich. Loo Ensign   do.   do.   do.
Nathl. Simons[31] Captain 4th Comy. 1 Battn. 3 Regt.
Roswell Dentry Lieut. & Jno. Ewing Ensign of Same
Joshua Fisher[32] Ensign 2 Comy. 2d Battn. 3d Regt.

[29] Benjamin Emmons was from New York. He settled on Dardenne prairie, but subsequently moved to St. Charles where he ran a hotel. He was a member of the constitutional convention of 1820 and afterward served in both houses of the state legislature.
[30] Probably William Craig, a Revolutionary War veteran from Virginia.
[31] Probably Nathaniel Simonds, an early settler on Cuivre River.
[32] Fisher settled on St. Cosme Creek in the Bois Brule bottom in 1799.

Chs. Saucier Lieut. 3 Comy. 2 Battn. 3d Regt.
Francis Coursoll[33] Ensign do.   do.   do.

23d. Henry Cassidy,[34] James Scull, Samuel Moseley
Judges of the Courts of Common Pleas and Quarter
Sessions for Dt. of Arkensas.

Samuel Treat a Justice of the Jeace for townships
of the Arkensas

James Scull, Captain Comy. of the Arkensas-Bat-
talion

Curtis Willborn Coroner of the district of the
Arkensas

24   Hail Talbert a Justice of the Peace for township of
Femme Osage in the district of St. Charles

26   James Brady Major Battn. 4th Regiment
James Evans[35] & Henry Widner Captains in Same.
Abraham Christ, Peter Statler, Edwd. Spear, Austin
Young[36] Lieuts Same

Jas. Ravencraft,[37] Wm. Duskins, Benja. Shell, and
Anthony Club Ensigns in the several Comys. of Battn.
4th Regt.

July 26. Danl. Duskin Adjutant of the 4th Regiment

---

[33] Probably Francis Coursault who was killed in a fight with the Indians near Roy's Fort in 1814.

[34] In 1815 Cassidy represented Arkansas County in the territorial legislature.

[35] Evans represented Cape Girardeau in the constitutional convention of 1820.

[36] Young settled on Byrd Creek in 1803.

[37] Ravenscraft represented Cape Girardeau County in the assembly in 1818.

30th. Frederick Reineker,[38] Justice of the Peace for the township of New Madrid, in the district of New Madrid. —

Robert McCoy,[39] a Justice of the Peace for Same

31 John Stanton a Justice of the Peace for the township of Breton, district of St. Genevieve

Walter Wilkinson a Justice for Same township

Elias Austin Elliott 2d Lieut. in St. Genevieve Troop of Cavalry in the room of Joseph Perkins resigned

Aug 9 Thomas D. L. Weeks a Justice of the Peace for the township of Cuivre, district of St. Charles.

22 Alexr. McNair Captain, Bernd. G. Farrar 1st Lieut. James Baird 2d Lieut. Jos. McKnight Cornet, Francis V. Bouis Purser of the St. Louis Independent Troop of Cavalry.

31 Danl. Colgan Senr. Justice of the Peace for township of St. Charles

Sepr 2d Silas Bent, Louis LeBeaume, Augte Chouteau, Bernard Pratte Judges of the Courts of Com Pleas & Quarter Sessions District of St. Louis.

4th Gabriel Long Ensign   3d Comy. 2d Battn. 1st Regt.
Hiacinthe Dehetre Capt 4th do. 2d do. 1st do.
J. M. Courtois Lieut   4 do. 2d do. 1st do.
Joseph Aubuchon Ensign 4th do. 2d do. 1st do.

---

[38] Probably Frederick Reinecke, of the firm of Steinbeck and Reinecke, German traders.

[39] Captain Robert McCoy came from Vincennes to New Madrid in 1787. He engaged in Indian trade. He served as a militia officer and commanded a Spanish galley on the Mississippi. In 1800 he was commandant in the Tywappity Bottom.

9   Ebenezer R. Hawley a Justice of the Peace for the township of St. Ferdinand, district of St. Louis.

11   Wm. Ewing Ensign 4th Comy. 1st Battn. 3d Regt.
      Jno. McCormick a Justice of the Peace for the township of Belle Vue district of St. Genevieve.
      David Curtis a Justice of the Peace for the township of New Madrid in the district of New Madrid

Sepr 13 Wm. Neeley[40] Pay Master to the 4th Regiment
      Prospect K. Robbins, a Justice of the Peace for the township of Dardenne, district of St. Charles.

17   Timothy Kibby, a Judge of the Courts of Com Pleas & Quarter Sessions, for the district of St. Charles.
      David Delaunay, Inspector General of the Militia, in the room of William Clark, resigned. —
      James Beatty[41] Adjutant of the 3d Regiment

19   Francis Saucier a Judge of the Courts of Com Pleas and Quarter Sessions for the district of St. Charles
      Samuel Griffith Captain 3d Comy. 2d Battn. 3d Regiment
      Governor Howard left Louisiana 19th Sepr. 1811. —

                    Secretary's Office
                 St. Louis Oct 1st 1811. —
                    Frederick Bates

[40] Neeley represented Cape Girardeau in the territorial council in 1812.
[41] James Beatty of Kentucky made a settlement near the headwaters of the Femme Osage and Dardenne in 1800.

A LIST OF CIVIL OFFICERS APPOINTED BY THE
GOVERNOR AND IN COMMISSION WITHIN
THE TERRITORY OF LOUISIANA ON
THE 1ST DAY OF OCTOBER, 1811[42]

TERRITORIAL OFFICERS

Office of Atty. Genl. vacant

Peter Didier,[43] Treasurer

Silas Bent, Auditor

Joseph V. Garnier, Clerk of the General Court

DISTRICT OF ST. CHARLES

Judges

Timothy Kibby, Frans. Soucier, Robert Spencer, Benj.
Smith ·

William Christy, Clerk of the Courts

Mackay Wherry, Shf.

Jas. Green, Coroner

Township Justices of the Peace

Portage des Sieux, Frs. Le Sieur, Eben. Ayres, Frs. Coursolle[44]

St. Charles, Jas Morrison, Elisha Goodrich, Wm. Christy,
Danl. Colgan, Sen.

Dardenne, Wm. McConnell, Abiel Farrensworth, Pros. K.
Robins

[42] Original in the Department of State, B. R. L., 3476.
[43] Pierre Didier was the first state treasurer of Missouri.
[44] François Coursault.

Femme Osage, Danl. Boone, Jno. B. Callaway, Benj. Cooper,[45] Hail Talbert

Upper Cuivre, Jos. Little, Christ. Clerk,[46] Robt. Simpson, Tho. D. L. Weeks

Lower Cuivre, Benj. Allen, Saml. S. Kennedy, Benj. Emmons

Henry Hight, Recorder, Judge of Probate & Noty. Public

To Admr. Oaths of Office

M. P. LeDuc, Mackay Wherry

Timothy Kibby, Audr. P. Accts.

District of St. Louis

Judges

Silas Bent, Augte. Chouteau, Bernd. Pratte, Louis Le Beaume, Samuel Hammond

Thos. F. Riddick, Clerk of the Courts

Alexr. McNair, Shf.

Jno. W. Honey, Coroner

Township Justices of the Peace

St. Ferdinand, Jno. Allen, Geo. Fallis, Tho. Musick, Danl. Bissell, Richd. Chitwood,[47] Eben R. Hawley

---

[45] Cooper was a Revolutionary War veteran who served in the Virginia-Illinois regiment. In 1808 he settled in the Boonslick Country but was forced to leave the Indian lands. He moved to Loutre Island, but eventually returned to the Boonslick Country, settling in Howard County. He was prominent in frontier fighting during the War of 1812.

[46] Christopher Clark.

[47] Richard Chittwood in 1797 settled on Maline Creek in the District of St. Louis.

Bon Homme, Richd. Caulk, Jas. McKay,[48] Andw. Kinkead[49]

Labbadie, Kinkead Caldwell, Jas. Stephens, Jno. G. Heth,[50] Geo. C. Sibley, Jas. H. Audrain,[51] Jno. Brownson

Joachim, Benj. Johnston, Jeduthun Kendal, Jas. McCullock, Phil. McGuire,[52] Benj. Baker, Jas. Rankin

St. Louis, Tho. F. Riddick, Peter Chouteau, M. P. Le Duc, Jos. V. Garnier, Fergus Moorhead, M. A. Rocque

Mary P. LeDuc, Recorder, Judge of Probate & Noty Public

William Christy, Regr. of Boatmen

To Admr. Oaths of Office

Tho. F. Riddick, Richd. Caulk, Bernd. Pratte, K. Caldwell, Samuel Hammond, M. P. Le Duc

Silas Hunt, Audr. P. Accts

DISTRICT OF ST. GENEVIEVE

Judges

Nathl. Cook

Thos. Oliver, Clerk of the Courts

Henry Dodge, Shf.

——————————, Coroner

---

[48] James Mackay.

[49] Andrew Kincaid in 1800 settled near Crève Coeur Lake.

[50] John G. Heath.

[51] Audrain was a Kentuckian who came to St. Louis in 1809 where he opened a tavern. He became an extensive landowner in the neighborhood of Fort Osage. He was a member of the family after whom Audrain County is named.

[52] McGuire was a member of the second territorial assembly.

Township Justices of the Peace

St. Genevieve, Thos. Oliver

Cinq Hommes, Isidore Moore, Joseph Donnohue

Belle Vue, Elisha Baker, Robt. M. Stephenson, Jos. Mc Cormeck

St. Michaels, John Callaway, William Dillon[53]

Big River, Jno. Andrews, Joseph Boring, John Baker

Breton, Jas. Austin, Michl. Hart, Darius Shaw, Robt. T. Brown, Wm. Mathers, Jno. Stanton and Walter Wilkinson

Thos. Oliver, Recorder, Judge of Probate & Noty. Public
To Admr. Oaths of Office

Otho Shrader, Thos. Oliver

Joseph Pratte,[54] Audr. P. Accts

DISTRICT OF CAPE GIRARDEAU

Judges

Stephen Byrd

Joseph McFerron, Clerk of the Courts

Jno. Hays, Shf.

Jas. Dougherty, Coroner

Township Justices of the Peace

Tywapity, Jno. Wellborn, Richard Mills, William Kelso

Cape Girardeau, Enoch Evans, John Abernathie, David Wade

---

[53] Dillon settled in the Murphy settlement on the St. Francis in 1799.

[54] Pratte was a large landholder who resided at Ste. Genevieve. He was interested in mining at Old Mine.

Byrd's, Wm. Matthews, John Davis, George Henderson
German, Frederick Ballinger, Benj. Shell, Fred. Linsbaugh, Sen.
St. Francis, Jacob Kelly

Geo. Henderson, Recorder, Judge of Probate & Noty. Public

To Admr. Oaths of Office

Joseph Mc Ferron

Geo Henderson, Audr. P. Accts

DISTRICT OF NEW MADRID

Judges

Peter A. La Forge

Joshua Humphreys, Clk. of the Courts

Jos. Lewis, Shf.

Robt. McKay, Coroner

Township Justices of the Peace

New Madrid, Tho. Evans, Jos. Lafernait, Fred Reineker, Robert McCoy, David Curtis
Big Prairie, Stephen Ross
Little Prairie, Geo Reeddell, Fr. Trenchard,[55] Will Connoway
Tywapity, Edwd. Matthews, Jr., Thos. Clarke

Michl. Amoureux, Recorder, Judge of Probate & Noty. Public

---

[55] François Trenchard settled on Lake Gayoso in the New Madrid District in 1802.

To Admr. Oaths of Office

Michl. Amoureux, Josa. Humphreys

Peter A. La Forge, Audr. P. Accts.

DISTRICT OF THE ARKENSAS

Judges

Henry Cassidy, James Scull, Saml. Moseley

Patrick Cassidy, Clerk of the Courts

Danl. Mooney, Shf.

Curtis Willborn, Coroner

This district not divided into Townships.

Justices of the Peace

Benjamin Fooy, Jno. McClain, Samuel Treat

Pat. Cassidy, Recorder & Judge Probate

Andw. Fagot, Noty. Public

To Admr. Oaths of Office

John Burke Treat, Benjamin Fooy, Pat. Cassidy

Joseph Stillwell, Audr. P. Accts.

Note — tenure of office. District Judges, ''during good behavior for four years''; Clerk of the General Court,
''During good behavior''; Notaries Public, ''during
good behavior for five years''; others during the pleasure of the Governor.

Secretary's Office
St. Louis Oct 1st 1811
Frederick Bates

A LIST OF LICENSES ISSUED TO TRADE WITH THE INDIANS WITHIN THE TERRITORY OF LOUISIANA
OCTOBER 1, 1810 — SEPTEMBER 30, 1811[56]

1810

Oct 14   Denis Julien with the Ioways & Sieux, for one year — Peter Chouteau Secy.

26   Elisha Lewis, on waters of Mississippi, for one year — H. Austin Security
Antoine Ceran, on the St. Francis for one year. Sam Solomon Security

1811

May 31   John Smith (T) & Co. on the Mississippi and its waters above the mouth of the Missouri, for one year, Wm. Christy, R. Easton Securities

24   James Aird, above the mouth of Missouri, for one year

July 2d   Henry Delaurier, on Missouri & its waters, one year, P. Lee[57] Security

15   Francis Deroin, on Missouri & its waters, one year, Aug Chouteau, [Security]
Louis Boudoin, on Missouri & its waters, one year, Aug Chouteau, [Security]
Brazeau & Buissonet, on Missouri & its waters, one year, Aug. Chouteau, [Security]
Francis Deroin, on Missouri & its waters, one year, Aug Chouteau, [Security]

[56] Original in the Department of State, B. R. L., 3474.
[57] Patrick Lee.

Joseph & Baptiste Lacroix, on Missouri & its waters, one year, Aug Chouteau, [Security]

Polite Dejardin, on Missouri & its waters, one year, Aug Chouteau, [Security]

Francis Rajotte & Co., on Missouri & its waters, one year, Aug Chouteau, [Security]

20th   Charles Monburn, on Missouri & its waters, one year, Aug. Chouteau, [Security]

23   Peter Godin on waters of White River
Sylvanus Philips on waters of St. Francis
Samuel Moseley on waters of Arkansas
Germain Charbonneau on waters of White River

Aug 6   Alex. Papin, Frs. Robidoux & Jacques Le Jeunesse, on the Missouri & its branches for one year Aug. Chouteau Security

8th   Primeau & L'Etourneau,[58] on Missouri & waters — Same Security

13th   William Rogers, on Missouri & waters — Same Security

19   Nathl. Irish on St. Francis & its waters 2 years, Edwd. Hempstead Secy.

Sepr 4   George Hunt, at Lead Mines on the Mississippi — Clement B. Penrose Security —

Sep 16   Jas. White & Wm. Preston trading under the name and firm of Jas. White & Co. by Geo. Wil-

[58] Probably Primo and Le Tourneau.

son their acting Agent, on the Mississippi and its waters, with the Sieux, Sacs & Foxes — for one year.

17   Jno. B. Bouvet,[59] on waters of the Missouri — one year — Pat Lee Secy.

18   Jas. Mc Farlane, on waters of Mississippi above the mouth of the river Missouri for one year Sam Solomon Security

Secretary's Office

St. Louis Oct 1st 1811

Frederick Bates

TO ALBERT GALLATIN

St. Louis Oct 17. 1811

Sir,

On the 20th of June I had the honor to write you that the Renaut-Agents had been making some attempts to *stay waste* within their imagined limits. Judge Shrader to whom the application for an Injunction was made, denied it, principally, as I understand, on account of their inability to shew boundaries. —

Having failed in these suits they have commenced actions of trespass for the recovery of damages against Wilkinson and others who had possession of the grounds before Henry Dodge the present tenant. These People have pleaded 'Justification under lease from John Smith (T)' and the court have ordered a survey (tho' the commis-

---

[59] Jean Baptiste Bouvet.

sioners had declined to do so) in order to ascertain the lines of Renaut.

I question the regularity of these proceedings: *or* it may perhaps be a matter of subsequent consideration for the Judges, whether an individual claim yet unadjusted, and without established limits, can, by any process of a territorial court, be brought into conflict with claims thus practically asserted by the Government. It would strike me that those who complain of trespass should come into court prepared to shew that they have suffered it. The ordinary course of justice, even in the present unsettled situation of real property, guards the possession without reference to the title, whereever that possession is warranted by the Acts of Congress: But where the right exists merely in the abstract, I cannot avoid viewing it as extraordinary, that a court of territorial jurisdiction, merely, should attempt the adjustment of what appears to be reserved to another tribunal. —

The Rents due to Government amount already to a considerable sum, probably six or eight thousand dollars, and a strange contest appears to have arisen, whether the *Agents* of *Renaut, John Smith (T)* or the *Government* shall receive them!

I have given to the Atty. General Mr Wash, every information on the subject, and desired his most diligent attention to it.

If Smith (T) in his haste to grasp these Rents should disclose evidences of his intrusion on the lands in question, or if these evidences should be obtained in any other manner, I have instructed the Atty. Genl. to institute the proper process against him without a moment's delay.

A LEASE

The undersigned Frederick Bates Recorder of Land Titles for the territory of Louisiana, authorized to that effect by the President of the United States does hereby covenant with James Bryan[60] & William Bates,[61] that, from and after the date hereof, for the term of twelve months, they shall be at liberty to occupy and work as Lead-Mine-Land, a tract, supposed property of the United States, to contain two hundred acres, situated, adjoining the Mineral Tract of Moses Austin at Mine A Breton in the district of St. Genevieve — It being expressly understood that the said tract shall be surveyed and marked as soon as possible, and in such a manner as not to interfere with any private claims depending before the board of Commissioners.

And the said James Bryan & William Bates do hereby engage and promise that they will pay to the said Recorder or to the person deputed by him for that object, for the use of the United States one tenth part of all the Mineral raised on the said tract or the amount thereof in Lead at the option of the said Tenants

These Covenants to be mutually binding on the contracting Parties, for the term of twelve months, as above mentioned unless the President to whom they are to be submitted shall disapprove of the same

Given under our hands at St. Louis the 26th day of October, Eighteen hundred Eleven.

Frederick Bates Seal

James Bryan   Seal

William Bates   Seal

[60] A son-in-law of Moses Austin.

[61] William Bates, a follower of Austin, in 1803 was living in Bellevue Valley.

AGREEMENT WITH PEYTON JOHNSON

Frederick Bates Recorder of Land Titles for the territory of Louisiana and empowered by the President of the United States to make Leases of Lead Mines within the said territory does hereby stipulate that Peyton Johnson shall be permitted to survey and mark two hundred acres of United States' Land situated on the East side of big River, about ¾ of a mile from said river; about four & a half miles above or to the right hand of the road leading from Mine A Breton to St. Genevieve and about one mile north of said Peyton Johnson's plantation, and that, as soon as he shall have executed a bond with good and sufficient security for the monthly payments of the rents herein after stipulated to be paid to the Government the said Peyton Johnson shall be at liberty to work the same as mineral Land, under the express Proviso that the lands so surveyed and marked shall not interfere with any claim or claims, depending before the board of Commissioners.

And the said Peyton Johnson does hereby engage and promise that he will pay to the said Recorder or to the person deputed by him for that object, for the use of the United States, at the end of every month is required, one tenth part of all the mineral raised on the said tract, or the amount thereof in lead, at the option of the said Peyton Johnson. —

These covenants to be mutually binding on the contracting parties, for the term of twelve months, from the date hereof, unless the President to whom they are to be submitted shall disapprove of the same

Given under our hands at St. Louis the 29th day of October, Eighteen hundred and Eleven. —

Witness   Frederick Bates Seal
James Givens   Peyton Johnson Seal

PERMIT TO EXPLORE MINERAL LANDS

Mr. Amable Partenay is hereby permitted to explore the mineral Lands of the United States within the district of St. Genevieve, and to make those diggings which may be necessary to ascertain the extent and richness of his discoveries.

It is understood, that if the undersigned retains the Agency in these matters, that Mr. Partenay shall have the first privilege of a Lease for the mines he may discover.

Given under my hand at St. Louis, the Sixth day of November, Eighteen hundred & Eleven

---

JOHN B. C. LUCAS TO JAMES MONROE[62]

Sir,   St. Louis December 15 1811

One of the offices of Judge of the Territory of Louisiana having vacated in the course of last month, by the expiration of the Commission of Judge Coburn, a sense of duty as well as a regard to the particular circumstance which I am in, — induces me to inform you, that since near five years during which Mr Coburn has been one of the Judges of this territory he has never ceased to reside with his family in the state of Kintucky on the ohio above Limestone Town, that he never came in the Territory but twice a year to attend the two terms of the Superior Court, after which he immediately left the Territory, som time went away before the term was expired and if at any time he detained to attend the Legislature, it was during so short

---

[62] The original is in the Department of State, B. R. L., 3482.

a time, that he never did stay in the Territory longer than one month at each term of the court, leaving at least ten month of absence every year, I further state that this year he has not even attended the court at may term — so that he has been since the Latter end of october 1810 until the commencement of october of this present year, without ever appearing in this territory. — ten or twelve courts of oyer and Terminer, for the trial of capital offenses have been holden in this Territory, during the time Mr Coburn was Judge, the Law requires that these Courts be presided by one of the Judges of the Superior Court, owing to his absence Mr Coburn never has attended any. — this has thrown upon the other two Judges of which I am one a greater proportion of Labour and responsibility than they ought to have born, beside these a variety of Business are to be done in vacation, of which Mr Coburn has likewise kept clear

I never absented my self from the Territory these six years past of purpose to take a journey to the states in the course of a few months, Since the death of Judge Shrader I find my self to be the sole Judge present — the propriety — that Judges and Legislators should be resident, is apparent enough independent of all the circumstances here related, a non resident Judge ressembles very much a sine cure officer; to my certain knowledge many old inhabitants of this territory have passed severe censures on the conduct of Judge Coburn I mean relatively to his non residence, they have exultingly remarked that republican officers are as little scrupulous as those of the former Spanish Government were, and that money is as eagerly sought after by the former without being more scrupulous than the Latter about the means of making it. —

A LEASE

The undersigned Frederick Bates Recorder of Land Titles for the territory of Louisiana, and Special Agent of the President of the United States for the leasing of Lead mines, does hereby covenant with James Bryan that from the date hereof he, said Bryan shall be at liberty to occupy and work as Lead Mine Land a tract supposed property of the United States, to contain three hundred — acres, situated on the S. E. fork of the Plattin, between the Settlements of Plattin & Big River, six miles from the former and four from the latter; it being expressly understood that the said tract shall be surveyed and marked as soon as circumstances will permit, and in such manner as not to interfere with any private claims regularly entered with the Recorder. And the said James Bryan does hereby engage and promise that he will monthly if required pay to the said Frederick Bates Special Agent as aforesaid or to the person deputed by him for that object, for the use of the United States, one tenth part of all the mineral raised on the said tract, or the amount thereof in lead.

These covenants to be mutually binding on the contracting parties for the term of twelve months — unless the President of the United States to whom they are to be submitted shall disapprove the same.

Given under our hands at St. Louis the 15th day of December, One thousand, eight hundred, eleven

Frederick Bates Seal
James Bryan   Seal

JOHN SMITH T TO BATES

Sir,   St. Louis 22nd Decm. 1811.

Wrong and injustice commenced on your part towards me with our acquaintance and you have persevered and still continue to persevere in you practices of oppression and injustice — I now call on you Sir for the injurys done me — from your standing I expect you will give me that prompt satisfaction justly my due on equal and fair terms — My friend the bearer will arrange on my part what ever may be necessary and by him I expect your answer.

TO JOHN SMITH T

Sir,   St. Louis Decr. 22d. 1811

Your note of this morning, delivered me by Docr Farrar has given me much surprize:

You charge me with wrong, injustice and oppression from the commencement of our acquaintance. It is due to truth and frankness to declare to you that I am totally unconscious of these things. Perhaps, if your charges had been special they might have been more susceptible of explanation. As they at present stand I am at a loss to conjecture to what particularly they allude.

22d[63]

A fair copy of the foregoing was presented to Doctor F. at my quarters at 2 oclock — He took an hour's time to consider of it — returned & declined to receive it — It was

[63] Bates attached this note to the copy of the above letter which he kept in his files.

then agreed that he would call again at 8 oclock — this delay was not at my instance; but it was understood that I would consult a friend or friends in the mean time with respect to the regularity of the Doctor's farther expectations. — He called between 8 & 9 — The same answer was presented to him — which he declined to receive — and promised specification tomorrow morning at 8 or 9 oclock. —

JOHN SMITH T TO BATES

Sir,   24th Decr. 1811.

In recurring to your conduct towards me I pass over the manner in which you removed me from the offices of judge of the Courts and that of Lt. Colo. of Militia in the District of St. Genevieve without the priviledge of an enquiry into my conduct — The brief authority with which you were at that time cloathed in the absence of a Governor and the arbitrary manner in which you exercised it carried conviction to every honest and independent mind that you were actuated by principles & practices which you would deem unjust and oppressive if practiced towards you — Of course you did not do by others as you would others should do by you —

That Monitor which the supreme being has placed in the breast of every man warns you of these injurys — You had the power tho not the right to exercise it in that manner — It was an official exercise of power which did not effect my property and in this respect I shall be satisfied with the public investigation and opinion. —

But Sir When the public agent attempts to shield himself under the cloak of his official character to do an individual personal wrong — to deprive him of his property —

such agent in his individual capacity ought & must be held responsible for his acts and behaviour — This is a principle maintained by the great Charter of our Natural Rights — The right of personal protection of (reputation, liberty) and property, is dictated by God to man even should it be at the hazzard of life itself — I state that you have wronged me in leasing my property at Mine Renault to a Messers Hart & Mathers known bankrupts from whom I can never recover a cent for the damages sustained thereby altho you have since acknowledged my title to be good, that the late Governor Lewis had intefered with your province as agent and that you would never lease an other tract!

You have wronged me in leasing the mine Shipboleth when from being recorder of land titles and exificior one of the Land Commissioners you must have known (as you did from personal information) that I claimed the tract and that my title papers were of record in your office in due time — It being provided by the 10th Section of the Act of Congress passed the 3d March 1811 that till after the decision of Congress thereon no tract shall be offered *for sale* the claim to which has been in due time and according to law presented to the recorder of land titles in the District of Louisiana and filed in his office for the purpose of being Investigated by the Commissioners, appointed for ascertaining the rights of persons claiming lands in the Territory of Louisiana — Can it be supposed that you have been authorised *to lease* such lands? —

You have injured me by a wanton pretence of power you never possessed by actually leasing my property to Messers. Dodge[64] Wilson and Craighead,[65] tho to evade cen-

[64] Henry Dodge.
[65] Alexander Craighead.

sure you have artfully inserted this clause in the lease Provided the same does not interfere with any private claim now depending before the board of Commissioners — You have declared to one of them that in case I should persist in maintaining my claim you would order out a sufficient military force to drive me from my possession whereby you have prevented my receipt of a bout ten thousand dollars justly my due by contract from the lessees

. If you dare to meet these accusations you dare to meet. me and extend to me that honourable satisfaction which you might ask from another and which is due from one gentleman to another.

My friend Docr. Farrar will arrange the manner time and place If you shrink from this test your gilt is confessed and you dare to commit acts of injustice and oppression which you have not the manhood to support and maintain.

[Note by Bates] recd. Satury. eveng. after Sunset the 28th Inst. —

BERNARD G. FARRAR TO BATES

Sir,   Sᴛ. Lᴏᴜɪs December 24th 1811.

I informed you last evening that I would call on you this morning at 8 o'clock, but being called on to visit Herculaneum renders it impossible Soon after my return I shall present to you Colo. Smiths communication. Delay on my part not intended.

TO JOHN SMITH T

Sir,   St. Louis Decr. 30. 1811

The only reply which I permit myself to make to your very extraordinary note of the 24th delivered by Doctor Farrar on the evening of the 28th is, that I owe to government alone, an account of my official conduct.—

A CERTIFICATE

Commissioner's Room,
[St. Louis], January 20. 1812

I Thomas F. Riddick Clerk of the Board of Commissions for ascertaining and adjusting the titles and claims to land in the territory of Louisiana do certify that on examination of the minutes of the board it appears that Frederick Bates Commissioner was present at the decision of three thousand Claims subsequent to the 1st of July 1809 and that all the claims have been disposed of by the board, either granted, confirmed, ascertained or reported.

JOHN COBURN TO JOHN GRAHAM, DEPARTMENT OF STATE, WASHINGTON, D. C.[66]

Dear Sir,   Ky. Mason. January 23d 1812.

Some time past I received your favor informing me of the friendly interest you took in the application I made to the Genl. Government, for a renewal of my Commission.

[66] Original in Department of State, B. R. L., 3485.

I shall always retain a grateful recollection, for this evidence of your friendly regard, and shall never cease to esteem, both the late and present Executive, not only for their political virtues, but the marks of confidence I have received from them — Devoted as I hope I am to the principles by which they have been governed, in the course of the administration of ten years past; my devotion is certainly not admonished by the acts of kindness which I have received.

I discover in your Letter, that you had supposed, I wished some assurances of appointment, previous to the express nomination by the President. Believe me, it never was my intention to produce such an impression on your mind, as such a wish on my part would have been improper and indelicate; I make this apology to you, in order, to satisfy you, that however desirous I might be for an appointment I would never adopt any improper means.

We are all anxiety to learn the result of the deliberations of Congress. You know that Kentuckians cannot remain lukewarm spectators of the interesting scenes now before the American people. As far as I can judge of the Western temper, it is for the most early and decisive measures, against G. Britain especially. We are inclined to think, that we shall never enjoy political happiness, while the British retain either their possessions in Canada or possess their present influence over our commerce. Some struggle must ensue, when we attempt to emancipate ourselves, from the shackle, under which we have too long labored. Perhaps that struggle may as well commence at this period as at any other; we have just causes of resistance, we certainly have borne the injuries we have received, with more than Christian forbearance; altho we have been patient under aggressions, we may cease to preserve the dignified character which our Government has justly merited, by a submission too much protracted.

It is perhaps time, that we should again recur to the principles of our revolution, that we should be brought closer to our own Government, and that those of our Citizens who may have wandered from the flock, should be brought back to the fold, and that we should distinctly separate wolves from the sheep.

We want a rallying period, a moment in which the true American principles shall be again brought to the test. The body politic is not unlike the body natural; it occasionally requires some degree of depletion, to throw off the humors accumulated either by intemperance, or any temperament improperly acquired. Excuse my politic lecture.

TO ALBERT GALLATIN

Sir,
                                    St. Louis Jany. 27. 1812

I have the honor to inform that the Report is at length completed and entrusted, for conveyance, to the care of Mr Penrose. It will probably reach the City about the 1st of March next.[67]

Until the present month no Patent Certificates have issued since the Return which I had the honor to make to you on the 5th day of Dec. 1810: — Because, during the investigation it was very inconvenient to proceed

[67] The report of the commissioners is in *American State Papers, Public Lands*, II, 388-603.

regularly with that work. It will now be in my power to take it up with a less divided attention.

With grateful recollections of the confidences heretofore reposed, I make so free as to offer myself for the Office of Register created during the last Session. I have continued to hope for you favorable opinions and in this affair have no other reliance.

Mr. Riddick will be very desirous of making his respects to you personally. Should you wish farther informations as to the business in which he was lately employed I am persuaded that he may be relied upon.

TO GOVERNOR HOWARD, ST. LOUIS

Sᴛ. Lᴏᴜɪꜱ Feby 23. 1812

Sɪʀ,

The friendly dispositions wch. you have had the goodness on various occasions to express towards me will perhaps justify the liberty wch. I am about to take. For some years past I have holden the offices of Secy. of the terry & Recorder of Land Titles always imagining that when the Sales of Lands actually commenced the several duties of these employments would be found incompatible — A Law of the last Session provides for the Appointment of a Register! and altho' it is not very probable, owing to the circumstances of the country, that this Officer will be very soon appointed, I have some time since become an Applicant. In the event of the President's determination to disunite these Offices — and if I should be indulged in a selection, I should prefer the Office of Register. It is a subject however on which I scarcely know how to address myself to the Administration, and should be greatly obliged by your making such a communication as, in your opinion will best promote these views.

TO ALBERT GALLATIN

ST. LOUIS Feby 27. 1812

SIR,

I have this day taken the liberty to draw on you in favor of my mother Caroline M. Bates for the sum of five hundred dollars, being the 'further allowance' due me as one of the commissioners for ascertaining & adjusting the rights of persons claiming lands in the territory of Louisiana as provided by an Act of Congress of 3d March 1811.

The Report was confided, for conveyance, to Mr Penrose early in the present month & has probably by this time been presented to you. I enclose a certificate that all the claims have been disposed of. I hope that this Dft will be deemed regular as my mother is much in want of money & could not very well, answer the consequences of a Protest.

TO ALBERT GALLATIN

ST. LOUIS Feby. 28. 1812

SIR

I have this day taken the liberty to draw on you in favor of Mc Knight & Brady[68] for the sum of Fifteen hundred dollars for my services as a commissioner for ascertaining and adjusting the Titles & Claims to lands

[68] In 1809 John McKnight and Thomas Brady came from Pittsburgh and opened a store in St. Louis.

in the territory of Louisiana, in the decision of three thousand Claims as expressed in the face of the draft & vouched by the enclosed Certificate.

TO JAMES PLEASANTS, JR., WASHINGTON, D. C.

Sir,   St. Louis March 8. 1812

The very high respects which I entertain as well by sentiment as habitually from my youth occasion me to intrude perhaps too frequently. I now entreat only one moment of your time. The friends of Alexander Mc Nair will probably mention him for military advancement in some of the new raised corps — a Regiment or a Battalion at the least. Do not mistake me. I am not presuming to recommend him either for the one or the other. He relies on abler Advocates. All I wish to say is, that I have known him for the last five years, and am not acquainted with a man more truly respectable. He was formerly in the regular army when very young and resigned his commission for civil pursuits in which he has acquired character as well as property. His military propensities perhaps predominate tho' he is at the same time conversant with civil business. This variety of fitness designated him at once as a Judge of the district court of St. Charles & Aid de camp to the Comr. in chief of the territory. He is at this time Sheriff of the district of St. Louis.

Major Mc Nair is a native of Pennsylvania, and sincerely attached, I have every reason to believe, to the republican institutions of our common country. He is indeed my personal friend; but in a general estimation of his character, I believe myself altogether free from any irregular biass arising from individual preposession. Hearing that his name would appear on the list of candidates I could not forbear adventuring this testimony of his merits.

TO SPENCER MONTAGUE WHARTON,
NEW ORLEANS

SIR,   ST. LOUIS March 12th. 1812

.   .   .   .

I have perhaps heard from Canada since you did. There is great preparation for war in that quarter, and I have no doubt that our government will give them time to complete their defences — for the stouter the resistance, the greater the honor of the conquest. But I am not in the secret & perhaps the great work is now going on, for we have all heard that it was the deep laid scheme of some of our wise men, that Canada should conquer itself in our behalf. . . .

TO JAMES MONROE

SIR,   ST. LOUIS March 12. 1812

I had the honor to receive ten days ago your letter of the 27th Decr. and by last week's mail the printed Census of the Inhabitants of the United States and of their territories.

It has been gratifying to review these papers in their complete and final form, and I offer you my best thanks for that courtesy which has given me the opportunity of doing so. They shall be preserved on the files of the Office as you require.

The Laws of the United States with which I was formerly supplied, were delivered to Governor Howard, on his arrival. In places less remote the want of these volumes would be less sensibly felt. If convenient to you, I should feel it as a singular favor, that you would order a set to be sent to me.

TO ALBERT GALLATIN

SIR,· ST. LOUIS March 30. 1812

I beg permission to say that on a review of the Patent Certificates heretofore issued it occurred to me that I might possibly have fallen into errors. To correct these if they exist, the more easily, and to guard against their future occurrance I have thought that some little delay could operate no substantial injury to any person. In the mean time, some of those already issued would be presented to you. — From your silence I should gather your approbation, and a direct communication would probably convey to me your censures.

If the Board was mistaken in giving Certificates other than under the 4th Sec of the act of 3d Mar 1807 I have followed their footsteps into the same mistakes in five instances only to wit in P. Certs. No. 11. 81. 90. 91. 92.

TO JAMES MONROE

SIR, ST. LOUIS Ap 1. 1812

In obedience to that provision of the organic law of this territory which requires the Secretary to make half yearly Reports, I have the honor to enclose a list of civil Appointments, — a list of appointments in the militia, — a list of licences granted for Indian Trade and a table of the civil Officers in commission.[69]

TO ALBERT GALLATIN

SIR,   ST. LOUIS April 25. 1812

It was not until the first of the present month that I had the honor to receive your letter of 26th October last.

John Smith (T) still attempts to carry his bold and extraordinary projects by menace and intimidation. He has established himself by the side of H Dodge on the Shibboleth-Mines[70] and at this moment maintains a joint possession with the tenants. It is not within my province to account for his continuance there. A deposition of the fact has been submitted to the Governor, a copy of which I enclose.

During the last week I have had much conversation with Messrs Dodge & Wilson[71] (the latter of whom together with Alexr. Craighead has joined in the covenants) as to their maintenance in possession and as to the payments of rents. On the latter subject there will be neither unnecessary delay nor difficulty of any kind, that I apprehend. But as I had not been honored with your orders as to the disposal of the lead or money, and

[69] The lists were not attached.

[70] The Shibboleth Mine was on Mineral Fork of Grand River about ten miles from Mine à Burton. Schoolcraft, *Scenes and Adventures in the Semi-Alpine Region of the Ozark Mountains of Missouri and Arkansas,* 168-175; *American State Papers, Public Lands,* III, 609-613.

[71] Nicholas Wilson was one of the representatives from Washington County in the second general assembly of Missouri Territory.

as either the one or the other would be equally safe in their hands as in mine, I have consented, at their instance that the payments shall be made in June next.

In the mean time the suit which Smith (T) has instituted against them for trespass on the premises (Date [?] 100,000 dols) will probably have been decided. I am summoned to attend the trial of this cause, at St. Genevieve, next month, with the papers appertaining to the lease, as well as with the records and papers in relation to the St. Vrain Claim:

I do not think that he will be hardy enough to alledge the want of power to make this lease (tho' Governor Howard has entertained some doubts on the subject, arising from a vagueness of expression in the law) for, from such a plea, tho' sustainable, he could derive no advantage, as his recovery of damages must depend, not on the irregular holding of the United States' tenants, but on his own actual previous possession under the laws. This cannot be shown. —

I have also had the honor to receive your letter of the 25th of March, remarking the defectiveness of several Patent Certificates. If this faultiness arise from any negligence of mine, I regret it extremely. At any rate, I shall, in future issue none except the Survey contain the clearest designations. —

TO JAMES PLEASANTS, JR.

SIR,   ST. LOUIS April 25. 1812

David Massey of Goochland has been about 12 Mos. in this country in search of business — for the last eight months he has been employed in the Clerk's office of St.

. Louis district, and under my very frequent observation. It is impossible to conceive a young man more undeviatingly .correct in his conduct or more irreproachable and blameless in his manners & deportment.

He has been seized with a military mania and burns to signalize himself in defence of his country. I make so free as to enclose a letter with respect to him which I lately received from Colo. Danl. Bissell.

If he is so fortunate as to obtain your patronage, I am sure that a commission will be transmitted, & I know his generous nature so well as to assure you, that your friendly interposition would be held in the most grateful remembrance.

TO ALBERT GALLATIN

Sir,

St. Louis May 30. 1812

I have had the honor to receive your letter of the 18th of last month, — and am much relieved by the detailed manner in which you have had the goodness to communicate your views as to the Land-Claims of this territory. Every intimation which has reference to my Office shall be most diligently attended to.

I have but lately returned from St Genevieve where I was summoned as a witness duces tecum[72] with the Records etca. in the suit, Smith (T) vs Dodge & others. The cause was not tried, owing to the Plaintiffs unreadiness. Whenever it does come on, I have no fear as to the result. Smith (T) has lately circulated Stories of my having made compromises with the tenants; as to receipt

---

[72] A writ commanding a person to appear in court bringing certain designated documents or things.

of Lead, prejudicial to the interests of the government.
I beg you Sir, to be assured that *I have made no compromises* and surely I had as little *inclination as authority*
to make any arrangements lessening rents already sufficiently moderate.

CONFIRMATION OF SALE OF SLAVES

Whereas James F. Hull esquire, authorized to that effect
by me, did, On the seventh day of March last, for and
in consideration of the sum of Nine hundred dollars paid
to him for my use by Frederick Bates, sell and deliver
over to the said Bates three negro slaves to wit, Sam, a
fellow, Polly a wench and their infant child Juno — Now,
know all men by these presents that I do ratify and
confirm the said sale and delivery, binding myself, my
Heirs, Executors and administrators to warrant and
defend the title to the said slaves against all legal claims
whatsoever. —

Given under my hand and seal at the town of St. Louis
the Sixth day of June, one thousand, eight hundred and
twelve

S Hammond (Seal)

Sealed and delivered
in presence of
A Mc Nair

Territory of Louisiana
District & Township of St. Louis

Before me the undersigned one of the Justices of the
peace in & for the Township of St. Louis aforesaid Personally came and appeared Alexander Mc Nair, Esqre.
who being duly sworn says that he was present when
Samuel Hammond signed & sealed the within Instrument

of Writing and that he the said deponent at the request of said Samuel Hammond did subscribe his name as Witness to the same.

A Mc Nair

Sworn to & Subscribed before me a Justice of the peace in & for the Township aforesaid.   Given under my hand this 26th day of June A. D. 1812

M. P. Leduc J. P

Recorded this 26th day of June A D 1812, Book C. Page 612.

M. P. Leduc   (Seal)

26th June 1812

Recorder

S. Hammond to F. Bates — Deed $1-00
Paid $1.00 to the Recorder 4 Aug. '12.

TO ALBERT GALLATIN

Sir,

St. Louis June 20. 1812

I have the honor to enclose for the information of the President a lease in renewal of that made last year to Messrs. Henry Dodge, Alexr. Craighead & Nicholas Wilson.

They now tell me that they expect to make the payments from the smeltings of their ashes which are estimated to be amply sufficient for that object. They think they have claims to indulgence and delay arising from the vexations of law suits and the continued intrusions to which they have been subject: But profess a readiness whenever the demand be insisted on, to deliver the lead.

WILLIAM C. CARR TO BATES

TRAVELLERS REST, [Kentucky], 9th July 1812.

DR SIR.

The last accounts that reached us of your situation as related to our red brethren were by no means pleasing. I hope however you are not all scalped· yet. I should be sorry to hear of your deaths —

Nothing is talked of here but John Pope[73] He has become a famous man in this land of political (in)tolerance. By the papers you will have learnt of his unfortunate fate at almost every town in Kentucky. perhaps before you get this — He was burnt in effigy at Limestone Washington, Mountsterling, Paris, Winchester, Lexington, Nicholasville[74] &c &c throughout the state as far as I have yet heard, as fast as the mail went, that brought the news of War —

At Lexington they refined on their punishments. On Saturday, being the Jubilee of our independence, He was only hung & burnt. But some remarks having been made as was, understood, about its having been done in the *night,* another effigy was made early on Monday morning in a grave yard, which being suspended from a gallows, with a purse grasped in his only hand, labelled in large letters, British gold; he was on this situation marched out of the burying ground & drum'd up and down town to the air of the rogues March on muffled drums. Not contented with this they then took him to the whipping post, had him whiped by two men with waggon whips,

[73] John Pope, United States senator from Kentucky, was violently opposed to the War of 1812. This caused his defeat when he stood for reelection.

[74] Towns in Kentucky.

shot him, and burnt him again. So that he was, at first hung burnt & buried, then raised from the dead drumed through town, whiped, shot hung, burnt & buried again —

This you will say is surely madness But sir such is the unspeakable horror in which his memory is held here, this proceedings was to be repeated next Monday, being court day. His friends are forced to see & hear this thing without a murmur: for believe me it is almost as much as a mans life & property are worth to open his mouth in opposition to their proceedings,—For only saying it was ungenerous to treat a man so, the person was instantly knocked down & forced to creep off —

I rejoiced to learn his sister Mrs. Trotter was then at Louisville, — Such spectacles would surely have harrowed up her very soul. She doats on her brother. . . .

TO MRS. CAROLINE M. BATES, GOOCHLAND, VIRGINIA

My Mother,   St. Louis July 19. 1812

.   .   .   .

I recollect, when I was very young you advised your children never to have a Slave, because, for the most part nothing but discipline could make them profitable. I have been induced to purchase — and have been so fortunate as to get a family which will not I hope, ever require harsh treatment. My lands are some miles from town & of course very little under my own superintendance & yet these blacks, without an overseer, are raising a most promising crop. I do not believe that if I were to devote myself to plantation business it would be more to my permanent advantage than any thing else I could pursue. The grounds are unconceivably fertile, both hill & bottom — the latter never overflows — And the Market is high for every thing which can be cultivated.

The rumour of Indian mischief is much more terrible abroad than at home. We have had a good deal of killing on the frontier. But the country is not in *general* danger. *My* employments confine me to the town & I shall gather neither *Scars* nor *Laurels.* . . .

TO WILLIAM C. CARR, TRAVELLERS' REST, NEAR LEXINGTON, KENTUCKY

Dr. Sir,   St. Louis July 31. 1812

Your letter on the 9th was received by last evening's mail. No, thank God! we are not yet scalped, and indeed it is only the extreme frontier which appears to be in any danger. Our villages are as safe as Lexington. Our 'red Brethren' must nevertheless get some *paternal* admonishings, before they learn to deport themselves like members of a decent family. It does appear to me that we carry this patriarchal notion rather too far. These wretches with whom we so familiarly claim brotherhood take no pride in the alliance. Divested of what few virtues they might have possessed as Savages without having acquired anything except the frauds and the hypocrisy of civilization, it is very *fond* in us to imagine that they will be governed restrained and impelled by motives similar to those which influence ourselves. Austere and haughty justice will alone answer. This harsh discipline suits slaves — and it suits Indians. I can fall down & worship the philanthropy of Mr Jefferson — And I can read the Republic of Plato too with very great delight; but I believe that the *one* as little as the other will be found compatible with the maxims and usages of the world at this day.

It must be, that you Kentuckians have been bitten by the *Mad Dogs of War.* If the Devil himself had fallen into your hands, you could not have devised for him severer punishments. If the *Effigy* be treated with this execration what, in Heaven's name will be your conduct to the illustrious Senator himself when he returns among you? But I suppose that this is all directed, in an abstract way, against the *political man,* and that Mr P[75] himself, after his resignation will be subject to no ill usage. I will believe that the *purse of gold* was thrown in, with his other punishments, gratuitously; for he can scarcely, I should hope, be suspected of any thing worse than a too obstinate adherence to his own opinions.

There is no calculating on the movements of the Missouri Folks, when once they get into safe harbour at Travellers' Rest'. There's yourself for one — and there's our very good friend Mr Riddick for another. I don't wonder at it at all — for I dream myself night & day about Kentucky or any other place rather than this hopeful village of ours. The place to be sure is good enough in itself but it wants peopling. —

Mc Nair is on duty with the Cavalry on the frontiers, near Fort Mason.[76] I gave him your order expecting that he would indorse the amount of my note on the execution

[75] Senator John Pope.
[76] Fort Mason was on the Mississippi River near modern Hannibal.

agt. Ramsay.[77] The whole affair is yet open. I do greatly fear that the Major does not make close arrangements. I was ready, as I told you I should be — and *am.*

The crops of your tenant near town are very good, as indeed are the crops of the country generally. My blacks at Bon Homme have done wonders. We shall have a vast abundance for those new Settlers who will probably come among us in the fall.

The People are looking forward with eager expectation to the time (I suppose you know that the 2d grade Act[78] has passed) when the deep and spacious foundations of *Liberty* and *Law* are to be laid by themselves. You will come to the country to study the new code. You must *necessarily* — for the machine will acquire such an increased impetus from the mania of reform which possesses the People that you will never comprehend its movements unless on the spot. Who do you think are Candidates for the delegation to Congress under the new Regime? Why, I'll tell you. There's Hempstead[79] the 'Heir presumptive' Gratiot,[80] the indefatigable — Easton[81] the * * * (I want epithets) and Provonchere[82] the forlorn hope.

[77] Thomas Ramsay was a 1st lieutenant in the regular army at the outbreak of the War of 1812. He was raised to the rank of captain on November 30, 1812. He was killed in a duel with Captain Wylie Martin near St. Louis on August 6, 1818.

[78] The Territory of Louisiana was changed to the Territory of Missouri on June 4, 1812. By this act the legislative power was vested in a bicameral "general assembly" composed of a legislative council of nine appointed for five years by the President, and a house of representatives elected for two years by the people of the territory. U. S., *Statutes at Large*, II, 743-747.

[79] Edward Hempstead.

[80] Charles Gratiot.

[81] Rufus Easton.

[82] Pierre Provonchère.

Mr Riddicks friends are speaking of him — and I entertain a very great confidence, that if he were on the ground
& would take some trouble in the affair, he might be
elected.

I am happy to hear of the health of Mrs Carr & your
little son. Please make my respects to the Ladies. Miss
Eliza thinks nothing of breaking her word. I understood
that she intended to have visited this country long ago.
But I suppose she is frightened by Indians, Earthquakes
& Epidemics like all the rest of the world. I do mightily
fear that Missouri will be nothing but a place of exile for
Robbers & Outlaws in a few years.

CIRCULAR TO ASSISTANTS FOR RECEIVING REPORTS OF BRITISH SUBJECTS

Sir,   St. Louis August 14. 1812

I enclose you a news Paper in which you will find a
notice to British Subjects, requiring them to report themselves, families, pursuits &c. &c. with two acts of Congress
respecting alien enemies, subjoined.

I have taken the liberty to name you to receive on my
behalf, the Reports of British Subjects, who may reside
within your district. —

If you should chance to have private information of
any who neglect to report themselves, I must request that
you will yourself report them to me, adding any facts
which may come to your knowledge as to their deportment
and conduct. You will please transmit the original
Reports weekly by mail, retaining exact copies thereof.
Should you decline the discharge of this trust, you will

have the goodness to signify it by first conveyance that another may be appointed.

LIST OF MILITIA APPOINTMENTS

Reorganization of the Militia, under an Act of the Congress of the United States providing for the Government of the Territory of Missouri approved June 4. 1812 —

1ST REGIMENT — COUNTY OF ST LOUIS

David Musick Lt colo. comdt. Tho F. Riddick Major of 1st Battalion Richard Chitwood Major of 2d Battn. Jeduthun Kendal[1] Maj. 3d Bat Peter Chouteau Maj. 4 Bat

COMPANIES OF 1ST BATTN.

1st William Smith Capt
    Hubert Guyon Lt
    Paul L Chouteau
           Ensign

2d Gregoire Sarpy Capt
    Joseph Bouju Lt
    ——— Ensign

3d Louis Coutoix Capt
    Louis Coutoix Lt
    Francis Roi Ensign

4th Zaphaniah Sappington
           Capt
    Thomas Sappington Lt
    William L. Long
           Ensign

COMPANIES OF 2D BATTN.

1st James Musick Capt
    Levi Lanzey Lt
    John Mc Donald Ensign

2d Hyacinthe Dehetre
           Capt
    J. M. Courtoix Lt
    Joseph Aubuchon
           Ensign

3d Jonathan Wiseman
                    Capt
    John Kinkead Lt
    Gabriel Long Ensign

4th John E. Allen Capt
     Joseph Lard Lt
     William Mc Downs
                    Ensign

COMPANIES OF 3D BATTN.

1st James McCullock Capt
     Jacob Collins Lt.
     John Horigne Ensign

2d Abner Vansant Capt
    David Briant Lt.
    Benja. Johnston Ensign

3d Thomas Williams Capt
    William Ink Lt
    ———— Ensign

COMPANIES OF 4TH BATTN.

1st Benja. Hatherley
                    Capt.
     Samuel Cantley Lt.
     Lewis Hall Ensign

2d Stephen Lanham Capt
    John S. Farrar Lt.
    John Sappington
                    Ensign

3d Auguste P. Chouteau
                    Capt
    ———— Lt
    ———— Ensign

2D REGIMENT — COUNTY OF ST GENEVIEVE

Nathl. Cook Lt. colo comdt — John Donohue Major of 1st
    Martin Ruggles Maj 2d Battn.

COMPANIES OF 1ST BATTN.

1st Thomas Oliver Capt
     John Mc Arthur Lt
     Joseph Hertick, Ensign

2d John B. Bossieur Capt
    James Rigdon Lt
    Joseph Amoureux
                    Ensign

3d   Richd. Moore Capt
     Thomas Riney Lt
     Thomas Patterson
                  Ensign

4th Francis R. Cissell Capt
     Mark Brooks Lt
     Samuel Mc Call Ensign

COMPANIES OF 2D BATTALION

1st Joseph Garrett Capt
     John Sinclair Lt
     Benja. La Chance
                  Ensign

2d   Andrew Miller Capt
     ———— Lt
     ———— Ensign

3d   Henry Poston Capt
     Robert Andrews Lt
     Joseph Winds Ensign

4th Thomas Sloan Capt
     ———— Lt
     ———— Ensign

5th William Holmes Capt
     Laken Walker Lt
     Isaac Murphy Ensign

STAFF OF 2D REGIMENT

Joseph Hertick Pay Master

3D REGIMENT — COUNTY OF ST. CHARLES

Danl. M. Boone Lt colo. comdt. Peter Journey Maj 1st
   & Jas. Morrison Maj 2d Battn.

COMPANIES OF THE 1ST BATTN.

1st John Mc Connell Capt
     Peter Teague Lt
     ———— Ensign

2d   Isaac Vanbibber Capt
     Anthony Head Lt
     William Cassio Ensign

3d   Samuel Gibson Capt   4th Nathl. Simonds Capt
     Isaac Hostetter Lt   Roswell Dusky Lt
     Samuel Lewis Ensign   Wm. Ewing Ensign

5th Elijah Collard Capt
     James Lewis Lt
     Jacob Groshong Ensign

COMPANIES OF 2D BATTN.   3D REGIMENT

1st William Hart Capt   2d   Robert Spencer Capt
     Stephen Hempstead Lt   John Fetteau Lt
     Osborn Knott Ensign   Joshua Fisher Ensign

3d   Samuel Griffith Capt
     Charles Soucier Lt
     Ebenezer Ayres Ensign

STAFF OF THE 3D REGT.

Henry Hight Judge Advocate
James Beatty Adjutant
Stephen Hempstead Quarter Master

4TH REGIMENT — COUNTY OF CAPE GIRARDEAU

Stephen Byrd Lt colo comdt — Geo F Bollinger Maj 1st
James Brady Major 2d Battalion

COMPANIES OF 1ST BATTALION

1st Joseph Young Capt   2d   George C. Miller Capt
     Austin Young Lt   Henry Bollinger
     Joseph Looney Ensign   (Son Dan) Lt
                                       Daniel Krytz Ensign

3d   Henry Widner Capt   4th David Whetstone Capt
     Abraham Krytz Lt   John Bollinger Lt
     ————— Ensign   Frederick Reap Ensign

COMPANIES OF 2D BATTALION

1st Abraham Krytz Capt
     Jacob Shepherd Lt
     Elijah Dougherty
                  Ensign

2d   Jesse Jeffry Capt
     Jacob Friend Lt
     John Friend Ensign

3d   James Ravenscraft
                  Capt
     Medad Randall Lt
     Elijah Randall Ensign

5TH REGIMENT — COUNTY OF NEW MADRID

John E Hartt lt colo comdt. Step. Ross Maj 1st Jos
Hunter Maj 2d Frs. Vaugine Maj 3d Battn.

COMPANIES OF THE TWO BATS. OF N. MADRID SETTLS. —

1st Elisha Winsor Capt
     Thos. Winsor Lt
     Joseph Shields Ensign

2d   Edwd. Matthews Capt
     Joseph Smith Lt
     James Lucas Ensign

3d   Samuel Cooper Capt
     Robert Boyd Lt
     Alexr. La Forge Ensign

4th Benja. Myers Capt
     John Walker Lt
     Joseph Westbrook
                  Ensign

COMPANIES OF THE ARKANSAS BATTALION

1st Daniel Mooney Capt
     Harrold Stillwell Lt
     Tenace Racine Ensign

2d   James Scull Capt
     Peter Lefevre Lt
     Charles Bougy Ensign

3d   Blassingham H McFarlane Capt
     John Lemmon Lt
     William Doyle Ensign

STAFF OF THE 5TH REGIMENT

Richd. H. Waters Judge Advocate   John Walker Adjutant

VOLUNTEER COMPANIES

CAVALRY

1st Hendy Dodge Capt   Jno Scott 1st Lt   E A Elliott 2d Lt   Jas C Young Cornet   Wm James Purser

2d Alexr Mc Nair Capt   Josha. H. Buckhart 1st Lt. Hiram Cordell 2d Lt   Alexr Lucas Cornet   A. E. Rheill Purser

3d Jas Callaway Capt   P. K. Robbins 1st Lt   Josha Dodson 2d Lt   Jno. B. Stone Cornet   Jona. Riggs Purser

MOUNTED RIFLEMEN

1st Jas. Rankin Capt   John Geiger Lt   Joseph Andrews Ensign   Joseph Hanks, Purser

2d Wm .H. Ashley Capt Strother Covington Lt William Harrison Ensign

3d Morris Young Capt   Thomas Wyley Lt   James Patterson Ensign   Robt Mc Williams Purser

4th Jno Hughes Capt   William Strother Lt   Thos Reid Ensign   Timothy Phelps Purser

5th Andrew Ramsey jr Capt   Jas Morrison Lt   William Ramsey Ensign   Peter Craig Purser

6th Samuel Phillips Capt   Philip Ross Lt   Robert Trotter Ensign

7th Joseph Conway Capt Richard Caulk Lt Thomas Caulk Ensign

INFANTRY

1st Joseph Millard Capt Stephen Martin Lt Anthony Bridger Ensign

ARTILLERY

Robert Lucas Capt John Mc Knight 1st Lt Joseph Henderson 2d Lt

Secretary's Office St Louis April 1st 1813

Frederick Bates Secy

of Missouri tery

Note — Alex. Mc Nair has been appointed Adj. Genl. & Inspector Genl. of the Militia — with the rank of colonel.

F. Bates Secy

ADDRESS OF CHEROKEES

To his Excellency Benjamin Howard Governor in & over the Territory of Missouri; Father we a part of the Cherekees tribe of Indians; have settled on the White River a water of the Mississippi by we presume, the consent of the Government of the United States, where we are indeavouring to cultivate the soil for our support & wish to live unintirrupted by the malicious white people; but the revurse; there are a few bad men combined together for the purpose of stealing our horses; & do steal them; to wit; Nicholas Trammel[83] Mote Askins

---

[83] This may have been Colonel Trammel who later had a farm on the Chariton road six miles from Franklin.

John Wells Joseph Carnes Robert Armstrong. Barnet Peter Tileo Thoms James John D. Chisholm Demis Chisholm Ignatious Chisholm Jessey Isaacks; John Williams Robert Trimble William Trimble; William Smith John Lafferty Senr. & Ace Musick,[84] [blank] Pain & Joseph Pain; all of which are on publick lands; we pray that they may be removed from amongst us; if it be consistent with Government; some of which characters have solicited us to join them in killing robing & burning the Houses of the honest & industrious part of the white inhabitance neare to us; which we wish to live peaceable with; to wit, Nicholas Trammel & Mote Askins; we have lost by those characters Twenty Horses in course of Twelve months & if some measures are not taken we shall in a short time be left destitut of property; & thereby prevented from persueing our Farms; & we no no way whereby we are to be redressed unless by; or through our father the governor of the white people; wherefore we pray your excellency may take such measures to remedy; & redress those evils as in your wisdom may seem meet to you; & as in duty bound will ever pray, &c

Soanetar X	Zoateltar X
Ayaokisby X	Clutakenner X
Quaoloqui X	Hanelar X
Bare foott X	Kewarsulusky X
Oakshellaner X	Aremokelar X

[84] Asa Musick was living in the Bon Homme settlement in 1797.

James Kolson X

his
Chikilly X Chief
mark

· his
Thomas X Graves
mark

his
Wolollenny X Doublehead
mark

his
Warhails X
mark

his
`James X Duvall
mark

his
John X Campbell
mark

his
Jòhn X Hill
mark

April 27th 1813

his
Zoalakqua X
mark

Aarchy X his mark

Thomas his mark X

his
Corn Tassel X
mark

Teleskeske X

Toallemar X

Bare Skin X

Difan

George Duvall X

Aitennoly X ··

Gitup X

Samuel X

Cotten X

Cokokattsky X

Choahar X

PART VI

Bates' Last Acting-Governorship

BATES' LAST ACTING-GOVERNORSHIP

ABSTRACT OF PROVISIONS

ISSUED TO A DETACHMENT OF MILITIA CALLED INTO SERVICE BY THE EXECUTIVE OF THE MISSOURI TERRITORY, STATIONED AT PORTAGE DES SIOUX IN THE DISTRICT OF ST. CHARLES FROM THE 6TH TO 30TH OF APRIL, 1813, UNDER THE COMMAND OF MAJOR JAMES MORRISON, UNDER THE CONTRACT OF WILLIAM MORRISON.[1]

1813 Dates	No. of Returns	No of Days Drawn For	No. of Men	No. of Complete Rations	Rations of Whiskey	Remarks
6 to 28	1			154		Issued to Captain Conway[2] and his Subaltern officers
" " "	2	22	45	990		Issued to Capt. Conway's Company
11 " 29	3	18	32	586		Issued to Capt. David Musicks[3] Company

[1] William Morrison, the Kaskaskia merchant, land speculator, and fur trader. Before Pike's journey into the Southwest Morrison made an unsuccessful effort to open trade with Santa Fé. See Gregg, *Commerce of the Prairies*, in *Early Western Travels*, XIX, 174.

[2] Joseph Conway served in the Indian wars during the American Revolution.

[3] David Musick participated in the Sink Hole fight on March 24, 1815. He commanded at Fort Cap au Gris on the Mississippi River a little below Fort Mason early in 1815.

,, ,, ,,	4			133	Issued to Capt Musick and his Subaltern officers
13 " 16	5			20	Issued to Capt. Rankin[4] & his Subaltern officers
" " "	6	4	20	80	Issued to Capt. Rankins Compy
14 " 28	7			81	Issued to Capt Spenser[5] and his Subaltern officers
" " "	8	15	52	780	Issued to Capt Spensers Compy
14 " 28	9	15	24	360	Issued to Capt James Musicks[6] Compy
28	10			105	Issued to Capt J Musick & his Subalterns
15 " 30	11			186	Issued to Major Dodge[7] and Capt Scott[8] & their Subaltern officers
" " "	12	16	38	608	Issued to Capt. Scotts Compy

[4] James Rankin was appointed captain of the mounted riflemen in 1814.

[5] Robert Spencer was appointed captain in the St. Charles County regiment in 1812.

[6] James Musick was a captain in the St. Louis County regiment.

[7] In 1814 Henry Dodge was appointed brigadier-general of militia.

[8] John Scott was a lieutenant in Dodge's company in 1812.

20	13	—	—	—	599	Issued to **Capt Spen**sers Company Working at the Battery in April
17 " 28	14	12	6	72		Issued to Capt. Vanbibers[9] Compy
20 " 29	15	10	1	10		Issued to one man of Capt D Musicks Compy
20 " 30	16	11	36	396		Issued to Capt. Ashleys[10] Compy
" " "	17			77		Issued to Capt Ashley & his Subaltern officers
21 " 30	18	10	1	10		Issued to one man of Capt Scotts Compy
" " "	19	10	1	10		Issued to one man of Capt Ashleys Compy
22 " 30	20	8	39	312		Issued to Capt Lucas[11] Compy
" " "	21			93		Issued to Capt Lucas & his Subaltern officers
19 " 29	22	10	1	10		Issued to one of Capt Conways Compy

[9] Isaac Van Bibber was a captain in the St. Charles regiment.
[10] William H. Ashley, afterward famous in the fur trade.
[11] Charles Lucas was appointed a captain of artillery in 1814.

7 " 29	23	22	34	748	Issued to the St. Louis ·Troop of Cavalry
28 " 29	24	2	9	18	Issued to two men of the St. Louis Troop of Cavly
15 " 29	25			120	Issued to the officers of the St. Louis Troop of Cavly
" " "	26			469	Issued to men of Capt J Musicks C o m p y working at the Battery for April .

5959 1068

I do Certify I have carefully examined the above Abstract with the original returns now in my possession and find it to be a true and correct Statement of Issues made to the Troops Stationed at Portage Des Sioux from the 6th to the 30 of April 1813 amounting to five thousand nine hundred and fifty nine Complete rations and ten hundred and sixty eight Gills of extra Whiskey

Signed Triplicates

5959   five thousand nine hundred & fifty nine

Frederick Bates Secy. of Missouri territory

Actg as Governor

TO CAPTAIN CHARLES LUCAS[12]

Sɪʀ,   Sᴛ. Loᴜɪs May 4th 1813

In order that we may have it in our power to repair the boat as expeditiously as possible, you are desired to continue those exertions, so promptly commenced, for the preservation of whatever may belong to her. — Colo. McNair will be at the Portage in a few days, when arrangements to meet the new aspect of things will be made. — In the mean time should your old encampment become untenable, you will assume a position on the main land, in the neighbourhood of the village.

LEASE OF A SALTPETRE CAVE

Williams Williams[13] having made a discovery of a Salt Petre Cave on the land of the U. States on the head waters of Saline Creek in the County of St. Genevieve — He is hereby permitted to work the same for the term of twelve months from this date — Provided the same be not claimed by any private person or persons — in which case this Permission to be null & void —

And the said William Williams does hereby engage to pay to the Recorder of Land Titles, quarterly, for the use of the Government, one tenth part of the Salte Petre which

---

12 Lucas was then in command of the St. Louis volunteer artillery company stationed on an island near Portage des Sioux.

13 William Williams was one of the first members of the Methodist Church at McKendree, Cape Girardeau County.

he shall make or cause to be made at the said cave. — Witness our hands at St Louis 12 May 1913

William Williams   Frederick Bates
                                        Recorder of Titles

ABSTRACT OF PROVISIONS

ISSUED TO A DETACHMENT OF MILITIA CALLED INTO SERVICE BY THE EXECUTIVE OF THE MISSOURI TERRITORY, STATIONED AT PORTAGE DES SIOUX UNDER THE COMMAND OF COLONEL ALEXANDER McNAIR, FROM THE 1ST TO THE 21ST OF MAY, 1813, AND UNDER THE CONTRACT OF WILLIAM MORRISON.

1813 Dates	NO. OF RETURNS	NO. OF DAYS DRAWN FOR	NO OF MEN	NO. OF COMPLETE RATIONS	RATIONS OF WHISKEY	REMARKS
1 to 18	1	18	22	396		Issued to Capt Callaways[14] Company
" " "	2			170		Issued to Capt Callaway and his Subaltern officers
2 " 21	3	19	59	1128		Issued to Capt Smiths[15] Company

[14] James Callaway, a grandson of Daniel Boone, was killed in a skirmish with the Indians in 1814.

[15] William Smith was a captain in the St. Louis regiment in 1812. Robert A. Smith held a similar place in 1814.

" " "	4				98	Issued to Capt Smith and his Subaltern of-cers
1 " 21	5	21	40	840		Issued to Capt Lucas Compy
" " "	6				125	Issued to Capt Lucas & his Subaltern officers
" " "	7					66	Issued to men of Capt Lucas Compy work-ing at the Battery
				2757	66	

I do Certify that I have carefully examined the above Abstract with the original returns now in my possession and find it to be a true and correct Statement of Issues made to the Troops Stationed at Camp Cuivre from the 1st to the 21st of May 1813 amounting to two thousand seven hundred and fifty seven Complete rations and Sixty Six rations of Extra Whiskey

Signed Triplicates

Frederick Bates, Secy. of Missouri Tery,

Actg. as Governor

ABSTRACT OF PROVISIONS

ISSUED TO A DETACHMENT OF MILITIA CALLED INTO SERVICE BY THE EXECUTIVE OF THE MISSOURI TERRITORY, STATIONED AT CAMP NEAR CUIVRE[16] IN THE DISTRICT OF ST. CHARLES UNDER THE COMMAND OF MAJOR HENRY DODGE, FROM THE 1ST TO THE [22ND] OF MAY, 1813, AND UNDER THE CONTRACT OF WILLIAM MORRISON.

1813 Dates	NO. OF RETURNS	NO. OF DAYS	DRAWN FOR NO. OF MEN	NO. OF COMPLETE RATIONS	RATIONS OF WHISKEY	REMARKS
1st to 22	1	22	42	924		Issued to Capt Scotts Company of mounted rifle men
" " "	2			328		Issued to Major Dodge Capt. Scott and their Subaltern officers
" " 18	3	18	36	648		Issued to Capt Ashleys Company
"	4	1	15	15		Issued to men of Capt Ashleys Company
22	5				409	
"	6	1	20	20		Issued to men of Capt Scotts Company
				1935		

16 The Cuivre River empties into the Mississippi about thirty miles north of the mouth of the Missouri.

I do Certify that I have carefully examined the above Abstract with the original returns now in my possession and find it to be a true and correct Statement of Issues made to the Troops Stationed at Camp Cuivre from the 1st to the 22nd of May 1813 amounting to one thousand nine hundred and thirty five Complete rations & four hundred & nine gills of Whiskey

Signed triplicates

Frederick Bates Secy. of Missouri

tery.

Actg. as Governor

ABSTRACT OF PROVISIONS

ISSUED TO THE INDIAN DEPARTMENT AT PORTAGE DES SIOUX, FROM THE 4TH TO THE 31ST OF MAY, 1813, UNDER THE CONTRACT OF WILLIAM MORRISON.

lbs of Pork	lbs of Flour	lbs of Beef	lbs of Salt	Gallons of Whiskey	Two hundred lb Pork — two hundred ninety six lb flour — Eleven hundred twenty one lb. Beef — two hundred seventy lb salt— three Gals. whiskey
200	296	1121	270	3	

I certify that I have examined the above abstract with the original returns now in my possession and find it to be a Correct Statement of Issues made to the Indian Department

Signed Triplicates

Frederick Bates, Secy of Missouri Tery., exercg. the Govt.

A PROCLAMATION

By Frederick Bates, Secretary of the Territory of
Missouri, and Exercising the Government.

Whereas the President of the United States has been
pleased to commission James Flaugherty, Benjamin
Emmons, Augustus Chouteau sen, Samuel Hammond, John
Scott (of St Genevieve) James Maxwell, William Neely,
George Cavener and Joseph Hunter, Members of the Leg-
islative council of this territory: I do therefore, as
enjoined by the 8th Sec of the Act providing for the gov-
ernment of the territory of Missouri, appoint the first
Monday in July next for the meeting of the General
Assembly, and require that the several branches of that
Assembly, convene at the town of St. Louis, on that day. —

In testimony whereof I have hereunto affixed the territorial Seal

— Seal —

Given under my hand at St. Louis the third day
of June in the year of our Lord one thousand,
eight hundred and thirteen, and of the Independence of the United States the thirty seventh

Frederick Bates

A PROCLAMATION

By Frederick Bates, Secretary of the Territory of
Missouri, and Exercising the Government.

Whereas, since the election of David Musick as a member of the House of Representatives for the county of St
Louis, in the General Assembly of this territory the said

David Musick has entered the military service of the United States, thereby, in the opinion of the Executive, vacating his seat in the House of Representatives: I do therefore require the Sheriff of the county of St Louis to cause an election to be holden at the Court House on the first day of July next, at which time and place there will be chosen by the People one Representative to supply the vacancy aforesaid: One of the Judges of the Court of Common Pleas and Quarter Sessions for the county will sit as Judge of the qualification of voters — and the election will continue open from nine O'clock in the morning till sunset. —

In testimony whereof I have hereunto affixed the territorial Seal

— Seal — Given under my hand at St Louis, the eleventh day of June, in the year of our Lord, one thousand eight hundred and thirteen, and of the Independence of the United States the thirty seventh

Frederick Bates

PART VII
The Bates Papers

JULY, 1813—DECEMBER, 1820

THE BATES PAPERS
July, 1813 — December, 1820

A PROCLAMATION

By William Clark, Governor of the Territory of Missouri, and Commander-in-Chief of the Militia thereof.

Whereas I have been informed by the House of Representatives that the seat of David Musick late a member of that House from the county of St Louis, has become vacant, by resignation: I do therefore require the Sheriff of the county of St Louis to cause an election to be holden at the Court House, on thursday next the twenty second instant, at which time and place there will be chosen by the People, one Representative to supply the vacancy aforesaid. One of the Judges of the Court of Common Pleas and Quarter Sessions for the county will sit as Judge of the qualifications of voters — and the election will continue open from nine o'clock in the morning till sunset. The Sheriff will make to me, Returns of the election, in the manner and form heretofore established — In testimony whereof I have caused the seal of the territory to be hereunto affixed. —

— Seal — Given under my hand at St Louis, the sixteenth day of July, in the year of our Lord one thousand eight hundred and thirteen, and of the Independence of the United States the thirty eighth. —

William Clark

By the Governor
Frederick Bates
Secy. of the Terry.

AN ALLEGORY

TO MY COUNTRY NEIGHBORS[1]

MY VERY GOOD FRIENDS,

Banks of the Missouri
VANCLUSE August 4th 1813

After every diligence which a man can bestow on his own affairs, ten to one but some little matters will at last slip through his fingers. Every day's experience teaches us this — Yet is the world full of generous hearted creatures, who are ever ready to trample down half your wheat fields in search of a cockle, while their own, good souls, are overrun by cuckold-Burrs. — Such is the charitable disinterestedness of mankind. It has seldom therefore, been my practice to ask your attention to any concerns of mine — Not but that on many occasions, I should have been very glad of your help; but I was never so unconscionable as to expect you to pull my oars, when your own boats were drifting down the current. — However, I have now an affair in hand, in which we are all equally interested, — for which reason I ask your attention to it with the greater boldness. — And because I love brevity, and that I need not keep you one unnecessary moment in suspence, I will tell you all at once that it is neither more nor less than certain complaints which I have to exhibit against a servant of yours. —

Every body knows what prejudices are so justly entertained against tale bearers, — and I certainly should not attempt to make mischief between *Master* and *Man*, except for good and sufficient cause: But the saucy impertinence

---

[1] This allegory was directed against Edward Hempstead who was trying to bring about the removal of Bates from the office of recorder.

of that Youngster who does your city-business, obliges me to tell you, after years of forbearance, that he is a *lying varlet* and a *sneaking Rascal.* — I grant you, that he has a good deal of pettyfogging instrumentality about him, and might have done very well, if you had confined him to those subordinate drudgeries in which he was once so profitably employed: But you must needs send him to *town* — and entrust him with messages to decent People, before he had learned to ape with any tolerable success the exterior deportment of a creditable breeding. You will perhaps be astonished to hear that those little comical parts of his character which recommend him so forcibly to your esteem, will stand a fair chance of being considered in town as *blemishes.* Virgil has a line on this subject — but as you don't read Virgil I'll not, just now, trouble you with it. Yet this I will say, that I have known a man clapt and applauded in one company, who has afterwards been hissed and kicked out of another, which happened to judge of merit by a different standard.

It may occur to you, on a first view, that it is *your* affair and not *mine* — and that I am endeavouring to come in for a share of those praises which I bestow so abundantly on those noble minded People who busy themselves in the affairs of others to the neglect and ruin of their own — Bear with me for a moment and I will convince you that I too have a Stake in the Hedge. You know that I am or rather that I formerly was, Steward, for a wealthy old Gentleman who leads for the most part a town life, and with whom your understrapper was sent to negociate about country matters. His flocks and herds graze the same pastures with yours, and for aught I can see to the contrary there is a perfect identity of interest between you. It

would seem that his worship sees the thing in the same
light for he has often told me, that if, at any time, I should
discover *Wolf-Trails* in the neighbourhood I must immediately leave my own work, tho' it should be in harvest-time
or hay making, to raise the Hue & Cry and put the settlement on its guard. Last winter, you all very well recollect,
we discovered a *great many* of these Trails. — They came,
for the most part from the north, and in that direction
there was a brushy wood extending to your very pastures
which facilitated their entrance and escape. — Now, my
good friends you perfectly well know what a humane, phil-
anthropical old Gentleman his worship *is* — and you may
have heard that for some years past he has taken an abundance of pains to domesticate those wild animals which he
found in the neighbourhood of his Estates — and that he
had actually succeeded so far as to put Bells on two gangs
of them whose Ranges were to the westward of his fields
and yours — Now, when these gaunt, howling Devils came
from the north, I thought I could not do better, tho' I had
not instructions from his worship as to the business; but
seeing that 'All our Dogs had clapt their tails between their
legs and cryed', for in fact a Dog is *not* equal to a Wolf,
I thought, I say that it might be a good arrangement to
assign to these Wolves with Bells of domestication about
their necks *'A position on our northern borders'*, quite in
advance of his worship's Estate and yours, by which an
impenetrable Rampart would have been established against
the irruptions of the famished hordes of the north. —

I had thought at first of employing the obvious means of
Pit-Falls and Steel-Traps, but on reflection I foresaw very
clearly that our own dogs would be the principal victims. —
Your metaphysical People may talk what they please

about their *committees of vigilance,* their *military cordons,* their *walls of Antoninus* or even of the famous *Chinese Wall,* the two latter of which were specially provided in former times to keep out the wild animals — I say that foolish People may prate of these things for *passtime,* but that my notion of vigilance is to set a Wolf to watch a Wolf & that no barrier will ever give such perfect and absolute security as a *Cordon of Pet Wolves.*

It is pleasant to hear Brutus lamenting that he can devise no means to exorcise that mischievous Spirit of Ambition which haunts night and day, the bosom of Caesar, short of the spilling of Caesar's blood — and so it is with all kinds of Beasts of prey — If indeed we could, by a set Speech, and a little cajolery, possess ourselves, in a tranquil way, of those lacerating implements with which they tear the fleeces, and sometimes the throats of our flocks, it might be very well, we might turn them to grass — it would only be a change of diet — and all difficulties would be accomplished, or as the Lawyers say, *Surcease,* between us. — 'But alas! they must bleed for it.' —

But before this hopeful project of mine had been actually put into execution, the Head Steward of his worship came upon the ground and accomplished the object which I had so much at heart, by *Other Means* less offensive to those benevolent dispositions which have been so strikingly manifested in every act of his Worship's life. Or rather he did *not* accomplish it; but as he sent back the Pet Wolves bustled about, considerably, and *talked* of accomplishing it, every liberal minded man was as grateful to him, you know, as if he had done the whole business. — And having performed this notable piece of service, the Head Steward left me again in the management of the Estate.

Now, my good friends, your understrapper ignorant and awkward as he may be, did perfectly well know of these acts and doings of the Head Steward. — And some time thereafter, when I was again in the transaction of his worships business in these parts, the aforesaid understrapper addressed to me a letter (for he knows that I dislike the company and conversation of Pettyfoggers) he did address to me a *letter* in which he gives me pretty fairly to understand that he had taken that position near his Worship, which the Devil, in the shape of a toad assumed some years ago, at the ear of a celebrated personage, who shall now be nameless, as I do not wish to revive old Scandals: — That in a tete a tete with his worship he had learned what were his future plans for clearing the woods of those beasts of prey by which they were infested — for, his worship, it seems, had at length become sensible that all further attempts to evangelize them must be a hopeless business. I was not indeed, very well satisfied with the dirty channel through which this information had been derived; but as I should lose half a day at least, by waiting on his worship in town — and as his worship has always been to me an open, generous and confiding patron, whose work I have done as much thro' *love* as *duty*, I lost not a moment in obeying the orders thus circuitously communicated.

Very Well! — And now for your understrapper. — He goes again to town on your business, handsomely compensated therefor, but generously determined to do mine for nothing at all, except for the pleasure of doing it. He tells his worship that I had not only changed the Ranges of the Pet Wolves but that I had also introduced them into the settlements, — formed an *alliance* offensive and defensive with them, and pretty broadly insinuates that I had become

absolutely and in fact a Wolf myself with nothing of the
Sheep remaining but the fleece of a Bell-Wether (which I
had killed at the head of one of the marauding parties),
thrown loosely over my shoulders. — What a lying stupid
booby it is. He represents to his worship besides that the
entire settlement is in a dreadful state of alarm on account
of this unnatural transformation and alliance and wishes
mightily to be informed whether his worship has sanctioned
a procedure so fraught with mischief and brutality — Well
knowing as I said before that the Ranges of the Pet Wolves
had *not* been changed, and that nothing like an alliance was
ever contemplated with them.

This my good friends is all that I had to say to you at
present. Truth has obliged me to speak some harsh things
of your understrappers. Justice and candour equally compel me to disclose to you whatever I may know to his
, advantage. There is one incident of that kind, which as it
stands very prominently, I will content myself with relat-
ing it as a Representative for the whole. Some years ago
he had grievously, and somewhat treacherously too, injured a person with whom he was then (but never since)
on terms somewhat intimate, he challenged that person to
the great trial, *by Battle* because he had the imprudence
to tell him in the presence of a few friends that he was a
Sneaking Rascal. Which was indeed the fact But now
comes that magnanimity which must crown him with unfad-
ing Laurels. Having thrown the gauntlet he began to re-
flect what might be the inconvenient, not to say dangerous
consequences of such a procedure — And recollecting too
that all the modern wrongs had modern remedies provided
for them & that this old mode of decision was exploded
from the Statute book, he heroically determined, humbly

to ask leave to enter a *non prosequi* — And indeed the request was made with so much tearful entreaty, that it could not, with humanity, be denied him. And this I am always ready to acknowledge in his praise, that few men, 'in the torrent, tempest and as I may say whirlwind of their passions' can in a moment like your understrapper, on the first suggestion of his prudence or his fears "acquire and beget a temperance which may give them smoothness." — But altho' this incident redounds to his *credit,* as a private, unknown and indeed *insignificant* individual, yet I must think that it ought to be set down among his disqualifications as a public man. And I leave it to your consciences or rather to your prudence as honest, thrifty and painstaking People whether a fellow so often degraded and disgraced by slaps in the face and other humiliations has not become unworthy of your protection and countenance. —

ALEXANDER CRAIGHEAD TO BATES

MINES 27th August 1813

DEAR SIR

A mulatto man who calls himself Tom Waters formerly of Detroit says you were acquainted with him there and know he was free — He has been sold by Doctr. Wilkinson[2] in this country and is now held as a slave — from what information I have gotten on the subject I have very little doubt of his fredom — If you know any thing about him will you be so good as to inform me by the return of the boy by whom this note will be handed.

Accept dear Sir the assurances of my high respect & Esteem.

2 Probably W. N. Wilkinson.

TO JAMES MONROE

ST LOUIS October 1st 1813

SIR,

I have the honor to transmit a packet containing the Legislative and Executive proceedings of the government of this territory, during the last six months — to wit —

Copies of the Acts of the General Assembly,
Copies of the Governor's Proclamations,[3]
Minutes of the Governor's appointments to office,
Minutes of Licences to trade with Indians.[4]

Also, a Table of the civil officers in commission on 30th Septr.

MILITIA APPOINTMENTS

BY THE GOVERNOR OF THE TERRITORY OF MISSOURI

APRIL 1—SEPTEMBER 30, 1813.

Ap 3d	Joshua Burckhartt	1st Lt.	of a company
	Hiram Cordell	2d Lt	of cavalry in
	Alexr. Lucas	Cornet	the county of
	A. E. Rheile	Purser	St Louis

William Christy Quarter Master of 1st Regiment

Joseph Conway	Capt	of a compy. of
Richard Caulk	Lt	mounted Rifle-
Thomas Caulk	Ensign	men — cty St Louis

[3] For the proclamations, see Bates' proclamation of June 3, and that of July 16, 1813.

[4] The list of licenses is missing.

9th. Martin Ruggles Major of 2d Battn. of 2d Regt
Joseph Hertick **Pay Master** of 2d Regiment

John Mc Arthur	Lt	1st comy. 1st
Joseph Hertick	Ensign	Bat. 2d Regt.

John Bossieur	Capt	
James Rigdon	Lt.	2d comy. 1st Bat 2d Regt.
Joseph Amoureux	Ensign	

13 Joseph Yardley Ensign 1st comy. 1st Bat 3d Regt
Robert Gray Ensign 3d comy. 1st Bat 3d Regt.

		of a comy. of
24 Jacob Pettit	Lt.	mounted Rifle-
Jesse Blackwell	Ensign	men cty of St Genevieve

April 29 Charles Lucas Capt of the St Louis comy. of Volr. Artillerists

30 Paul L. Chouteau Lt 2d comy. 1st Bat 1st Regt.
Frederick Geizer Ensign 2d comy. 1st Bat 1st Regt.

May 14 Joshua H. Burckhartt	Capt	of the St
Hiram Cordell	Lt	Louis comy of
Absalom Link	Ensign	cavalry

24 Burwell J. Thompsom	Capt	6th comy. 2d
James F. Mutry	Lt	Bat 2d Regt
E. D. Devillemont	Ensign	

Thomas Mc Laughlin	Lt	4th comy. 2d
Zachary Goforth	Ensign	Bat 2d Regt.

William Harrison	Lt	2d comy. 2d
Stephen Austin	Ensign	Bat 2d Regt.

30 Paul L. Chouteau Captain 2d comy. 1st Bat 1st
Regt.

June 19 Henry Battu Ensign 2d comy. 1st Bat 1st Regt.

Francis Coursolle	Capt	of a comy. in the settlement of Sans Dessein
Joseph Bivarq	Lt	
Louis Dehetre	Ensign	

July 22 George Jameson | Capt | of a comy. in 2d Battn 4th Regt.
Charles Logan | Lt |
William Ingram | Ensign |

George Jameson	Capt	of a comy. in 2d Battn 4th Regt.
Charles Logan	Lt	
William Ingram	Ensign	

Aug. 21 Henry Battu 3d Lt of 2d comy. 1st Battn of 1st
Regt.

Martin Ruggles	Capt	of a comy. of mounted Infantry on a service of 60 days
Phil Mc Guire	Lt	
James Mc Cullock	Ensign	

Sept 2d (see above)

Thomas Williams	1st Lt	of a comy. of mounted Infantry on a service of 60 days
Robert Wash	2d Lt	
George Henderson	Ensign	

3 (see above)

13 Hardy Ware Ensign of 3d comy. 3d Battn 1st
Regt.

Manuel Lisa	Capt	of a volr. comy Infantry 1st Battn of 1st Regt —
Barw. Berthold	Lt	
Francis Guyol	Ensign	

Secretary's Office Oct 1. 1813
Frederick Bates

A MEMORANDUM

Mr. Partenay has this day reported to me [Bates] a discovery between Mine A Breton & the Old Mines — and is considered as having the first right to the lease, when I am empowered to support the covenants which I might make with him —   St Louis Oct 1st 1813

TO EZEKIEL ABLE[5]

Commissioner's Office
St Louis Nov 9. 1813

SIR,

On the application of Charles Payton & Henry Burning I have appointed the 15th day of December next, to receive farther testimony in the claim of the Legal Representatives of Joseph Doublewye[6] for 800 Arpens of Land, on the waters of the St Francis, in the county of Cape Girardeau at which time you can attend, if you think proper.

TO JAMES PLEASANTS

ST LOUIS Nov 12th 1813

SIR,

I have no sort of right to trouble you so frequently as I have lately done. I feel the indecorum and yet have not been able to resist the impulse. I entreat your liberal constructions of these liberties, and ask your attention for a few moments to a subject which occasions me much anxiety. — Since my coming to this country in the year 1807

---

5 The father-in-law of William H. Ashley.

6 Joseph Doublewye dit Deblois, an Indian trader. The name was also spelled De Blois. He was an early resident of Ste. Genevieve.

as a Commissioner of Land Claims, I have suffered all those attacks, open and concealed which might be counted on among a set of fraudulent and rapacious speculators. — These I have for the most part disregarded, — not deeming it proper to descend to low minded altercation. — Every species of machination has been attempted. If a man of more than ordinary consequence presented himself I have been obliged to treat him in another manner. When a challenge has been offered (by Colo. Jno Smith) I have applied for advice to an officer of rank, in the line of the army, with whose concurrence, I have informed my antagonist, that I was accountable only to the government for a discharge of my public duties.

Despairing after a long course of abortive experiment of accomplishing their purposes by private slanders, or open intimidations, they have at last adopted that which (if there be any cause of complaint) I conceive to be the correct course, an application to Mr Tiffin,[7] or perhaps to the President himself — But they do not intend that I shall know the grounds of the accusation nor the names of the witnesses brought forward to support it. They will present to Mr Tiffin some monstrous exaggeration & probably expect that the Delegates assurances will be deemed sufficient evidence of its truth. I gather however from the anticipated triumph of the Party and the vindictive garrulity of Judge Bent[8] in particular that the charges have been sworn to and transmitted by *Mr Hempstead,* of whom I gave you some account, in an allegorical way, in August last, — Mr B is himself no speculator — but he is the crea-

[7] Edward Tiffin was the first governor of Ohio. In 1812 President Madison appointed him commissioner of the general land office.
[8] Silas Bent.

ture of Hempstead — & affects to have recd injuries from me in order to mask the under part which he is acting with the appearance of independence. But I am speaking of others when I should be defendg myself — As I said before I am unacquainted with the accusation.

I know of but one charge that can be brought against me with any colour of truth. — It is this — That the Papers of the Recorders Office have not always dur[in]g a press of business been kept in that exact order which ought certainly to be preserved in the files of a public office — But there are reasons for this — the necessity of frequent reference to originals, in the investigation of titles — the incessant application of claimants themselves — And above all the tiresome & impudent enquiries of one class of speculators who have no regular concern with the business. It has been very falsely said, but whether or not it makes a part of the accusation, I am altogether ignorant, that I *threatened* a Land Claimant, — telling him '*I will remember you Sir, for this*' These Pismires will sting you to death. Mr Pleasant, I am incapable of such conduct — If I had descended so low, I should never have the confidence to meet the eye of a man of honour or to address myself to you I have no recollection 'of the circumstance to which it can possibly allude *Errors* I may have committed, but *deliberate injustice never.* I do not ask you however to vouch for me but I do entreat, that you will procure me a *hearing* — some little investigation, before I suffer the final censures of the Government. Mr. Tiffin is a just man & I ask nothing but justice. . . .

[P. S.] I have lived long enough to be but little surprized at whatever may happen but The conduct of this man is unaccountable — I have known him in this country for the last six years — He appeared correct & prudent — He was poor & I thought him honest Being in the exercise of the govt. I bestowed on him several offices of honor & of profit — I never injured him and yet all on a sudden he bursts forth my inveterate enemy

Sometimes too, merely for the purpose of creating anxiety & trouble a Cl[aiman]t will demand a Paper which he well knows is not in the office but in his own possession. It was the very frequent practice of my Predecessor to redeliver Papers after having recorded them. — I have also done it, but the parties are informed that if they are not forth coming at the time of the decision the claim may be declared abandoned. Originals are sometimes necessary for the detection of frauds.

TO AMABLE PARTENAY

Sir,
St. Louis Feby 26. 1814

Mr Scott has delivered me your letter of the 24th with its accompaniments. As I am not invested with the powers necessary for your maintenance in possession it has been impossible for me to make the lease which you ask. — Together with Mr Scott, I waited on Governor Clark for the purpose of being informed of the cooperations which I might count on from the Executive Department, when we were told by the Governor that he should not, under present arrangements, interfere in the affair. I certainly consider you as having the first privilege; but unless the President give power to his Agents to perform their covenants, I shall be careful of bringing upon myself those humiliations which I formerly suffered.

WILLIAM STEVENSON[9] TO BATES

BELLE VUE March 5th 1814

Sir, The scarcity of Salt, together with the difficulty of obtaining it, in this part of the community has induced a Number of the Inhabitants of Belle Vue, to make a trial for Salt water in this Township, there being several extensive licks, which furnish ground to think there may be a body of Salt water in the Earth, Wherefore a number of Shares has been subscribed, A committee appointed to make choice of a place or places to dig at An agent to superintend the digging A well, or wells, who commenced some time past, at two different places and there is a probability of geting Salt water at one of the places, which is thought to be on public land, and Whereas I have been informed that there are some designing men who are only waiting for the discovery to be made — when they intend to obtain a lease and drive off the Company who have been at the trouble and expence to make the discovery if we should be so fortunate as to obtain Salt water, It is the desire and expectation of the share holders to have the priviledge of renting from the United States, and carrying on the business themselves I have therefore troubled you with the above Sketch and trust and hope you will not grant any lease to any one, should there be application made but to the Company or their Agent, — . . .

P. S. The Name of the lick where there is the greatest probability for Salt Water is Chicago —

[9] Probably William O. Stevenson of Bellevue Valley near Potosi. He acted as agent for the company.

TO THE SECRETARY OF THE TREASURY[?]

St. Louis June 12th 1814. —

Sir,

Soon after the receipt of your letter of 5th April, I went to Ste. Genevieve and submitted, personally to the examination of Mr Scott[10] all the Papers which have relation to the leases of Dodge,[11] Wilson[12] & Craighead.[13] — As the superior court was then in session, Mr Scott had not leisure to consider the case. I left in his hands whatever might be necessary for the forming of an opinion, which he has this morning sent me in writing — a copy of which I have the honor to enclose. — I beg leave to remark that I submitted no such points [as] the District Atty has quoted in his opinion — I wrote nothing & spoke sparingly & in general terms, folding down & shewing him that part of your letter which immediately concerned the business — The question of the Presidents right had slept since the silence of the Govt. on suggestions of that sort made some years ago by the late Gov Howard. The Dist. Atty. has copied fr[om] the books principles of Genl Law, — These I suppose are indisputable — but whether or not they apply to the case in hand might perhaps make another question. —

I have conversed with Genl. Dodge, one of the Partners as to an amicable adjustment — Nothing is yet conclusively done — he wishes first to see Mr Wilson, who has just arrived from Tennessee.

I advertised the Shibboleth Mines as you directed. — A Partenay alone gave in proposals, a copy of which I

10 John Scott.
11 Henry Dodge.
12 Probably Nicholas Wilson.
13 Alexander Craighead.

enclose. Notwithstanding the liberality of his offer, I could not make the contract as Jno. Smith (T) is in possession and determined I understand to retain it until Govt. adopt more compulsory process than has yet been employed — In Nov 1812 under alleged right derived from the act of 13 June preceding he made an Entry of 1000 arps. (under the St Vrain concession) to include the lands then actually in possession of the U States tenants   Indeed the most of the U. S. mines in the late county of Ste. Genevieve are in the same situation.   Colo. Smith availing himself of the lenity and forbearance of the President has seldom failed, on the discovery of Lead, to make an immediate location, and to assume the rights of a legitimate proprietor.   This has been long known to the Govt.   I enclose a Schedule of his claims of this description of which he has been acquiring the possn. fr time to time since the year 1807.

Mc Kee's Branch	250
New Diggings	1000
Mine A Robina	300
On the Branch above Renaut Mine	300
Doggett's Mines	300
On Branch of Mine Fork	200
Mc Kee's Discovery	200
Mill Seat on branch of Big River	50
Mine A Liberty	359 52/100
Mine Shibboleth	1300
Belle Fontaine	1200
Bon Femme Salt Spring (St. Charles)	64 St Chs.
A Salt Spring between Bon Femme & Salt Cr	64 St Chs.
Grand Monitur Salt Spring	64 St Chs.
Le Moine Salt Springs	70 St Chs.

A Salt Spring above Sugar Loaf.............	25	New Madrid
1st Lead Mine on the waters of White River	36	New Madrid
2d Lead Mine on waters of White River....	64	New Madrid
Grand Lead Mines of White River................	54	New Madrid
Mines, supposed of the precious metals....	13⅓	Arkansas

Entered 30 Nov 1812 under Act of 13 June precedg.

Whatever may be the abstract validity of the St Vrain concession it seems strange to me that Colo Smith should have right to locate before its allowance by the Govt. The District Atty. seems to be of the opinion, however, that a possession & entry of claim however tortuous and penal secures him from molestation until the final decision. This reasoning if admitted to be correct would overthrow every idea wch. I had before entertained on the subject. — The Law does not presume that any entries will be made of claims which do not fall within the general scope of confirmation or of Grant. — Besides by the act of 3d March 1807 the abstract 'right, title, or claim' to Lands in Orleans or Louisiana is not to be affected by those summary & efficient means which the President is empowered to make use of, for the removal & punishment of Intruders. From which I clearly infer that he may incur the penalties, pecuniary & corporeal provided by act of 26 Mar 1804 for the punishmt. for his illegal & forcible intrusion even during the [duration] of his abstract pretentions. . . . [14]

[14] Three lines of the manuscript are illegible.

In fact I imagined that such directed and recorded acknowledgments on the part of the Intruder was the best evidence for his conviction, if you should think proper to order a prosecution under the act of the 3d March 1807. —

JOHN H. WEBER FOR AMABLE PARTENAY TO BATES

Dr Sir,

Mine a Burton Septb 28th 1814

I hasten to inform you of a most wanton and cruel outrage committed on my person yesterday while at Silvers's Mine. — Conformable to the Lease obtained from Government I went on, the 21st Inst. to take possession in the name of the U. S. of Silvers's Mines, as one of the Mines included in said Lease. I put up a Notice of which the enclosed is a copy which as soon as put up, was tore down by Jno. Scott, who insisted that I should shew my authority, before he would allow that I should put up any Notices there; — he made use of the most abusive Language at the same time, as well to Government as myself, but offered no violence, owing no doubt to the precaution I had taken of having two persons with me. —

Yesterday however, while I was by myself, peaceably riding through said Mines, in quest of a chain-carrier as I had began surveying, I was surrounded by Jno Scott and others, forcibly dragged off my horse, knocked down with a stick or club, and beat in a most shocking manner with clubs & sticks — John Scott who was the ringleader observing ''that was the way he would give possession.''

I sincerely hope Government will show some energy on this occasion and make an example of all those that were engaged in the wanton abuse, while I was acting under the orders of Government. — Now is the Time or never, if Government will not act with rigour now, they may as well abandon the idea of laying claim to any Lead Mines in this country, when the first ruffian can dispute the same with them with impunity, and would maltreat their officers, if they were sent against him. —

They continue (Scott & Swon)[15] to receive all the Mineral that is raised at Silvers's Mines and always will, unless forcibly put out of possession. —

I should have commenced a suit for assault & battery against Scott &c. but find that it is useless, there being no Jail in this county, consequently they would refuse giving Bail. —

I have taken possession of all the other Mines. — Colo. Jno. Perry pretends to claim Shous's Mines by virtue of a concession tho' he has not shewn me his concession

Will you please inform me, whether you have stipulated any Time with Mr. Perry, in which he was to finish smelting what he has on hand at Shous's Mine? Also with Messrs. Brown & Henry, and what length of Time you have accorded them? I wish to know, that I may regulate myself accordingly.

COPY OF THE EXECUTIVE JOURNAL FROM APRIL 1 TO SEPTEMBER 30, 1814

MISSOURI TERRITORY

Ap. 5 Louis Lebeaume, a Judge of the Court of Com Pleas for Washington Cty

Robert A. Smith Capt of 1st Comy. of 1st Battn of 1st Regiment

15 Probably William Swan who in 1804 was a settler at New Madrid.

15 George Wilson Surveyor for the County of St Louis

Joseph Story   Surveyor for the County of New Madrid

22d.   Robert Spencer Major of 2d Battn. of 3d Regiment

Wright Daniel   a Judge of the Court of Com Pleas for Arkensas

Henry Battu Lieutenant 2d Comy. 1st Battn of 1st Regt.

27.   Jacob Pettitt   Capt   ⎤
       Jno. Perry   Lieut.   ⎬ 1st Comy. 1st Bat 6th Regt.
       Stephen F. Austin   Ensign   ⎦

       Jesse Blackwell   Capt   ⎤
       Anthy Wilkinson   Lt   ⎬ 2d Comy. 1st Bat 6th Regt.
       Benja. Horine   Ensign   ⎦

       Robert T. Brown   Capt   ⎤
       James H. Moutry   Lt   ⎬ 3d Comy. 1st Bat 6 Regt.
       Drury Gooche   Ensign   ⎦

       Joshua Morrison   Capt   ⎤
       Zachariah Goforth   Lt   ⎬ 1st Comy 2d Bat 6th Regt.
       Thomas McLaughlin   Ensign   ⎦

       Timothy Phelps   Capt   ⎤
       Wm. Read   Lt   ⎬ 2d Comy. 2d Bat 6th Regt.
       James Gray   Ensign   ⎦

       Job Westover   Capt   ⎤
       John Baker   Lt   ⎬ 3d Comy. 2d Battn. 6th Regt.
       Joseph Wood   Ensign   ⎦

Ap. 29. Archd. Huddleston Lt 3d Comy. 2d Bat 2d Regt.

William Mc Farland Adjutant of 2d Regiment

Same a Justice of the Peace for township of St Michael in the county of Ste Genevieve

June 1st Wm. Stevenson a Judge of the Court of Com Pleas for Washington Cty

Bartholomew Cousin Surveyor of the county of Cape Girardeau

23d Joseph Brazeau a Licence to trade with the Teton & Yankton Sieux at Cedar Island on the Missouri for one year

Patrick Cassidy Clerk of the Court of Com Pleas of Arkensas county

Lemuel Currin Coroner for the county of Arkensas

Saml. Miller, Zach Philips Andw. Fagot, James Currin Fred Notrebee Jno. Carnehan, Jno. Billingsley Jno Mc Illmurray Isaac Cates, Saml. Cates Justices of the Peace within Arkensas county

Wm. Russell a Justice of the Peace for sett[lemen]t. on Current River New Madrid

Jno Maupin Capt — Joshua Brock Lt 2 Co. 4th Bat 1st Regt.

Daniel Mooney Major 1st Battn. of 7th Regt.

Alexr. Kendrick	Capt	1st Comy. 1st
Wm. Glass Sen	Lt	Battn. 7th
Wm. Dunn	Ensign	Regt.

June 23			
James Scull	Capt	2d Comy. 1st
Peter Lefevre	Lt	Battn. of 7th
Charles Bougy	Ensign	Regt.

Saml. Moseley Capt, Lemuel Currin Lt 3d Comy. 1st Bat 7th Regt.

Blassingham H. Mc Farland Major 2d Battn. of 7th Regt.

Edwd. Hogan	Capt	1st Comy. 2d Batt. 7th Regt.
Jno Payatte	Lt	
Joseph Duchassin	Ensign	

James C. Newell	Capt	2d Comy. 2d Batt 7th Regt.
Benja. Murphy	Lieut.	
George Rankin	Ensign	

Wm. Berney	Capt	3d Comy. 2d Batt 7th Regt.
Isaac Cates	Lieut.	
Saml. Gates	Ensign	

27 Prospect R. Robbins Surveyor for County of St Charles

30 Peter Mc Comack a Justice of the Peace for the township of Platen in County of Ste. Genevieve

July 7. Louis Bijou & Chs. Sanguenette jr a License to trade with the Aricaras & Sieux Indians, on the Missouri for one year.

Louis Letourneau a Licence to trade with the Poncas Indians on the Missouri, for one Year.

July 20. Charles Gratiot a Justice of the Peace for township of St. Louis Cty of St Louis

23d Daniel M. Boone Lt Colo. Comdt. of the 3d Regiment

26 George Tompkins Ensign 2d Comy. 1st Bat 1st Regt.

28 Jno. W. Thompson Adjutant of the 1st Regiment

Aug. 3. Jno. W. Thompson   Capt ⎫ of St Louis
       Alexr. Lucas   1st Lieut ⎬ T r o o p   o f
       Absalom Link   2d Lieut ⎭   Cavalry

Jno Miller Capt of 3d Comy. 2d Bat 1st Regt.

Alexr Papin & Co. Licence to trade S. W. of the Missouri & on Platte for one year

    5 Jno Hawkins Surveyor for the County of Washington

   13. Benja. Cooper Major 3d Batt of 3d Regt.

       Wm. McMahen   Capt   ⎫ 1st Comy. 3d
       Sarshell Cooper   Lieut. ⎬ Batt 3d Regt.
       Benja Cooper jr   Ensign ⎭

       James Alexander   Capt   ⎫ 2d Comy. 3d
       Jno Morrow .   Lieut. ⎬ Bat. 3d Regt.
       Amos Barnes   Ensign ⎭

       Wm. Head   Capt   ⎫ 3d Comy. 3d
       David Mc Quitty   Lieut ⎬ Batt 3d Regt.
       Jno. Berry   Ensign ⎭

   15 Wm. C. Carr 3d Lt of 4th Comy. of 2d Bat of 1st Regt.

Edw. Hempstead Capt of a Comy. of Militia. —

ORGANIZATION OF THE MILITIA OF THE TERRITORY OF MISSOURI, OCTOBER 1, 1814

William Clark Gov. & commr. in ch. — Henry Dodge Brigadier General   Alexander Mc Nair Adjutant Genl. & Inspector.

1ST REGIMENT — COUNTY OF ST. LOUIS

.... Lt colo. comdt. — Tho F. Riddick Major of 1st. Richd. Chitwood Major of the 2d. — Jeduthun Kendall Major of the 3d. & Peter Chouteau Major of 4th Battn.

COMPANIES OF THE 1ST BATTALION

1st Robert A Smith Capt — Hubert Guyon Lt — Frederick Geizer Ensign

2 Paul L. Chouteau Capt — Henry Battu Lt — George Tompkins Ensign

3d Louis Courtoix Capt — Louis Courtoix jr Lt — Francis Roi Ensign

4 Zeph Sappington Capt — Thos. Sappington Lt — William L. Long Ensign

COMPANIES OF 2D BATTALION

1st James Musick Capt — Elisha Patterson Lt — Green Baxter Ensign

2d Hyacinth Dehetre Capt — J. M. Courtoix Lt — Joseph Aubuchon Ensign

3d John Miller Capt — John Kinkead Lt — Gabriel Long Ensign

4 John E. Allen Capt — Joseph Lard Lt — Wm. McDowns Ensign

COMPANIES OF THE 3D BATTALION

1st James McCullock Capt — Jacob Collins Lt — John Horine Ensign

2d Abner Vansant Capt — David Brook Lt — Benja. Johnston Ensign

3d Thos. Williams Capt — William Ink Lt — Hardy Ware Ensign

COMPANIES OF THE 4TH BATTALION

1st Benja. Hatherley Capt — Saml. Cantley Lt — Lewis Hall Ensign

2d John Maupin Capt — Joshua Brock Lt — Jno. Sappington Ensign

3d Augte Chouteau Capt —

Regimental Staff — John Washington Thompson Adjutant

2D REGIMENT — COUNTY OF STE GENEVIEVE

Nathl Cook Lt colo comdt. Jno. Donohue Major of 1st Jno. Callaway Major of 2d Battalion

COMPANIES OF 1ST BATT

1st Thomas Oliver Captain — Jno. McArthur Lt Jos Hertick Ensign

2d Jno Bossieur Capt — James Rigdon Lt — Jos Amoureux Ensign

3d Richd Moore Capt — Tho Riney Lt — Tho Patterson Ensign

4 Frs. B. Cessell Capt — Mark Brooks Lt — Saml McCall Ensign

· COMPANIES OF 2D BATT

1st William Dillon Capt — William Sims Lt — Benja. La Chance Ensign

2d Andw. Miller Capt — Isaac Murphy Lt — John Burnham Ensign

3d   Henry   Poston   Capt — Archd.   Huddleston   Lt —
Alexr. Craighead Ensign

Regimental   Staff—Joseph   Hertick   Pay   Master — Wm
McFarland Adjutant

3D REGIMENT.—COUNTY OF ST. CHARLES

Daniel M. Boone Lt colo. comdt. — Peter Journey Major
of the 1st   Robert Spencer   Major   of the 2d *and*
Benja. Cooper Major of the 3d Battalion —

COMPANIES OF THE 1ST BATT

1st John Mc Connell Capt   Peter Teague Lt — Joseph
Yardley Ensign

2   Isaac Vanbibber Capt   Anthony Head Lt — William
Cassio Ensign

3d   Saml Gibson Capt Isaac Hostetter Lt   Robert Gray
Ensign

4th Nathl Simonds Capt   Roswell Dusky Lt — Wm
Ewing Ensign

5   Elisha Collard Capt   James Lewis Lt — Jacob
Groshong Ensign

COMPANIES OF 2D BATT

1st William Hartt Capt   Osborn Knott Lt   Ralph
Flaugherty Ensign

2d   Henry Hight Capt   Sylvestre Pattie Lt   Charles
Dennis Ensign

3d   Saml. Griffith Capt   Charles Soucier Lt — Eben
Ayres Ensign

COMPANIES OF THE 3D BATT

1 Sarchel Cooper Capt Wm. Mc Mahan Lt — Benja Cooper Jr Ensign

2d Jas Alexander Capt Jno. Morrow Lt — Amos Barnes Ensign

3d William Head Capt David Mc Quitty Lt — John Berry Ensign

Frs. Coursolle Capt Jos Rivard Lt Louis Dehetre Ensign of a comy. at Sans Dessein —

Regimental Staff — Henry Hight Judge Advocate — Jas. Beatty Adjt. Stephen Hempstead Q Master. —

4TH REGIMENT — COUNTY OF CAPE GIRARDEAU

Stephen Byrd Lt colo. comdt. Geo F Bollinger Major of 1st James Brady Major of 2d Battn

COMPANIES OF 1ST BATT

1st Abrm. Byrd — Capt — Austin Young Lieut. Andrew Byrne Ensign

2d Geo C Miller Capt — H. Bollinger son of D[an] Lt — Daniel Krytz Ensign

3d Wm. Johnson Capt — John Baker Lt. — Thos. Izner Ensign

4th Adam Ground Capt — Adam Shell Lt — John Ground Ensign

COMPANIES OF THE 2D BATT

1st Abm. Dougherty Capt — Jacob Shepherd Lt — Elijah Dougherty Ensign

2d   Jesse Jeffry Capt — Jacob Fryend Lt — John Fryend Ensign

3d   James Ravenscraft Capt — Medad Randall Lt — Elijah Randall Ensign

4   Geo Jameson Capt — Charles Logan Lt — Wm. Ingram Ensign

Regimental Staff Samuel Dunn Pay Master — Erasmus Ellis Surgeon

5TH REGIMENT — COUNTY OF NEW MADRID

Jno. E. Hartt — Lt colo. comdt. Stephen Ross Major of 1st & Jos Hunter Major 2d Battalion

COMPANIES IN THE TWO BATTALIONS

Elisha Winsor Capt — Thos. Winsor Lt — Joseph Shields Ensign

Edwd Matthews Capt — Jos Smith Lt — James Lucas Ensign

Saml Cooper Capt — Robert Boyd Lt — Alexr La Forge Ensign

Benja Myers Capt — Jno Walker Lt — Joseph Westbrook Ensign

Edwd Tanner Capt — Andw. Robertson Lt — Danl. Stringer Ensign

Jno Hines — Capt — Alexr Willard Lt — Jacob Gibson Ensign

Regimental Staff Richd H. Waters Judge Advocate Jno Walker Adjutant

6TH REGIMENT — COUNTY OF WASHINGTON

Wm H. Ashley Lt colo comdt. Andrew Henry Major of the 1st Martin Ruggles Major of 2d Battalion

COMPANIES OF THE 1ST BATT

1st Jacob Pettitt Captain — William James Lieut. Stephen F. Austin Ensign

2d Jesse Blackwell Capt Anthony Wilkinson Lieut. Benja. Horne Ensign

3d Robert F. Brown Capt James H. Moutree Lieut. Drury Gooche Ensign

COMPANIES OF 2D BATT

1st Joshua Morrison Capt Zach Goforth Lt Thomas Mc-Laughlin Ensign

2d Timothy Phelps Capt William Reed Lt James Gray Ensign

3d Job Westover Capt John Baker Lieut Joseph Wood Ensign

7TH REGIMENT — COUNTY OF ARKENSAS

Anthony Haden Lieut. colo. comdt. — Danl. Mooney Major of 1st .... Major of 2d Battalion

COMPANIES OF 1ST BATT

1st Alexr. Kendrick — Capt William Glassen Lieut. William Dunn Ensign

2d James Scull — Capt Peter Lefevre Lieut. Charles Bougy Ensign

3d Samuel Moseley — Capt Lemuel Currin Lieut. .... Ensign

COMPANIES OF 2D BATT

1st Edward Hogan Capt   John Payatte Lieut.   Joseph Duchassin Ensign

2d Jno. C. Newell Capt   Benja. Murphy Lieut.   Geo Rankin Ensign

3d William Berney Capt   Isaac Cates Lieut.   Saml. Gates Ensign

VOLUTEER COMPANIES

CAVALRY

.... Capt — Jno. Scott 1st Lt — E. A. Elliott 2d Lt Jas C. Young Cornet Wm. James Purser

.... Capt .... 1st Lt — Joshua Dodson 2d Lt Jno B Stone Cornet   Jona. Riggs Purser

John W. Thompson Captain — Alexander Lucas 1st Lieut. Absalom Link 2d Lieut.

MOUNTED RIFLEMEN

James Rankin Capt   Jno Geiger Lieut.   Joseph Andrews Ensign   Joseph Hanks Purser

Morris Young Capt   Thomas Wyley Lieut.   James Patterson Ensign   Tho McWilliams Purser

John Hughes Capt   William Strother Lt   Thos Reed Ensign   Timy. Phelps Purser

Samuel Philips Captain   Philip Ross Lieutenant   Robert Trotter Ensign

INFANTRY

Joseph Conway Captain — Richard Caulk Lieutenant Thomas Caulk Ensign

Joseph Millard Captain — Stephen Martin Lieutenant
Anthony Bridger Ensign

Manuel Lisa Captain — Barthelemy Berthold Lieutenant
Francis Guyol Ensign

ARTILLERY

Charles Lucas — Captain — John McKnight 1st Lieut.
Joseph Henderson 2d Lieut.

Secretary's Office St Louis Oct 1st 1814
Frederick Bates

TO JOHN WASHINGTON THOMPSON

Whereas I have been informed by the House of Representatives the county of St Louis, has become vacant by the death of the [incumbent]

I do therefore require you to cause Election to be [held] at which time there will be chosen by the People, in the [County of St. Louis, a representative]

In testy whereof I have caused the seal &c. [to be attached]

Given under my hand 8th Decr 1814 —

TO RUFUS EASTON,[16] WASHINGTON, D. C.

Dec. 10. 1814.

Yr letter of 16th Nov was recd this morng. — It gives me much pleasure on several accts. — I had some anxiety

---

[16] Rufus Easton came to St. Louis with Governor Harrison in 1804. He became a judge under the act creating the Territory of Louisiana, but was not reappointed in 1806. He was the first postmaster of St. Louis and for a time acted as United States attorney. In 1814 he was elected delegate to congress from Missouri Territory.

as [to] the construction Mr Pleasants might put on the frequency of my application to him, on behalf of my friends as well as on my own acct. There is perhaps not another man for whom I feel such deeply rooted respects. — And if I had no other incitement to an honorable conduct, than the hopes of his good opinion, it would be an all sufficient inducement. —

Those interested in Lands have been constantly desirous of knowing my opinion as to the interpretation of the first section of the act of 12th of April last. — As the business of my office cannot, in the very nature of things, (& by order of Govt too) progress faster than the surveys, I have maintained a cautious silence. — Several questions were lately put to me with more than usual earnestness on these subjects, when I was obliged to say to them that if the law was obscure they ought to apply to you for a declaratory act. —

The death of Seth Emmons[17] left a vacancy in the House of Representatives to supply which Mr Lucas & Dr Farrar are the Candidates. The canvass will be very warm — the event doubtful. — If Lucas succeeds, he will probably try titles with greater politicians than the Dr. at the next Genl Elections, — and it cannot be doubted that I wish him success very heartily. — Wm. C Carr is surely the most impudent man alive. He pretends to think hardly of me for purchasing the lot on the hill and is persecuting LeDuc with the most poisoned animosity. How he has become Compr[omised] in this affair is altogether unconceivable — At the time he accepted the conveyance from Clamorgan, he well knew as I can from his Bro in law, that this very

17 Seth Emmons represented St. Louis in the first territorial council of Missouri.

Clamorgan had long before conveyed the lot in question to the late Secy. Browne. When I purchased of the Representatives of Browne I was totally ignorant of the fraudulent attempt to deprive them of their property by the 2 deed to Carr. Had I known of them I might with perfect propriety have made the purchase; yet it is very likely that I should not have done so, as it is always best to avoid contest with low minded People. — It is said that Mr Carr will make a misrepresentation of this business in order to prevent my reappointment to the Secretaryship, — This I take to be mere bluster to impress our village People with the notion that he really thinks himself injured — Yet the thing has been told in sober seriousness by one of his friends to one of mine — Altho' it is always desirable to meet our *enemies* in sunshine or at least in day light, I will not like Ajax in Sir Wm. Draper[18] insist upon the thing as a *Sine qua non*, provided I am permitted to meet their *accusations*. — And this I am very certain you will enable me to do.

0

PERMIT TÓ EXPLORE FOR LEAD MINES

ST. LOUIS Decr. 18. 1814

Mr Jno Perry is hereby permitted to explore the United States' untenanted Lands within the County of Washington for the purpose of discovering Lead Mines. Should he make the discovery he is at liberty to ascertain their extent & richness by such operations as are usual & necessary for those objects — And as soon as may be convenient

[18] Draper is remembered mainly because of his controversy with Junius.

thereafter transmit an acct. of his proceedings to this office
that he may obtain a Lease for the same

Frederick Bates, Recr L Titles
& Agent for Lead Mines —

TO AMABLE PARTENAY

St. Louis April 1st 1815.

Sir,

Whatever may be the hardships which you suffer from
interruption in your possession of the mines, I cannot
answer your letter of the 14th March, until you comply
with the condition on which the President is willing to
approve the Leases. — I wrote you expressly in January
last that the approbation was conditional — My words are
these '*The President has indeed approved the Lease on
condition the payment of the rents be secured in a satisfactory manner.*' And now you say you are willing to do
so when I require it. — Sir, I did require it in my letter
of 24th Jany. and do again require it. —

The responsibilities which I owe to the commissioner
of the General Land Office oblige me to be thus explicit.

PERMIT TO OCCUPY MINERAL LAND

St. Louis April 24th 1815.

James Gray,[19] Jno. Stoddard and Joseph Wheat, having
as they alledge discovered a Lead Mine on the Lands of
the United States, on the waters of Big River about eight

---

[19] In 1800 he was living near the mouth of the Meramec. In 1814
he was an ensign in the Washington County regiment.

miles from mine Shibboleth & 20 from Herculaneum adjoining the claim of Jno. Thurman are hereby permitted to ascertain the richness and probable extent of said mine, by the usual operations — if the said discovery be really on the lands of the United States —

On the following conditions to wit — That said persons shall keep and render to this Office a just and true acct. of the mineral raised or to be raised — & pay therefor the usual rents to the government —

That they shall report the result of their search, to this Office within one month — at which time a lease will be given in the usual manner, on said persons giving satis-factory security — Provided others have not better claims.

If the permission be not renewed the said James Gray for himself & Partners promises & obliges himself to deliver the Premises to the Recorder of Land Titles if so required to do, after the expiration of one month. —

Frederick Bates

Witness present. —   Recorder L. Titles

Edw. Bates   James Gray

EDWARD BATES[20] TO FREDERICK BATES

Sᴛ. Loᴜɪs Decr. 18th. 1815

Mʏ Dᴇᴀʀ Bʀoᴛʜᴇʀ

From the excellent weather we have had you will arrive at Washington sooner than was at first expected. Yet I should not write to you so soon if I had not been particularly requested to do so by Mr Connor and several

[20] Edward Bates was a seventh son. He served six months in the War of 1812. At the age of twenty he came to St. Louis. He studied in the law office of Rufus Easton and was admitted to the bar in 1816. He was soon made district attorney. He rose rapidly in his profession and

others — You heard before your departure that Judge
Lucas and Colo. Chouteau intended to offer a square of
ground for the erection of the public buildings of the
County and that the lot they had pitched upon lies on the
hill near the Court house, a situation which they contend
is the most eligible about the town — Mr. Connor has determined with the warm concurrence of all the large land
holders at the upper end of the town, to offer a large lot
at the south east corner of his tract, and as all of them
are much interested, they seem to think if you have any
particular wishes on the subject that the making known
of your opinion and views might have some influence on
the commissioners appointed to manage the business on
the part of the County; the bill for the appointment of
commissioners was to pass its third reading today — I
think there will be large offers made at both ends of the
Town, and perhaps subscriptions opened — I told the gentlemen who conversed with me on the subject that I did
not think you would take any part in the affair, but as they
were very solicitous I agreed to inform you of the above
facts

The Legislature is very busily employed in altering and
abolishing former provisions, and in passing *supplemental
bills* but they create very little, and in fact their character
for prudence and wisdom is not at all advanced in my estimation. They are again making great changes in the
judiciary system — and have introduced 'an occupying
claimant Law' with the same villainous features as its Kentucky model

But this letter was not intended as a letter of news, it
is written merely on the above request.

became a national figure. His highest honor was a position in the Lin-
coln cabinet.

JOHN G. HEATH TO BATES[21]

SIR

SAINT LOUIS 14th January 1816.

The Chairman of the Land Committee has required proof that the Settlers (i e the early settlers) at Boonslick[22] did actually settle by permission of the then Executive Magistrate of this Territory. They have frequently stated to me, and I find they state it also in their petition to Congress that you then exercised the Government It is impracticable to send to those people and procure any thing on the subject, in time to forward it to Washington before Congress will adjourn.

Therefore if it really be fact as stated in said petition will you satisfy the committee in that behalf? — Perhaps it also known to you that those people have suffered very much by the late war maintained their ground & servered as malitia enrolled in actual service &c. — The Gov-s forming them into Batalions & companies & their having been a second time received into the Jurisdiction of the Territory. Any friendly aid rendered will doubtless be gratefully acknowledged by those people. . . .

NB We do not want W Clark our Governor any longer — I have no doubt this would be freely subscribed by nine tenths of the Territory — also Govn & Superintendent — two men.

---

[21] Bates was then in Washington, D. C.

[22] In 1807 Nathan and Daniel M. Boone, sons of Daniel Boone, with three others manufactured salt in central Missouri, which region henceforth was known as the Boonslick Country. The region was beset by Indians in the War of 1812. The settlers defended themselves by building blockhouses and by forming volunteer companies.

NOTES ON A LAND BILL FOR THE STATE OF LOUISIANA AND THE TERRITORY OF MISSOURI[23]

WASHN. March 17. 1816. —

The first section provides for the confirmation of incomplete Grants of the French and Spanish Governments — The Acts of Congress (See Land Laws p. 305 Sec 1. p. 316 Sec 4) appear to be founded on strict principles of Law — that is of position right on the part of the claimants and of obligation on that of the government. — It was necessary for a confirmation that the claimant should have inhabited and cultivated the land of which he had been put into the possession under the concession, order or warrant. This was required by the Spanish usages to which our Law of 3d March 1807 (4 Sec) refers. — The claimants had good titles — And the Government in issuing the Patents only gave evidence of those titles. — But these principles were considerably relaxed, or rather they were altogether done away by the Act of 12 of April 1814. This Act demands nothing of the party — it only inquires whether or not the warrant or order of survey had been executed at the time of the actual change of the flag — that is when Wilkinson & Claiborne at N. Orleans & Maj Stoddard at St Louis took possession of the country. However gratuitous this liberality of Congress might have been, Justice does now seem to require a farther provision that its operation may equally reach all the legitimate objects of it. No provision has yet been made, such as the first section of this bill provides for the holders of unexecuted warrants. The sovereign sanctions of the country had been given in

[23] This was prepared by Bates for James Clark of the congressional committee on the public lands.

their favour, and nothing but a ministerial act of a subordinate Spanish officer remained to be done — Nothing
was wanted but the process verbal of survey — Let that
process verbal be dispensed with — And let our surveyors
do that which the Spanish surveyor had not time to perform — And which at last, is merely an official routine
consequent on the incohation [inchoation] of the claim.
This provision with the limitation which the 1st Sec of the
Act establishes will make the liberality of the American
Government consistent. —

The second section of the bill provides for the grant,
under Settlement Right Provisions [of] such lands as had
been improved or cultivated on or before the 10th Mar
1804 [It] does not occur to me why this date should not
have been rather 20 Augt. 1804 as by the existing Laws,
cultivation at that time has been made the basis of grant
(See Act of June 13. 1812). The former Laws (See Land
Laws P. 305 Sec 2. P. 311 Sec 1 P. 315 Sec 2 — Sec 3 of
Act of June 13. 1812 — Sec 4 of Act of 3 March 1813 — Sec
2d. of Act of 12 April 1814) required that these acts of
ownership should have been performed both prior to and
on certain given days to wit, in first instance, 20th Dec.
1803, time of the transfer at Orleans & in the second instance, 10 March 1804 time of the transfer at St Louis.
It is proposed by this section of the bill to dispense with
the continuation of the improvement & require only that
it should have been either on or prior to those days respectively assumed for the state of Louisiana & ter of Missouri
and to extend the donation in all cases to the quantity of
640 acres or a mile square. As to the first object of this
section I would only remark that this class of claimants
is principally composed of persons whose settlements were

broken up by the incursions of the Indians and by other casualties incident to a frontier no part of which was deemed to be secure until the transfer to the U States. As to the second object of the section, I believe it to be true that the comparatively inconsiderable number of persons who claimed less than 640 acres [were] themselves compelled by the then existing arrangements. They would have claimed more, had they not thought themselves bound to proportion their quantity to the number of their families. It was *not* then the voluntary act of the claimant but the principles of our own Laws as they were understood by the Treasury department. Mr Gallatin on the opinion of Mr Breckenridge the Atty. General instructed the commissioners to graduate these claims as to quantity according to the ratio established by the Spanish Usages. This was understood, at the time in Upper Louisiana and for the most part disregarded by the People who thought it a harsh construction of the Law. Some few however entered according to this ratio believing that no more would ultimately be granted — And those conscientious people are perhaps at this day as much entitled to the full quantity as those who will receive it under the 4th Sec of the act of 3d March 1813

The third section provides for opening the office as well for original notice as for the introduction of evidence. It would seem that opportunities for entering claims had been already afforded (See Land Laws P. 306 Sec. 4. — P. 312 Sec 3 — P. 317 Sec 5. — Sec 7 of Act of 13 June 1812) Yet I know the fact to be that there are yet some few claims not entered, owing in some cases to the ignorance of the ' holders. — Neither speaking, writing nor understanding our language, they have not known the forms of business — and not unfrequently have been ignorant of the necessity for entry created by our Laws. A liberal justice to an acquired province would, I think, dictate the arrangements made by this section — And I am sure expediency would imperiously demand them — for altho' barred by the Laws they would not fail at some future period to load your tables with Petitions for individual relief —

Thus much ad to the entry of notices — But as to the introduction of testimony, the necessity of such a provision is, it seems to me enforced by every consideration of justice and of right. The 3d Sec of the act of 13 June 1812 extended the time of cultivating the donation claims till 20 Augt. 1804 with the supposition, no doubt, that whereever the fact existed, the proofs of that fact was now the record. In some few cases however, it is otherwise — for in recording the testimony previously to that time, nothing of a more recent [date] than the time then limited, was, in the ordinary course of business, entered on the minutes. If it sometimes appear on the record, it was at the earnest instance of the claimant or his agent. The first Section of the act of 3d March 1813 will be found not to permit the introduction of testimony to meet the extension provided for by the act of June 1812 And I trust it is sufficiently obvious that claimants in that situation should be permitted to prove themselves entitled to those benefits which it was the intention of that act to confer. —

TO JOHN A SHAW,[24] WASHINGTON, D. C.

WASHINGTON CITY April 9. 1816.

SIR,

I have heard with much regret that in the late consolidation of the army, you lost that station which in the

[24] John A. Shaw was a Pennsylvanian. He entered the United States

opinion of your friends you had filled with so much propriety and usefulness.

In the reduction of great establishments the occurrence of hardships of this kind is unavoidable. — Time may correct the caprices of fortune — Do not despair — Accident — a change of scene — some new modification, will, I greatly hope, from time to time, restore to the service of their country those meritorious men who contributed so largely to the successful termination of the late war. — I have been solicited by persons who do not know the absolute obscurity in which I live, to assist in your restoration. I have nothing to offer you but my good wishes. We have known each other for years in the western country — and the undeviating rectitude of your conduct, as far as I was acquainted with it, or could presume to judge of it, was acknowledged by all —

It will give me great pleasure to hear of your future welfare.

TO THE COMMISSIONER OF THE LAND OFFICE, WASHINGTON, D. C.

[Washington], Nov 10. 1816

With permission I will recapitulate the contracts with Partenay

On the .15th Sept 1814 the Agent by order of the President thro' the comr. of Land Dept. leased to Amable Par-

---

Army as an ensign in the 1st infantry in 1809. He became a second lieutenant in 1812 and a first lieutenant in 1814. He received an honorable discharge on June 15, 1815, but was reinstated on May 17, 1816, serving henceforth in the light artillery.

tenay the following Lead Mines in the county of Washington

Mine A Straddle	300 acres	
Mine A Burton	200 acres	
*Mine A Bourassar	800 acres*	18241
Shous's Mine	200 acres	
*Little Diggings	200 acres	40910
*Martins Mines	200 acres	529592
Sievers Mines	800 acres	
		588,743

As it was expected that he would not gain the possession in less than 5 days — this Contract was made to extend to 20 Sepr. 1815 — On the 30th day of that month he settled his accts with the Agents for all the mineral recd up to that day — to wit for 588,743 pounds recd. from the Mines marked with asterisks which at $4 per thousand amounts to — $2354..97 cts. — The Covenants were renewed after this payment, for the then follg 12 mos. at 350 cts. per thousand previously to the expiration of which term to wit on the 24 Sepr. 1816 — A Partenay settled with the Agent for 463,477 pds. of Mineral which at 350 cts amts to $1622 — Overpd. 3 Ds. carrd to his Cr. The Lease has been again renewed subject to pleasure of the President [subject to][25] the same rents & to include a late Discovery called Maçons Diggings — In this last contract James Scott[26] is a joint contractor with Partenay —

From this recapitulation it appears, (and I declare upon honor that I believe the statement to be just & true) that I have received at difft times from Partenay the sum of

---

[25] The original manuscript is here illegible.
[26] James Scott was living at Mine à Burton in 1802.

$3979. .97 cts. — and no more — The monies may not have
be[en] actually paid at the times stated — Sometimes on
settlement. I have been satisfied with *good assurances* on
an early future day —

The revenues from these mines are indeed inconsiderable. Sir, it is not my fault — *I have made no unworthy
compromises — No misapplications of the public money.*
When the Government think proper to take possession of
what is rightfully their own, the Revenues will necessarily
be very considerable. — At present your Agent is *de-
famed* — And your tenant but the treatment which he
has received has been of a character too shameful to be
here repeated — it was communicated at the time. —

[Bates' note of explanation]. This statement I gave in to
the actg. officers of the Treasury when I was in Washington — They owed me money on a general settlement — for
services & compensations in other capacities — not expences of Agency. —

TO JAMES SCOTT AND AMABLE PARTENAY

ST. LOUIS February 1st. 1817. —

GENTLEMEN,

There is one article of your covenants with which you
have not yet complied — to wit the rendering of quarterly
Accounts — I ask that this may be attended to without
delay — And I moreover require that the first quarters
payment of rents be also made — In Mr Scott's punctuality I have every reliance — but Mr Partenay ought to
have recollected that he yet owes an Acct. of the unfinished
business of his former Lease, as well as a few hundred
Dollars, which I have advanced for him to the Govern-

ment. — I am in very great want of Money. — If I do not hear from you within a reasonable time, I must take measures to avoid those censures which I might expect to receive from those by whom I am employed. . . .

[P. S] The President has not yet explicitly *approved* — And if he discovers this want of punctuality, the probability is that he will *disapprove.* —

PERMIT TO EXPLORE MINERAL LAND

Office of the Recorder of Land Titles
St. Louis April 29. 1817.

Major Langham,[27] is permitted to explore and ascertain the extent and richness of a supposed Lead Mine, of which he is alledged to have been the first discoverer, if (and is believed) situated on the public Lands of the United States. — Sections 19. 20. 17. 18 — or parts thereof — Township 41 N. of Base Line — Range one E of 5. P. Meridian — On both sides of Meramec. For some time past this office, tho' its powers in that respect have not been revoked, has made no Leases of Lead Mines — If this should be found to be an object worth attention, I will endeavour to procure for Major Langham as favorable an arrangement as the circumstances of the case may warrant. — In the meantime this is intended to secure him from intrusion and to exempt him from any penalty to which he might be liable under the Laws of U. S. without Licence from the President.

Frederick Bates

27 Probably Angus Lewis Langham, who was one of the promoters of a town called Osage at the mouth of the Petite Osage. It proved to be an ephemeral enterprise.

EDWARD BATES TO FREDERICK BATES

McCreary's, 75 miles from
KASKASKIA, Aug:18. 1818.

My Dr. Brother,

We left Shawanee Town on the day before yesterday,[28] mother and sister are in pretty good spirits & tolerable health — Notwithstanding the extreme badness of the roads — which I believe is always the case here after hard rains. They came down by water — I brought the horses across, and altho' the voyage was disagreeable yet upon the whole there was no great matter to complain of — We had no accident on the whole trip till we left the Ohio, since when we have broken 3 swingletrees but our knives soon got a substitute

I am fearful our carriage horses will *fag* as we find little or nothing to feed them with but green corn *stalks & all* — We shall come on slowly, 20 or 25 miles a day & shall probably keep the Kaska: road altho' the longest, being told it is better for carriage, and affords better accommodations. I long to be at home & you may be sure I shall be at St Louis as soon as my horses will bring me. From *Shawanee,* I have taken Ben,[29] (*yr. Blacksmith*) as our driver — he is not experienced but is very careful & does well — The boat left Shawanee the same day we did — James goes round with the negroes & is accompanied by a Mr. Brown who, I believe will be much assistance to him — I write this

[28] In July, 1817 Edward Bates went to Virginia to dispose of the Belmont estate. He remained there for about a year. In July, 1818 he started for St. Louis with his mother and a sister. His brother James followed with the slaves. Edward Bates to Frederick Bates, September 1, September 29, and October 13, 1817, July 19 and August 18, 1818, Bates Papers.

[29] One of the slaves.

Just to let you know when to look for us — as to our affairs
you will have to wait till we meet. . . .

P. S. This is Wednesday but I am not sure whether the
18th 19th or 20th of the month — . . . .

Boucoup Aug: 21st ,18 — (Friday) — We shall probably
be at St: Louis some time on monday next — High waters
have retarded us a little — The flies are very bad but our
horses stand it wonderfully — A gentleman going directly
to St. Louis (who will out travel us) has been good enough
to promise a conveyance for this —

A SALE OF SLAVES

Know all men by these presents that I Samuel Sydnor
of the county of St Louis in the territory of Missouri, for
and in consideration of the sum of four hundred..................
dollars to him in hand paid by Frederick Bates and also for
and in consideration of the friendship which has subsisted
your earliest infancy between Nancy Bates the wife of said
Frederick, and the said Samuel, he the said Samuel B
Sydnor has bargained, sold and delivered — and by these
presents does bargain, sell and deliver to the said Frederick Bates for the sole use and benefit of the said Nancy
his wife a negro Girl named Lucy about six years old, to be
held in trust for the said Nancy Bates her heirs, or the
assigns of herself and husband forever.

And the said Samuel B. Sydnor does covenant with the
said Frederick Bates, as Trustee as aforesaid that the title
to the said Lucy is unincumbered, and that he will warrant
and defend the title to the said Slave against all claims
whatsoever. — Given under my hand in the county of St
Louis the second day of March, 1820. —

Samuel B Sydnor   (Seal)

JOSHUA BARTON[30] TO BATES

DEAR SIR,   ST. LOUIS September 14th 1820.

Since I saw you in town I have had an attack of the fever and ague, of which however I have recovered — that together with the indisposition of my brother Isaac has prevented my coming out to see you as I proposed.

As the meeting of the Legislature is at hand, you will excuse me for again introducing the subject I spoke to you on. I am informed by McNair & others from the upper country that it is the wish of many of the members from that quarter you should run for the Senate, and the same wish I have heard frequently expressed by very respectable gentlemen of this place. Col. Cook is a candidate & wil beat Benton.

As to yourself I do believe there is no difficulty if you can give your own consent to be run.

A SALE OF A SLAVE

Know all men by these presents that I Samuel B. Sydnor for and in consideration of the sum of four hundred dollars to me in hand paid by Frederick Bates, have bargained sold and delivered and by these presents do bargain sell and deliver to the said Frederick Bates, a Negro Woman Slave, named Sylvia, in full and absolute property of said Bates his Heirs and assigns

---

[30] Joshua Barton, a brother of Senator David Barton, was associated with Edward Bates in the practice of law. He was secretary of state for Missouri in 1821, but resigned to become United States attorney for Missouri. He was killed in a duel with Rector on June 30, 1823.

And the said Samuel B. Sydnor does hereby covenant with the said Frederick Bates, that the title to the said Slave Sylvia is unencumbered, and that the said Slave is sound in her health and bodily constitution — all which he will warrant and defend. Given under my hand in the county of St Louis in the State of Missouri, this Fifth day of December one thousand eight hundred and twenty

Witness   Samuel B Sydnor

   John Ward

PART VIII
The Later Years

THE LATER YEARS

EDWARD BATES TO FREDERICK BATES

Dr. Brother,   St. Louis May 15. 1823.

Mr Leduc being about to visit you in a few days, I take
the occasion to write you, lest circumstances should frus-
trate my intention of calling upon you the last of this week
or first of next. The pressure of business in the Supreme
Court, at St Charles lately, and now here, and my daily
hope of seeing you in town, have prevented me from making
you acquainted with a matter which it much concerns me
you should know. I am to be married[1] on the last thursday
in this month (a fortnight from today), and hope you &
my good sister will grace the occasion with your presence.
It is not the intention to make any display on the occasion,
but as the family connexion is pretty large, and I have
invited several of my personal friends, of course there will
be a considerable crowd. You will not only gratify me
but comply with the wishes of the family by attending.
It is likely you will see me before you receive this, yet I
have thought it best to write for fear of accidents.

I have also desired Mr Leduc to hand you a letter enclosed to me by Wm Russell[2] which I suppose relates to
the delivery of certain patent certificates for surveys in
Arkansas, and correction of the list of confirmed claims
in that Country, which he says is defective, in as much as
he alleges that some 10 or 15 confirmed claims in which he

---

[1] Edward Bates married Miss Julia D. Coalter.
[2] William Russell filed three hundred and nine claims, but only
twenty-three of these were confirmed.

is interested now are omitted on the list. He has written to me to attend to this business, & I have promised to apply to you for that purpose

He urges me to apply for all the Arkansas certs. *in which he was agent* (with a few exceptions). But it was impossible for me to ascertain his agency without a laborious search, and your assistance, which I could not ask you to give; the matter is at present deferred. . . .

You can cross the Missouri at Lewis' ferry — the worst of the road is on this side, and the distance not more than 12 or 14 miles.

A SALE OF SLAVES

Know all men by these presents that I Benjamin L. Todd of the county of Pike county in the state of Missouri, for and in consideration of the sum of six hundred and fifty dollars to me in hand paid by Frederick Bates of the county of St Louis in the state aforesaid, hath bargained sold and delivered and by these presents do bargain sell and deliver to said Frederick Bates One negro woman slave named Winney with her three female children Hannahrette, Mary and Harriott — to have and to hold the said four slaves to him the said Frederick Bates his Heirs and Assigns forever — And I the said Benja L. Todd do covenant with said Frederick Bates that I have had until this transfer a full, free and unencumbered property in said Slaves and that I will defend the title against all claims or pretensions to said Frederick Bates his Heirs Assigns. Given under my hand this Second day of March AD 1824.

Witness   Benjamin L. Todd (SS)

   Chas[?] Kinkead

EDWARD BATES TO FREDERICK BATES

My Dr. Brother,   St. Louis 30 June 1824

As Mr Moore is just taking his departure for yr. house, I take the opportunity to drop you a line. We were much surprised to learn that you had declined taking the tour of the State, which it was thought you had determined upon. The policy of inactivity I think is very questionable; but of this, doubtless you are the best judge. We have been expecting you in town daily — Some seem anxious to see you on political grounds merely — some on business in relation to yr. office, and I for various reasons.

I believe it is since you were last in town that I have received the appointment of District Attorney. The ordinary duties of that Station are more immediately within my line than yours, but the recent passage of the land law (allowing claimants to commence actions in the District Court) will throw upon me a mass of business, the correct management of which will require a knowledge of facts and principles with which you are far better acquainted, than any other man in the State. The transaction of this business I think, will be worth to me several thousand dollars, and being of a public nature, calculated to attract the attention of the public & the Government, I feel particularly anxious to be enabled to do the business in such a manner as may be creditable both to myself and those whom I represent. With these views, I beg you to direct your attention somewhat to that subject; for, in truth, the hope of acquitting myself handsomely in this thing, is bottomed very much upon the expectation of obtaining information and instruction from you. Perhaps, after you have seen the act, I may go so far as to request a written statement of yr. views on the subject with a reference to the various laws and regulations with which I know you to be entirely familiar. I have had a very slight view of the act, and believe that it does not contain any enlargement of the principles on which confirmations can be founded, but merely provides for doing now in court, what might have been formerly done before the commisrs. or the recorder.

I hope to see you soon on this & other subjects, in which yr. society may be useful as well as pleasant to me.

My family is in perfect health except that my wife is very subject to severe head ache which she has at this moment, but wch. seldom lasts long. I am too busy in court affairs to indulge at present in any political speculations. Present my best respects to Mrs. B. & kiss the *light infantry* for me. . . .

[P.S.] Thanks for the catsup.

GEORGE GRAHAM TO BATES

General Land Office
Washington, D. C., Aug. 21, 1824

Sir

I have the pleasure of acknowledging the receipt of your letter of the 24 Ulto. with a list of the claims confirmed by the Board of Commissioners.

I would call your attention to the undermentioned cases in which the tracts relinquished to the U. S. under the Act of 17 Feby 1815 do not agree with the confirmations, and will thank you to give such explanations as the several cases may require — Viz

Location
Certif[icat]e

No. 111	in favor	of	Benjn Fooy under John Hogan		C o n firmed
"	139	"	"	" Isaac Fooy	as being in
"	140	"	"	" Elizabeth Jones	the County
"	237	"	"	" Caty Gallowhorn	of A r k a n-
"	477	"	"	" Edwd Proctor	sas
"	514	"	"	" Augustine Gonzales	
"	515	"	"	" Jno F. Almendros	
"	164	"	"	" John Brooks	
"	224	"	"	" Charles Lucas	
"	232	"	"	" Jas Brady under Williamson	
"	275	"	"	" John Tucker	
"	276	"	"	" Stephen Quimby	C o n firmed
"	306	"	"	" William Hacker	as being in
"	318	"	"	" Stepn Byrd under J. Bowden	the County of Cape
"	341	"	"	" Jacob Millikin	Girardeau
"	346	"	"	" E Hogan under Millikin	
"	353	"	"	" John Wellborn	
"	379	"	"	" Abm Bird Senr.	
"	458	"	"	" Robt Lane	
"	505	"	"	" Charles Hogan	

"   104 and 105 issued to John B. Chartier on his having surrendered two lots in the Village of
Little Prairie — No lots in that Village appear to have been Confirmed to him.

"   113 in favor of Conrad Wheat Junr for *640* acres
but the only Confirmation in his favor is for
450 arpens.

Location Certife No. 342 issued in the name of Jacob
                  Serego but the confirmation is to Jacob
                  Lerego
"   "   No. 371 in favor of James Noiris for
                  300 arpens — the only tract that ap-
                  pears to have been Confirmed to him
                  Contains *351* arpens and is stated to be
                  in Cape Girardeau County
"   "   No. 388 issued in favor of Louis Baby
                  for 250 arpens, when but 200 arpens
                  appear to have been Confirmed to him.

EDWARD BATES TO FREDERICK BATES

My Dr. Brother,   St Louis Aug: 24. 1824.

I am much concerned to hear of the sickness of yrself
& family, particularly at a time when we were in daily
expectation of seeing you in our City, & congratulating
you on your easy & honorable election. Many of the
good folks desire me to salute you *Excellent.* . . .

It is amusing to observe what strange stories can be
devised, & what wonderful contrivances invented by the
descending, to break their fall. Genl: A. & his most
ardent supporters will have it that you have not been
so easily elected over him, by the spontaneous wishes of
the people, nor on your own solid popularity; but for
sooth, that I, even I, E. B. *the great!* did wickedly &
maliciously write & compose divers wise, artful & cunning
epistles and did most secretly & with great diligence &
labor scatter & disperse them throughout the land,
whereby the hearts of the people were suddenly turned
& corrupted — the mighty laid low, and the humble
exalted, yea to the pinacle of power. "Big man me!"

If my letters could put the Gen: down (& by the bye I wrote none) he must be weaker than any of us supposed.

What I wrote you the other day about Gamble,[3] was far from being dictated by any wish to obtrude upon your rights or duties — I merely meant to say that I think him *fit* for the office, and under present circumstances, I know the office to be particularly well *fitted* for him. He moved from Franklin here in hopes of, at once getting a good practice, this has not yet been realized, and being conscious of superior talents to several who stand, as yet, above him at our bar, I think he is somewhat depressed. He was & deserved to be at the head of the bar in the upper Country, where his chief acquaintance is.

DAVID BARTON[4] TO BATES

WASHINGTON 6th February 1825

D SIR

I have received yours of 7 ult concerning Col. Reeves, and shall be happy in an opportunity of aiding him in the attainment of his object, should an occasion occur. Without alluding to this application of Reeves, I regret to find such a number of applications for office from Missouri. You would be surprised to see some of my letters upon that subject from men who spell and write as badly as the Osage Agent.

[3] Bates appointed Hamilton Rowan Gamble secretary of state. He had a long and honorable legal and public career. In 1846 he was a member of the legislature. In 1851 he was elected judge of the supreme court by an overwhelming majority, in spite of the fact that he ran on the whig ticket in a democratic state. In 1861 he was provisional governor of Missouri.

[4] United States senator from Missouri.

We have had some able discussion upon the bill to suppress piracy. Mr Tazewell[5] has done due honor to Virginia for chasing him to the Senate. After striking out such parts of the bill as proposed clandestine war upon Spain, the bill has been ordered to a 3d reading. From the threat of the silly King of Spain, to revoke the cession of Florida if we do not retract our acknowledgement of the Mexican and South American Independence, and from the collisions likely to arise with respect to the host of pirates who have sprung out of the revolutions of those countries, a war with Spain seems probable at no distant day.

Mr Clay, you see, has determined to support Mr Adams for the Presidency.

I think he is perfectly right in so doing — tho' it is rather leaving some of his over zealous friends in Missouri, in the lurch; but that is probably their fault and not his. If Gen. Jackson's indiscreet friends here are to be taken as specimens of his Court & favorites, during his reign, may that reign never commence.

I send you a no. of Niles[6] containing much matter, which I pray you to take as part and parcel of this letter.

TO SAMUEL WOODSON AND CHAUNCEY SMITH[7]

EXECUTIVE OFFICE ST. CHARLES Feb 8th. 1825

GENTLEMEN,

A paper was recd. at this office, some time ago (handed perhaps by Mr. Smith) recommending Jabez Warner as

[5] Littleton Waller Tazewell, United States senator from Virginia, 1824-1833.
[6] *Niles' Register.*
[7] Members of the general assembly from Jefferson County.

Judge of Probate for the county of Jefferson. — I cannot consent to this course. — If the General Assembly had thought proper to have made that Office elective by the People, they had full power and would certainly have done so. — But then they would, at the same time have prescribed an observance of all the usual forms. — The People would have had due *notice* — there would have been managers, to see among other things that no unqualified persons were admitted to the Polls, — and Clerks to take down the names of the voters — And in all respects there would have been *an open competition.* The public sentiment when fully and fairly expressed will always be binding on me on subjects of expediency — but a hasty and ex parte exhibition of names will not always influence my public conduct; especially in cases where I am enjoined by the laws to exercise my own best judgments and discretions.

As the matter now stands the nomination is with the Governor, and the responsibility is *his.* — I assume that responsibility — The People of Jefferson, I know very well, can have no deliberate wish to take upon themselves the powers confided by law to the Executive — And it is to be supposed if they made such an attempt, that at least, all persons not qualified to vote on other occasions would be excluded from a participation in a procedure so unprecedented. I do myself believe that Mr. Warner is very well qualified for the office — but that he better deserves it than any other Citizen of Jefferson is not pretended —

I wish there to be no misunderstanding. — When I consulted you it was for information — and with a wish too, to consult, as far as possible, your inclinations — After your disagreement in opinion, and after the withdrawal of the names which you had respectively offered me (Messrs. Lewis & Hammond) I think it right to follow the dictates of own understanding, and nominate to the Senate an individual whom neither of you have either recommended or supported, — and one too, who shall not seem to be imposed upon me by Petitions very hastily gotten up.

MARIE PHILIP LEDUC TO BATES

DEAR SIR,   ST LOUIS Febry. 14th, 1825

I now receive your letter of the 9th instant on the subject of the Patent Certificates; Mr. Hunt, as I wrote to you will wait till you come to Town to have an understanding with you about them: but should he use legal means to get them, how can it be resisted — he nevertheless would have to enter into bond with sufficient security for the redelivery or fees dues thereon. — but this cannot be his views, for he said that he is of opinion that those P.C. ought not to have been prepared, that is I believe null and void — I will not in the mean time lose sight of our interest.

Please, accept my most sincere thanks for the trouble you have taken, in my nomination of Judge of Probate I heard enough here of the intrigues which were practised to procure it to another.

PIERRE CHOUTEAU TO BATES

DEAR SIR   ST LOUIS April 3d. 1825.

Having understood that Mr Reeves our lieutenant Governor was one of the Commissioners appointed by

Government to locate a road from this State to new mexico I take the liberty to request of you the favor of writing to him in behalf of my nephew René Paul[8] as a proper person to be employed by the Commissioners as principal surveyor in that Expedition you being acquainted with him & his talents as an Engineer being now so well established I think it unnecessary to say any more to you on the subject I must however observe that his knowledge of the Spanish language may become very useful to the party in Getting into the Spanish provinces.

Please to accept My best wishes for your welfare.

BATES' EXPLANATION OF HIS ATTITUDE TOWARD LAFAYETTE'S VISIT TO ST. LOUIS[9]

During the session of the legislature I informed the two Houses of the intention of General Lafayette to visit this state in the month of April or May, that they might if they thought proper cause him to be received as the Guest of the nation. — They made no order, they gave to me no instructions. — My judgment entirely coincides with theirs — They as well as myself, entertain for the Genl. the most perfect respect — but surely he has had already sufficient evidences of that cordiality & good will which a free and enlightened People are always disposed to show to their friends — and of that homage too, which ought to be rendered to the illustrious assertor of the equal rights of Mankind. — His devotions at the holy sepulchre of Washington — his visits to our renowned

[8] A St. Louis merchant.
[9] Lafayette visited St. Louis April 29, 1825.

Ex President — his transits thro' our Atlantic cities — his laborious attendance in the halls of our national Legislature, with sundry et ceteras might one would think be sufficient to exhaust the patience of the Genl. — Spare him I pray you — the subject is sufficiently understood & sufficiently cited — There is no personal sacrifice we would not make on this occasion — but enough of pageantry — something is due to principle — and I am afraid that amidst this ostentation and waste, the wounds of our revolution, etc., which yet survive, many of them in poverty or but lately relieved might cause those Veterans to make comparisons very little to the credit of the nation. As an individual it would be altogether immaterial whether I kissed the hem of his garment or not — As the Governor of the State I shall not wait on him since the Genl. Assembly has not thought proper to give the first impulse. It has however been suggested that he may personally take it into his head to search me up, either at St Chs or on the hills of Bon Homme. He would find me at neither place, — for I have long since promised my family to visit some friends about that time.

THE END.

INDEX

33-34; investigation of losses by Indian depredations in the War of 1812, I, 33-34; report on claims, 1816, I, 34; record as recorder of land titles, I, 34; joined by his mother, Edward, and a sister, II, 306-307. *The Later Years, 1820-1825:* II, 311-324; urged to become candidate for the United States senatorship, I, 36; II, 308; purchase of slaves, II, 307, 308-309, 314; investments, II, 36; marriage, I, 36; Thornhill, I, 37; family, I, 37; campaign for the governorship of Missouri, I, 37-38; II, 315, 318; governor, I, 38-39; II, 320-324; on appointments, II, 321; veto of measure to prevent dueling, I, 38; attitude concerning Lafayette's visit to St. Louis, I, 38-39; II, 323-324; death, I, 39; Edward Bates' estimate of him, I, 39-40. *See also.* Board of land commissioners, and John Smith T.

Bates, Frederick, Jr., I, 37.
Bates, James Woodson, I, 3.
Bates, John I., I, 3.
Bates, Lucia Lee, I, p. VII, pp. 36, 37.
Bates, Lucius Lee, I, 37.
Bates, Margaret Maria, I, 3.
Bates, Nancy Opie Ball, I, 36-37.
Bates, Richard, I, 3, 315, 316, 317, 341-343.
Bates, Sarah, I, 3.
Bates, Susannah, I, 3, 5, 83.
Bates, Tarleton, I, 3, 5, 50, 51.
Bates, Thomas Fleming, I, 3-5.
Bates, William, II, 205.
Bates, Woodville, I, 37.
Battu, Henry, II, 269, 280, 284.
Baxter, Green, II, 284.
Bayard, James Asheton, II, 128.
Beatty, James, II, 194, 236, 287.
Beatty (Beaty), Joseph, I, 331, 332; II, 25.
Beauvais, St. Geminin (St. James), I, 145, 324; II, 38.
Beckett, William R., I, 289-290.

Belford, Francis, II, 33.
Bellefontaine, I, 162-163, 169, 229, 272.
Bellefontaine Factory, I, 219-220, 224-225, 337.
Bellefontaine races, II, 14.
Bellevue, I, 111.
Benoist, François Marie, I, 324.
Bent, Silas, I, 321, 323; II, 162, 190, 193, 195, 196, 271.
Benton, Thomas Hart, II, 308.
Berger, Peter, II, 33.
Berney, William, II, 282, 290.
Berry, John, II, 283, 287.
Berthold, Barthelemy, II, 269, 291.
Bibb, Richard G., I, 195, 329.
Big Soldier, II, 166-167.
Bijou, Louis, II, 282.
Billingsley, John, II, 281.
Bird, Absalom, II, 317.
Bissell, Daniel, I, 164, 169, 196, 266.
Bissonett, Charles, II, 32.
Bivarq, Joseph, II, 269.
Black Hawk War, I, 118.
Blackwell, Jesse, II, 268, 280, 289.
Blair, Robert, I, 329.
Bleakley, John, II, 105, 129.
Blondeau, Maurice, II, 86.
Board of land commissioners, Louisiana Territory, I, 29-30, 93-97, 99, 127, 134-135, 137, 158-161, 165-166, 220-221, 252-253, 282-283, 298, 301; II, 7-13, 19-22, 42-44, 47-54, 70-73, 77-79, 92-93, 129, 135-136, 138-139, 147, 152, 162, 165-166, 172-173, 179, 184-185, 188-189, 214, 216-217, 218-219, 221, 224, 316-318.
Boatmen, I, 241.
Bocher, David, II, 27.
Boilvin, Nicholas, I, 167-168, 169, 171-172, 179, 182, 199, 222, 226, 247, 334-335; II, 40, 103-104, 106-107.
Bois, Antoine B., I, 334.
Boisbriant, Sieur de, I, 276.
Bollinger, Frederick, I, 326.
Bollinger, George F., II, 236, 287.

CPSIA information can be obtained at www.ICGtesting.com
Printed in the USA
LVOW10s1027230714

395661LV00010B/95/P